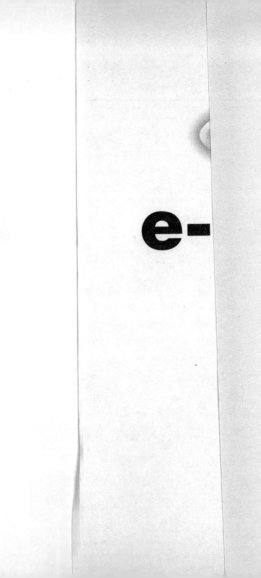

**the best
& worst
of internet
humour**

e-tales

CASSELL&CO

Cassell & Co
Wellington House
125 Strand
London
WC2R 0BB

British Library Cataloguing-in-Publication Data

A catalogue entry for this book is available
from the British Library.

ISBN 0–304–35727–8

Distributed in the United States
by Sterling Publishing Co. Inc.
387 Park Avenue South
New York, NY 10016–8810

Designed by Richard Carr
Printed in Great Britain by Mackays of Chatham PLC, Chatham, Kent

Contents

Introduction

>> E-mail has changed our lives. For thousands, perhaps even millions of us, the day begins as follows – sit at desk, switch on computer, switch on kettle while waiting for computer to boot up, log on and – hey presto! E-mail housekeeping here we come, but, first of all, who's sent us jokes this morning? Look at these first, sift the best ones and forward them all via our e-mail joke network. And we'll forward anything: dirty jokes, excruciating jokes, stories true or stories tall, revealing personality tests, amazing facts, amusing word games, buttock-clenchingly awful puns … Many of the amazing facts are utter rubbish, of course, and many of the 'true' stories are in fact false – but who cares? It's better than working!

You'd be surprised at some of the contributors to *e-tales* – people like Jeremy Paxman, for example, who wrote in the *Spectator* diary that the best thing about e-mail is the jokes it disseminates. (We are not revealing which of his jokes we've included here, however, because that would be telling!) Michael Grade, another of our prolific contributors, says that the best thing about e-mail is that good jokes and stories don't get destroyed in the re-telling by people who *think* they're comedians.

E-mail jokes are a great way of making new friends and keeping old ones, and, to that end, the publishers would like to offer particular thanks to the following: Paul Ward (for having the idea in the first place), Anita Land (for providing great jokes in such glorious abundance that a second book of *e-tales* will almost certainly be necessary) and David Milsted (for organizing and structuring the final text). Thanks are also due to Brook Land, Sonya Zuckerman, Jane Lush, Paul Jackson, Lorraine Esdaile, Kay Burley, Brenda Finlay and to everyone who supplied jokes and stories for this volume. You know who you are …

So, enjoy *e-tales* and make new friends!

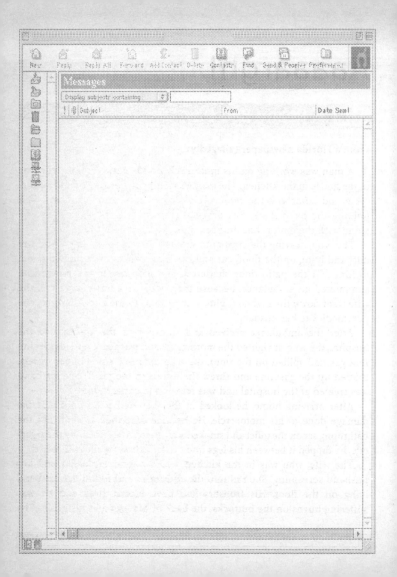

Aaaaargh!

From a Florida newspaper (allegedly) ...

A man was working on his motorcycle on his patio and his wife was in the house in the kitchen. The man was racing the engine on the motorcycle and somehow, the motorcycle slipped into gear. The man, still holding the handlebars, was dragged through a glass patio door and along with the motorcycle dumped onto the floor inside the house.

The wife, hearing the crash, ran into the dining room and found her husband lying on the floor, cut and bleeding, the motorcycle lying next to him and the patio door shattered. The wife ran to the phone and summoned an ambulance. Because they lived on a fairly large hill, the wife went down the several flights of long steps to the street to direct the paramedics to her husband.

After the ambulance arrived and transported the husband to the hospital, the wife uprighted the motorcycle and pushed it outside. Seeing that gas had spilled on the floor, the wife obtained some paper towels, blotted up the gasoline and threw the towels in the toilet. The husband was treated at the hospital and was released to come home.

After arriving home, he looked at the shattered patio door and the damage done to his motorcycle. He became despondent, went into the bathroom, sat on the toilet and smoked a cigarette. After finishing the cigarette, he flipped it between his legs into the toilet bowl while still seated.

The wife, who was in the kitchen, heard a loud explosion and her husband screaming. She ran into the bathroom and found her husband lying on the floor. His trousers had been blown away and he was suffering burns on the buttocks, the back of his legs and his groin. The wife again ran to the phone and called for an ambulance.

The same ambulance crew was dispatched and the wife met them on the street. The paramedics loaded the husband on the stretcher and began carrying him to the street. While they were going down the stairs to the street accompanied by the wife, one of the paramedics asked the wife how her husband had burned himself. She told them and the paramedics started laughing so hard, one of them tipped the stretcher and dumped the husband out. He fell down the remaining steps and broke his arm.

Accidents to Male Genitalia

When a 40-year-old man arrived at a hospital asking to see a doctor specializing in "men's troubles", he was shown to a cubicle. There, he gingerly unwrapped three yards of foul-smelling, stained gauze from around his scrotum, which had swollen to twice the size of a grape-fruit.

On further inspection, it was discovered that his left testicle was missing completely and, embedded within the swollen, tender and weeping wound, were a number of dark objects which the patient confessed were one-inch staple nails from an industrial staple gun. It transpired that the man spent lunchtimes alone in the workshop, where he regularly enjoyed the sexual thrill of placing his penis on the moving canvas fan belt of a piece of machinery. One day, the excitement had caused him to lose his concentration and the fan belt had snatched his scrotum into the fly-wheel, throwing him several feet across the floor and removing his left testicle. Rather than go to hospital, he self-adminis-tered first aid using a staple gun and then continued work when his colleagues returned. It was two weeks before he got around to visiting the hospital.

A man arrived at a hospital wearing an overcoat and with blood dripping down his leg. When he removed the coat, the doctor saw he had a geranium inserted in his penis. The man had got the flower in without any difficulty, but when he tried to remove it, the 'hairs' on the stem of the flower had dug into the urethra and ripped it to shreds.

A policeman in Staffordshire returned home from a night shift to his wife preparing breakfast. For some unknown reason, he wrapped a slice of bread around his penis, at which point the dog leapt up and took a bite out of it. The man required cosmetic surgery to repair the damage.

A 34-year-old New Yorker injected a cocaine solution into his penis to heighten his sexual pleasure. After enjoying intercourse with his girlfriend on not one, but two occasions, he noticed that his erection was still in its full glory. Having struggled to sleep through the night, he awoke to find his boner still standing proud. Due to his concern that the police discover his possession – and indeed use – of an illegal substance, he decided against visiting his doctor.

However, after three days of enduring headaches and nausea caused by the constant trouser swelling, he went to the hospital in search of help. He was immediately admitted and referred to a specialist who diagnosed

```
cow tales....
>             (__)                        (__)
>             (oo)                        (oo)
>      /-------\/
>     /  |     ||           ------------------------
>    --------------
>
>    Cow in water          Cow in trouble
```

a "lack of oxygen to vital blood streams" in his body as the cause of his sickness. He was given numerous drugs to combat the swelling and infection but shortly afterwards developed blood clots in various parts of his body, ultimately leading to the onset of gangrene.

As a result of his condition, he lost both of his legs, nine fingers and his penis.

A student (American, I believe) studying in Ireland took up rugby. As his first season progressed, he and his companions were eventually scheduled to play a team that had a reputation for violent play.

Considering that they weren't the most talented outfit to grace the field, they decided to accept the challenge with a "do or die" mentality, hoping that the game would eventually swing in their favour.

It didn't. To make matters worse, David, their star player, dislocated his pelvis after a particularly ferocious tackle. The player was clearly in a lot of pain so everyone stood back to allow the medic, in one swift movement, to pop the leg back into the socket. David released a long, blood-curdling scream.

To their horror, they realized that one of his testicles had been jammed in the socket and was now firmly held in the place between the femur and pelvis.

Incidentally, David managed to rip a vocal chord as a consequence of his screaming.

! 🛈 Flaming Gerbil

'Actual article from the *LA Times*'*

In retrospect, lighting the match was my big mistake. "But I was only trying to retrieve the gerbil," Eric Tomaszewski told bemused doctors in the Severe Burns Unit of Salt Lake City Hospital. Tomaszewski and his homosexual partner Andrew (Kiki) Farnom had been admitted for emergency treatment after a felching session had gone seriously wrong.

"I pushed a cardboard tube up his rectum and slipped Raggot, our gerbil, in," he explained. "As usual, Kiki shouted out 'Armageddon', my cue that he'd had enough. I tried to retrieve Raggot, but he wouldn't come out again, so I peered into the tube and struck a match, thinking that the light might attract him."

At a hushed press conference, a hospital spokesman described what happened next. "The match ignited a pocket of intestinal gas and a flame shot out of the tubing, igniting Mr Tomaszewski's hair and severely burning his face. It also set fire to the gerbil's fur and whiskers, which in turn ignited a larger pocket of gas further up the intestine, propelling the rodent out like a cannonball. Tomaszewski suffered second-degree burns and a broken nose from the impact of the gerbil, while Farnom suffered first- and second-degree burns to his anus and lower intestinal tract."

Editor's note: Not, in fact, an actual article from the *LA Times* or any other newspaper. No hospital in the USA has ever reported treating a "felching incident" in A&E.

```
....and more cow tales....
>                 (__)                              (__)
>                 (oo)                              (oo)
>          /————————\/                      /-oooooo-\/
>    * o|        ||                    * ooooooooo
>       ||————||                    ooooooooooooo
>    ooo^^      ^^                  ooooooooooooooooo
>
>    Cow taking                     Cow in deep
>     a shit                           shit
```

Age Concerns

! ◎ Boredom in Old Age

Two elderly ladies are sitting on the front porch, doing nothing. One old lady turns to the other and asks, "Do you still get horny?"

The other replies, "Oh sure I do."

The first old lady asks, "What do you do about it?"

The second old lady replies, "I suck a Life Saver."

After a few moments, the first old lady asks, "Who drives you to the beach?"

! ◎ Failing Powers

A 75-year-old man went to his doctor's office to get a sperm count. The doctor gave the man a jar and said, "Take this jar home and bring me back a semen sample tomorrow."

The next day, the 75-year-old man reappeared at the doctor's office and gave him the jar, which was as clean and empty as on the previous day. The doctor asked what happened and the man explained "Well, doc, it's like this. First I tried with my right hand, but nothing. Then I tried with my left hand, but still nothing. Then I asked my wife for help. She tried with her right hand, then her left, still nothing. She even tried with her mouth, first with the teeth in, then with her teeth out, and still nothing. We even called up Arleen, the lady next door and she tried too, first with both hands, then an armpit and she even tried squeezing it between her knees, but still nothing."

The doctor was shocked! "You asked your neighbour?"

The old man replied, "Yep, but no matter what we tried we still couldn't get the damn jar open!"

! ◍ Grandpa's Nightcap

A man goes to visit his 85-year-old grandfather in the hospital.

"How are you grandpa?" he asks.

"Feeling fine," says the old man.

"What's the food like?"

"Terrific, wonderful menus."

"And the nursing?"

"Just couldn't be better. These young nurses really take care of you."

"What about sleeping? Do you sleep OK?"

"No problem at all – nine hours solid every night. At 10 o'clock they bring me a cup of hot chocolate and a Viagra tablet . . . and that's it. I go out like a light."

The grandson is puzzled and a little alarmed by this, so rushes off to question the Sister in charge.

"What are you people doing?" he says. "I'm told you're giving an 85-year-old Viagra on a daily basis. Surely that can't be true?"

"Oh, yes," replies the Sister. "Every night at 10 o'clock we give him a cup of hot chocolate and a Viagra tablet. It works wonderfully well. The hot chocolate makes him sleep and the Viagra stops him rolling out of bed."

! ◍ Just Holding It

Two elderly people live in a nursing home and spend their afternoons together watching TV. They would lie in bed and she would hold on to his pecker, not doing anything, just holding it.

One day she is walking down the hall and passes the room of another female resident and sees her boyfriend lying on the bed and this other woman is holding on to it.

She storms into the room shouting, "I thought we had something going for us, is she better looking than me? Is she younger? What does she have that I don't?"

The old man says, "Parkinson's."

! Oral Sex

A young fellow was about to be married and was asking his grandfather about sex. He asked how often you should have it. His grandfather told him that when you first get married, you want it all the time . . . and maybe do it several times a day. Later on, sex tapers off and you have it once a week or so. Then as you get older, you have sex maybe once a month. When you get really old, you are lucky to have it once a year . . . maybe on your anniversary.

The young fellow then asked his grandfather, "Well how about you and Grandma now?"

His grandfather replied, "Oh, we just have oral sex now."

"What's oral sex?" the young fellow asked.

"Well," Grandpa said, "she goes to bed in her bedroom, and I go to bed in my bedroom. And she yells, 'Fuck You', and I shout back, 'Fuck you too.'"

! Problems Down There

Three men were discussing ageing on the steps of the nursing home.

"Sixty is the worst age to be," announced the sixty year old.

"You always feel like you have to pee. And most of the time, you stand at the toilet and nothing comes out!"

"Ah, that's nothing," said the seventy year old. "When you're seventy, you can't take a crap anymore. You take laxatives, eat bran – you sit on the toilet all day and nothing comes out!"

"Actually," said the eighty year old, "eighty is the worst age of all."

"Do you have trouble peeing too?" asked the sixty year old.

"No . . . not really. I pee every morning at 6 a.m. I pee like a race horse – no problem at all."

"Do you have trouble taking a crap?" asked the seventy year old.

"No, not really. I have a great bowel movement every morning at 6:30." With great exasperation, the sixty year old said, "Let me get this straight. You pee every morning at six o'clock and take a crap every morning at six thirty. What's so tough about being eighty?"

To which the eighty year old replied, "I don't wake up until ten."

```
 ....and more cow tales....

>               (___)
>              (  oo
>              /\__|
>             |  \\|       q
>             |   \\====|
>             |___\\===|\
>              \    |_____  \   (
>         _____/\        \=\/
>         \====/\=======/  /==_____
>  // \   /\\\ | | / /  //\----\\
>  //    \/__|\\/ /|=|  //   \    \\
>  ||    @ __||/ //-\   ||    @   ||
>   \\     //|_|=\_/    \\        //
>    =====            =====
>
>            Bicy-Cow
```

Signs That You're Getting Old

You can live without sex but not without glasses.

Your back goes out more than you do.

You quit trying to hold your stomach in, no matter who walks into the room.

You buy a compass for the dash of your car/truck.

You are proud of your lawn mower.

Your best friend is dating someone half their age, and isn't breaking any laws.

You sing along with the elevator music.

You would rather go to work than stay home sick.

You enjoy hearing about other people's operations.

You no longer think of speed limits as a challenge.

People call at 9:00 p.m. and ask, "Did I wake you?"

You answer a question with, "Because I said so."

You send money to PBS.

The end of your tie doesn't come anywhere near the top of your pants.

You take a metal detector to the beach.

You wear black socks with sandals.

You know what the word "equity" means.

You can't remember the last time you laid on the floor to watch TV.

Your ears are hairier than your head.

You talk about "good grass" and you're referring to someone's lawn.

You get into a heated argument about pension plans.

You got cable for the weather channel.

You have a party and the neighbours don't even realize it.

You agonize over a broken air conditioner.

People send you this list.

Taking Precautions

An old man in his eighties got up and was putting on his coat.

His wife said, "Where are you going?" He said, "I'm going to the doctor."

And she said, "Why? Are you sick?"

"No," he said. "I'm going to get me some of those new Viagra pills."

So his wife got up out of her rocker and was putting on her sweater and he said, "Where are you going?"

She said, "I'm going to the doctor too."

He said, "Why?"

She said, "If you're going to start using that rusty old thing again, I'm going to get a tetanus shot."

The Banker's Balls

A little old lady went into the Bank of Canada one day, carrying a bag of money. She insisted that she must speak with the president of the bank to open a savings account because, "It's a lot of money!"

After much hemming and hawing, the bank staff finally ushered her into the president's office (the customer is always right!). The bank president then asked her how much she would like to deposit.

She replied, "$165,000!" and dumped the cash out of her bag onto his desk.

The president was of course curious as to how she came by all this cash, so he asked her, "Ma'am, I'm surprised you're carrying so much cash around. Where did you get this money?"

The old lady replied, "I make bets."

The president then asked, "Bets? What kind of bets?"

The old woman said, "Well, for example, I'll bet you $25,000 that your balls are square."

"Ha!" laughed the president. "That's a stupid bet. You can never win that kind of bet!" The old lady challenged, "So, would you like to take my bet?"

"Sure," said the president. "I'll bet $25,000 that my balls are not square!"

The little old lady then said, "Okay, but since there is a lot of money involved, may I bring my lawyer with me tomorrow at 10:00 a.m. as a witness?"

"Sure!" replied the confident president.

That night, the president got very nervous about the bet and spent a long time in front of a mirror checking his balls, turning from side to side, again and again. He thoroughly checked them out until he was sure that there was absolutely no way his balls were square and that he would win the bet.

The next morning, at precisely 10:00 a.m., the little old lady appeared with her lawyer at the president's office. She introduced the lawyer to the president and repeated the bet: "$25,000 says the president's balls are square!"

The president agreed with the bet again and the old lady asked him to drop his pants so they could all see. The president complied. The little old lady peered closely at his balls and then asked if she could feel them.

"Well, okay," said the president. "$25,000 is a lot of money, so I guess you should be absolutely sure." Just then, he noticed that the lawyer was quietly banging his head against the wall.

The president asked the old lady, "What the hell's the matter with your lawyer?"

She replied, "Nothing, except I bet him $100,000 that at 10 a.m. today, I'd have the Bank of Canada's president's balls in my hand."

! Unruffled

An elderly Jewish lady is leaving the garment district to go home from work. Suddenly a man who has been walking towards her stands in front of her, blocks her path, opens up his raincoat and flashes his wares in all their sordid glory.

Unruffled, she takes a look and remarks, "This you call a lining?"

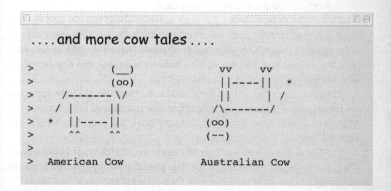

```
....and more cow tales ....

>               (___)              vv      vv
>               (oo)              ||----||   *
>      /--------\/                ||      | /
>     /  |        ||              /\-------/
>   *  ||----||                  (oo)
>      ^^        ^^               (~~)
>
>   American Cow                Australian Cow
```

Air Travel

Aer Lingus Flight 101 was flying from Heathrow to Dublin one night, with Paddy the pilot and Declan the co-pilot. As they approached Dublin airport, they looked out the front window.

"B'jeesus," said Paddy. "Will you look at how feckin short that runway is."

"Yer not feckin kiddin, Paddy," replied Declan.

"Dis is goin ter be one a' the trickiest landings you are ever goin ter see," said Paddy.

"Yer not feckin kiddin, Paddy," replied Declan.

"Right Declan. When I give the signal, you put ta engines in reverse."

"Right, I'll be doing dat."

"And ten you put the flaps down straight away."

"Right, I'll be doing dat."

"And ten you stamp on tem brakes as hard as you can."

"Right, I'll be doing dat."

"And ten you pray to ta Mother Mary with all a' your soul."

"Right, I'll be doing dat."

They approached the runway with Paddy and Declan full of nerves and sweaty palms. As soon as the wheels hit the ground, Declan put the engines in reverse, put the flaps down, stamped on the brakes and prayed to Mother Mary with all his soul.

With roaring engines, squealing tyres and lots of smoke, the plane screeched to a halt centimetres from the end of the runway, much to the relief of Paddy and Declan and everyone on board. As they sat in the cockpit regaining their composure, Paddy looked out the front window and said to Declan, "Dat has gotta be the shortest feckin runway I have EVER seen in my whole life."

Declan looked out the side window and replied, "Yeah Paddy, and the feckin widest, too."

Customer Assistance

An award should go to the United Airlines gate agent in Denver for being smart and funny, and making her point, when confronted with a passenger who probably deserved to fly as cargo.

A crowded United flight was cancelled. A single agent was rebooking a long line of inconvenienced travellers. Suddenly an angry passenger pushed his way to the desk. He slapped his ticket down on the counter and said, "I HAVE to be on this flight and it has to be FIRST CLASS."

The agent replied, "I'm sorry sir. I'll be happy to try to help you, but I've got to help these folks first, and I'm sure we'll be able to work something out."

The passenger was unimpressed. He asked loudly, so that the passengers behind him could hear, "Do you have any idea who I am?"

Without hesitating, the gate agent smiled and grabbed her public address microphone. "May I have your attention please?" she began, her voice bellowing throughout the terminal. "We have a passenger here at the gate WHO DOES NOT KNOW WHO HE IS. If anyone can help him find his identity, please come to the gate."

With the folks behind him in line laughing hysterically, the man glared at the United agent, gritted his teeth and swore, "Fuck you!"

Without flinching, she smiled and said, "I'm sorry, sir, but you'll have to stand in line for that, too."

! 📎 Lights

Thirty minutes before a plane landed, its cabin lights came on, indicating to the flight attendants that breakfast could be served.

One of the passengers, upset because he was awakened, growled, "Who turned on the fucking lights?"

"Oh, no, sir," the nearest flight attendant replied. "Those are the breakfast lights. You missed the fucking lights."

! 📎 Progress

Two moose hunters from Texas are flown into a remote lake in Alaska. They have a good hunt, and get a large moose each. When the plane returns to pick them up, the pilot looks at the animals and says, "This little plane won't lift all of us, the equipment and both of those animals – you'll have to leave one. We'd never make it over the trees to take off."

"That's baloney," says one of the hunters.

"Yeah," the other one agrees, "you're just chicken … we came out here last year and got two moose and that pilot had guts. He wasn't afraid to take off!"

The pilot gets angry and says, "Hell! If he did it, then I can do it! I can fly as well as anybody!"

They load up, taxi at full throttle and the plane almost makes it, but doesn't have the lift to clear the trees at the end of the lake. It clips the tops of the trees, flips, then breaks up, scattering the baggage, animal carcasses and passengers all through the brush.

Still alive, but hurt and dazed, the pilot sits up, shakes his head to clear it and says, "Where are we?"

One of the hunters rolls out from under a bush, looks around and says, "I'd say … about a hundred yards further than last year!"

Second Visit

The pilots of a PanAm 747 listened to the following exchange between Frankfurt Ground and a British Airways 747 (Speedbird).

Speedbird: "Good morning Frankfurt, Speedbird 206 clear of the active."
Ground: "Guten morgen. Taxi to your gate."

The BA 747 pulls onto the main taxiway and stops.

- G: "Speedbird, do you not know where you are going?"
- S: "Standby ground, I'm looking up the gate location now."
- G: (with typical German impatience) "Speedbird 206, have you never been to Frankfurt before?"
- S: (coolly) "Yes, in 1944, but I didn't stop."

Security Check

I was at the airport, checking in at the gate, when the airport employee asked,
   "Has anyone put anything in your baggage without your knowledge?"
   I said, "If it was without my knowledge, how would I know?"

He smiled and nodded knowingly, "That's why we ask."

! 🗅 Squawks

"Squawks" are problem listings that pilots generally leave for mainten-ance crews to fix before the next flight. Here are some squawks submitted by US Air Force pilots and the replies from the maintenance crews:

(P)=PROBLEM (S)=SOLUTION

(P) Left inside main tire almost needs replacement
(S) Almost replaced left inside main tire

(P) Test flight OK, except autoland very rough
(S) Autoland not installed on this aircraft

(P) #2 Propeller seeping prop fluid
(S) #2 Propeller seepage normal – #1, #3 and #4 propellers lack normal seepage

(P) Evidence of leak on right main landing gear
(S) Evidence removed

(P) Friction locks cause throttle levers to stick
(S) That's what they're there for

(P) Number three engine missing
(S) Engine found on right wing after brief search

(P) Aircraft handles funny
(S) Aircraft warned to straighten up, "fly right" and be serious

(P) Target Radar hums
(S) Reprogrammed Target Radar with the lyrics

Aladdin Updated

! Cork

Two guys are in a locker room when one guy notices the other guy has a cork in his ass.

He says, "How d'you get a cork in your ass?"

The other guy says, "I was walking along the beach and I tripped over a lamp. There was a puff of smoke and then a red man in a turban came oozing out. He said, "I am Tonto, Indian Genie. I can grant you one wish."

And the other said, "No shit."

! Lucky Sod

A guy is strolling down the street in London when he comes across an old lamp. He picks it up, rubs it vigorously, and out pops a genie. The genie offers to grant him one wish, to which the guy replies "I've always wanted to be lucky."

The genie grants his wish. So off the bloke strolls, wondering how this will change his life, when he spies £10 on the footpath. Not a bad start, he thinks. As he picks it up, he notices a betting shop across the road. He strolls over, looks through the racing lists and sees a horse named Lucky Lad at 100/1 in the 4th at Ascot. He puts the £10 on the nose, and what do you know, the horse strolls it.

Feeling on a bit of a roll, he heads to the local illegal casino, fronts up at the roulette table and puts all his winnings on "lucky seven". Round and round the wheel spins, and "bang!" – lucky seven.

Now he's really flying ... what better way to celebrate than to head to the local brothel for a bit of horizontal folk dancing. He knocks and enters, when all of a sudden he is showered with streamers and handed a glass of champagne. The madame of the establishment puts her arm around him and says, "Welcome sir! We have much pleasure in informing you that you are our lucky 1000th customer and you have won the right to enjoy the pleasures on offer from any girl who works here, absolutely free of charge."

The bloke says that he's always fancied making it with an Indian girl . . . so he's ushered into one of the rooms when in strolls the most gorgeous sub-continental he has ever seen. Not much time passes before clothing is strewn around the room and the Karma Sutra (pp 101 to 532) is being well and truly tested.

At one point the guy pauses and says to the girl, "You are one of the most beautiful women I've ever seen in my life. I can't believe how lucky I am. But there is one thing I don't really like about Indian women. I don't like that red spot that you all have on your forehead."

The Indian girl looks him in the eye and says, "Sir, I am here to please you and succumb to your every desire. If you wish to see it gone, then please scratch off my caste mark."

So the bloke goes at it with his fingernail. All of a sudden he leans back and starts killing himself laughing.

"What's wrong, what's wrong?" asks the Indian girl.

To which the bloke replies, "You're never going to believe this, but I've just won a BMW!"

The Voice

A man walks along a lonely beach.
Suddenly he hears a deep voice: DIG!
He looks around: nobody's there. I am having hallucinations, he thinks.

Then he hears the voice again: I SAID, DIG!

So he starts to dig in the sand with his bare hands and after some inches, he finds a small chest with a rusty lock.

The deep voice says: OPEN!

OK, the man thinks, lets open the thing. He finds a rock with which to destroy the lock, and when the chest is finally open, he sees a lot of gold coins.

The deep voice says: TO THE CASINO!

Well the casino is only a few miles away, so the man takes the chest and walks to the casino.

The deep voice says: ROULETTE!

So he changes all the gold into a huge pile of roulette tokens and goes to one of the tables, where the players gaze at him with disbelief.

The deep voice says: 27!

He takes the whole pile and drops it at the 27. The table nearly bursts. Everybody is quiet when the croupier throws the ball.

The ball stays at the 26.

The deep voice says: DAMN!

Amazing But True(ish)

❗ 🔖 1999 Official Darwin Awards

The Official Darwin Awards are given annually to those people who have performed the greatest service to the human gene pool – by removing themselves from it.

🗑 Living on Zionist Time

1999 Darwin Awards Winner Confirmed True by Darwin

(5 September 1999, Jerusalem) In most parts of the world, the switch away from Daylight Saving Time proceeds smoothly. But the time change raised havoc with Palestinian terrorists this year. Israel insisted on making a premature switch from Daylight Savings Time to Standard Time to accommodate a week of pre-sunrise prayers. Palestinians unequivocally refused to "live on Zionist Time".

Two weeks of scheduling havoc ensued. Nobody knew the "correct" time. At precisely 5:30 Israel time on Sunday, two coordinated car bombs exploded in different cities, killing three terrorists who were transporting the bombs. It was initially believed that the devices had been detonated prematurely by klutzy amateurs. A closer look revealed the truth behind the untimely explosions. The bombs had been prepared in a Palestine-controlled area and set on Daylight Saving Time. The confused drivers had already switched to Standard Time. When they picked up the bombs, they neglected to enquire whose watch was used to set the timing mechanism.

As a result, the cars were still en route when the explosives detonated, delivering to the terrorists their well-deserved demise.

Firefighters Ignite!

1999 Darwin Awards Runner-Up Confirmed True by Darwin

(15 July 1999, Tennessee) Seven firefighters from the Sequoyah Volunteer Fire Department, located in rural Hamilton County north of Chattanooga, decided to impress their chief by surreptitiously setting fire to a house, then heroically extinguishing the blaze. The men apparently hatched the plan in order to help Daniel, a former firefighter, return to duty.

Unfortunately, Daniel's career plans were irreversibly snuffed when he became trapped while pouring gasoline inside the house. Surrounded by smoke and flames, he was unable to escape and died inside the burning house on June 26. His six accomplices are facing 87 years in prison for conspiracy, arson and burglary.

American Sex Laws

- In the quiet town of Connorsville, Wisconsin, it's illegal for a man to shoot off a gun when his female partner has an orgasm.

- It's against the law in Willowdale, Oregon, for a husband to curse during sex.

- In Oblong, Illinois, it's punishable by law to make love while hunting or fishing on your wedding day.

- No man is allowed to make love to his wife with the smell of garlic, onions or sardines on his breath in Alexandria, Minnesota. If his wife so requests, law mandates that he must brush his teeth.

- Warn your hubby that after lovemaking in Ames, Iowa, he isn't allowed to take more than three gulps of beer while lying in bed with you – or holding you in his arms.

- Bozeman, Montana, has a law that bans all sexual activity between members of the opposite sex in the front yard of a home after sundown – if they're nude. (Apparently, if you wear socks, you're safe from the law.)

- In hotels in Sioux Falls, South Dakota, every room is required to have twin beds. And the beds must always be a minimum of two feet apart when a couple rents a room for only one night. And it's illegal to make love on the floor between the beds.

- The owner of every hotel in Hastings, Nebraska, is required to provide each guest with a clean and pressed nightshirt. No couple, even if they are married, may sleep together in the nude. Nor may they have sex unless they are wearing one of these clean, white cotton nightshirts.

- An ordinance in Newcastle, Wyoming, specifically bans couples from having sex while standing inside a store's walk-in meat freezer.

- A state law in Illinois mandates that all bachelors should be called master, not mister, when addressed by their female counterparts.

- In Norfolk, Virginia, a woman can't go out without wearing a corset. (There was a civil-service job – for men only – called a corset inspector.)

- However, in Merryville, Missouri, women are prohibited from wearing corsets because "The privilege of admiring the curvaceous, unencum-bered body of a young woman should not be denied to the normal, red-blooded American male."

- It's safe to make love while parked in Coeur d'Alene, Idaho. Police offi-cers aren't allowed to walk up and knock on the window. Any suspi-cious officer who thinks that sex is taking place must drive up from behind, honk his horn three times and wait approximately two minutes before getting out of his car to investigate.

- Another law in Helena, Montana, mandates that a woman can't dance on a table in a saloon or bar unless she has on at least three pounds, two ounces of clothing.

- Lovers in Liberty Corner, New Jersey, should avoid satisfying their lustful urges in a parked car. If the horn accidentally sounds while they are frolicking behind the wheel, the couple can face a jail term.

- In Carlsbad, New Mexico, it's legal for couples to have sex in a parked vehicle during their lunch break from work, as long as the car or van has drawn curtains to stop strangers from peeking in.

- A Florida sex law: If you're a single, divorced or widowed woman, you can't parachute on Sunday afternoons.

- Women aren't allowed to wear patent-leather shoes in Cleveland, Ohio – a man might see the reflection of something he oughtn't.

- No woman may have sex with a man while riding in an ambulance within the boundaries of Tremonton, Utah. If caught, the woman can be charged with a sexual misdemeanour and "her name is to be published in the local newspaper". The man isn't charged nor is his name revealed.

❗ 🔋 Ask a Silly Question ...

These were actual answers given on "Family Fortunes":

Name something a blind person might use – *A sword*
Name a song with moon in the title – *Blue Suede Moon*
Name a bird with a long neck – *Naomi Campbell*
Name an occupation where you need a torch – *A burglar*

Name a famous brother and sister – *Bonnie & Clyde*
Name a dangerous race – *The Arabs*
Name an item of clothing worn by the three musketeers – *A horse*
Name something that floats in the bath – *Water*
Name something that you wear on a beach – *A deckchair*
Name something red – *My cardigan*
Name a famous cowboy – *Buck Rogers*
Name a famous royal – *Mail*
Name a number you have to memorize – *7*
Name something you do before going to bed – *Sleep*
Name something you put on walls – *Roofs*
Name something in the garden that's green – *Shed*
Name something that flies and doesn't have an engine – *A bicycle with wings*
Name something you might be allergic to – *Skiing*
Name a famous bridge – *The bridge over troubled waters*
Name something a cat does – *Goes to the toilet*
Name something you do in the bathroom – *Decorate*
Name an animal you might see at the zoo – *A dog*
Name something associated with the police – *Pigs*
Name a sign of the zodiac – *April*
Name something slippery – *A conman*
Name a kind of ache – *Fillet 'O' Fish*
Name a kind of food that can be brown or white – *Potato*
Name a famous jacket potato topping – *Jam*
Name a famous Scotsman – *Jock*
Name another famous Scotsman – *Vinnie Jones*
Name something with a hole in it – *Window*
Name a non-living object with legs – *Plant*
Name a domestic animal – *Leopard*

Country & Western Classics

These are NOT made up. These are the actual titles of The Worst (or Best) Country and Western Song Titles of All Time:

1. Get Your Biscuits In The Oven And Your Buns In Bed

2. Get Your Tongue Otta My Mouth 'Cause I'm Kissing You Goodbye

3. Her Teeth Was Stained, But Her Heart Was Pure

4. How Can I Miss You If You Won't Go Away

5. I Can't Get Over You, So Why Don't You Get Under Me?

6. I Don't Know Whether To Kill Myself Or Go Bowling

7. I Got In At 2 With A 10, And Woke Up At 10 With A 2.

8. I Hate Every Bone In Your Body Except For Mine

9. I Just Bought A Car From A Guy That Stole My Girl, But The Car Don't Run, So I Figure We Got An Even Deal

10. I Keep Forgettin' I Forgot About You

11. I Liked You Better Before I Knew You So Well

12. I Still Miss You Baby, But My Aim's Gettin' Better

13. I Wouldn't Take Her To A Dog Fight, 'Cause I'm Afraid She'd Win

14. I'll Marry You Tomorrow But Let's Honeymoon Tonite

15. I'm So Miserable Without You, It's Like Having You Here

16. I've Got Tears In My Ears From Lying On My Back While I Cry Over You

17. If I Can't Be Number One In Your Life, Then Number Two On You

18. If I Had Shot You When I Wanted To, I'd Be Out By Now

19. Mama Get A Hammer (There's A Fly On Papa's Head)

20. My Head Hurts, My Feet Stink And I Don't Love Jesus

21. My Wife Ran Off With My Best Friend, And I Sure Do Miss Him

22. Please Bypass This Heart

23. She Got The Ring And I Got The Finger

24. You're The Reason Our Kids Are So Ugly

! Directory Enquiries

The following are real conversations Directory Enquiries operators had with callers, as revealed in interviews with staff at the Cardiff Telecomms Directory Enquiries Centre.

C = Caller; O = Operator.

C: I'd like the number of the Argoed Fish Bar in Cardiff, please.
O: I'm sorry, there's no listing. Is the spelling correct?
C: Well, it used to be called the Bargoed Fish Bar but the B fell off.

C: I'd like the number of the Scottish knitwear company in Woven.
O: I can't find a town called 'Woven'? Are you sure?
C: Yes. That's what it says on the label – Woven in Scotland.

C: I'd like the RSPCA please.
O: Where are you calling from?
C: The living room.

C: The water board please.
O: Which department?
C: Tap water.

O: How are you spelling that?
C: With letters.

C: I'd like the number for a reverend in Cardiff, please.
O: Do you have his name?
C: No, but he has a dog named Ben.

C: The Union of Shopkeepers and Alligators please.
O: You mean the Amalgamated Union of Shopkeepers?
C: Er, yes.

and finally,

On one occasion, a man making heavy breathing sounds from a phone box told the worried operator: "I haven't got a pen so I'm steaming up the window to write the number on."

! Doctors' Notes

AMERICAN DOCTORS' NOTES ON PATIENTS' CHARTS (ACTUAL NOTES – UNEDITED!):

1. Patient has chest pain if she lies on her left side for over a year.

2. On the 2nd day the knee was better and on the 3rd day it disappeared completely.

3. She has had no rigors or shaking chills, but her husband states she was very hot in bed last night.

4. The patient has been depressed ever since she began seeing me in 1993.

5. The patient is tearful and crying constantly. She also appears to be depressed.

6. Discharge status: Alive but without permission.

7. Healthy appearing decrepit 69-year-old male, mentally alert but forgetful.

8. The patient refused an autopsy.

9. The patient has no past history of suicides.

10. Patient has left his white blood cells at another hospital.

11. Patient's past medical history has been remarkably insignificant with only a 40-pound weight gain in the past three days.

12. Patient had waffles for breakfast and anorexia for lunch.

13. Between you and me, we ought to be able to get this lady pregnant.

14. Since she can't get pregnant with her husband, I thought you might like to work her up.

15. She is numb from her toes down.

16. While in the ER, she was examined, X-rated and sent home.

17. Occasional, constant, infrequent headaches.

18. Patient was alert and unresponsive.

19. Rectal exam revealed a normal-size thyroid.

20. She stated that she had been constipated for most of her life, until she got a divorce.

21. I saw your patient today, who is still under our car for physical therapy.

22. Patient was seen in consultation by Dr X, who felt we should sit on the abdomen and I agree.

23. Large brown stool ambulating in the hall.

24. Patient has two teenage children, but no other abnormalities.

25. Patient appears responsive, but unable to communicate with me.

26. Bladder is under control, but cannot stop urine from seeping.

27. Heart problem is fixed. Patient died at 10:07 this morning.

28. Complains of chest pain occasionally. Otherwise just a pain.

29. Patient is always telling me about her pains and problems. This remains a significant pain to me.

30. The blood work-up showed no antibodies present. Need the rest of the blood to be sure, however.

31. If it weren't for the fact that the patient is dead, I would say he was in perfect health.

32. Testicles are missing on this woman.

Hong Kong Subtitles

The following are actual English subtitles used in films from Hong Kong:

- I am darn unsatisfied to be killed in this way.
- Fatty, you with your thick face have hurt my instep.
- Gun wounds again?
- Same old rules: no eyes, no groin.
- A normal person wouldn't steal pituitaries.
- Darn, I'll burn you into a BBQ chicken.

- Take my advice, or I'll spank you a lot.
- Who gave you the nerve to get killed here?
- This will be of fine service for you, you bag of the scum. I am sure you will not mind that I remove your toenails and leave them out on the dessert floor for ants to eat.
- Quiet or I'll blow your throat up.
- I'll fire aimlessly if you don't come out!
- You daring lousy guy.
- Beat him out of recognizable shape!
- Yah-hah, evil spider woman! I have captured you by the short rabbits and can now deliver you violently to your doctor for a thorough extermination.
- I have been scared silly too much lately.
- I got knife scars more than the number of your leg's hair!
- Beware! Your bones are going to be disconnected.
- The bullets inside are very hot. Why do I feel so cold?
- How can you use my intestines as a gift?
- Greetings, large black person. Let us not forget to form a team up together and go into the country to inflict the pain of our karate feets on some but of the giant lizard person.
- You always use violence. I should've ordered glutinous rice chicken.

How to Get a McJob

This is an actual job application someone submitted at a McDonald's fast-food establishment AND THEY HIRED HIM!

NAME: Greg Bulmash

DESIRED POSITION: Reclining. HA! But seriously, whatever's available. If I was in a position to be picky, I wouldn't be applying here in the first place.

DESIRED SALARY: $185,000 a year plus stock options and a Michael Ovitz-style severance package. If that's not possible, make an offer and we can haggle.

EDUCATION: Yes.

LAST POSITION HELD: Target for middle management hostility.

SALARY: Less than I'm worth.

MOST NOTABLE ACHIEVEMENT: My incredible collection of stolen pens and post-it notes.

REASON FOR LEAVING: It sucked.

HOURS AVAILABLE TO WORK: Any.

PREFERRED HOURS: 1:30-3:30 p.m., Monday, Tuesday and Thursday.

DO YOU HAVE ANY SPECIAL SKILLS?: Yes, but they're better suited to a more intimate environment.

MAY WE CONTACT YOUR CURRENT EMPLOYER?: If I had one, would I be here?

DO YOU HAVE ANY PHYSICAL CONDITIONS THAT WOULD PROHIBIT YOU FROM LIFTING UP TO 50 LBS?: Of what?

DO YOU HAVE A CAR?: I think the more appropriate question here would be "Do you have a car that runs?"

HAVE YOU RECEIVED ANY SPECIAL AWARDS OR RECOGNITION?: I may already be a winner of the Readers Digest Prize Draw.

DO YOU SMOKE?: Only when set on fire.

WHAT WOULD YOU LIKE TO BE DOING IN FIVE YEARS?: Living in the Bahamas with a fabulously wealthy supermodel who thinks I'm the greatest thing since sliced bread.

Actually, I'd like to be doing that now.

DO YOU CERTIFY THAT THE ABOVE IS TRUE AND COMPLETE TO THE BEST OF YOUR KNOWLEDGE?: No, but I dare you to prove otherwise.

SIGN HERE: Scorpio with Libra rising.

! Law and Order Around the World

It's the law ...

Most Middle Eastern countries recognize the following Islamic law: "After having sexual relations with a lamb, it is a mortal sin to eat its flesh."

- In Lebanon, men are legally allowed to have sex with animals, but the animals must be female. Having sexual relations with a male animal is punishable by death.
- In Bahrain, a male doctor may legally examine a woman's genitals, but is forbidden from looking directly at them during the examination. He may only see their reflection in a mirror.
- Muslims are banned from looking at the genitals of a corpse. This also applies to undertakers; the sex organs of the deceased must be covered with a brick or piece of wood at all times.
- The penalty for masturbation in Indonesia is decapitation.
- There are men in Guam whose full-time job is to travel the countryside and deflower young virgins, who pay them for the privilege of having sex for the first time. Reason: under Guam law, it is expressly forbidden for virgins to marry.
- In Hong Kong, a betrayed wife is legally allowed to kill her adulterous husband, but may only do so with her bare hands. (The husband's lover, on the other hand, may be killed in any manner desired.)
- Topless saleswomen are legal in Liverpool, England – but only in tropical fish stores.

- In Cali, Colombia, a woman may only have sex with her husband, and the first time this happens her mother must be in the room to witness the act.
- In Santa Cruz, Bolivia, it is illegal for a man to have sex with a woman and her daughter at the same time.
- In Maryland, it is illegal to sell condoms from vending machines with one exception: prophylactics may be dispensed from a vending machine only "in places where alcoholic beverages are sold for consumption on the premises."

! 📎 Letters to Hackney Council

Can you please tell me when our repairs are going to be done as my wife is about to become an expectant mother.

I want some repairs doing to my cooker as it backfired and burnt my knob off.

The toilet is blocked and we can't bath the children until it is cleared.

The man next door has a large erection in his back garden which is unsightly and dangerous.

Will you please send someone to mend our broken path as my wife tripped and fell on it and she is now pregnant.

Our kitchen floor is very damp and we have two children and we would like a third so will you please send somebody round to do something about it.

Would you please repair our toilet. My son pulled the chain and the box fell on his head.

Mrs Smith has no clothes and has had none for over a year. The clergy have been visiting her.

I need money to buy special medicine for my husband as he is unable to masturbate his food.

In reply to your letter, I have already cohabited with your officer with no results so far.

I am pleased to inform you that my husband, who was reported missing, is dead.

Mrs Adams has asked me to collect her money as she is going into hospital to have her overtures out

Sir, I am forwarding my marriage certificate and two children – one of which is a mistake as you will see.

My husband is diabetic and has to take insolence regular but he finds he is lethargic to it.

Unless I get my husband's maintenance money soon, I shall be obliged to live an immortal life.

The children have been off school because there is a lot of measles about and I had them humanized.

You have changed my little boy into a little girl. Will this matter?

Please forward my money at once as I have fallen into errors with my landlord and the milkman.

Mrs Brown only THINKS she is ill, but believe me she is nothing but a hypodermic.

In accordance with your instructions, I have given birth to twins in the enclosed envelope.

I want my sick pay quick. I have been in bed under the doctor for a week and he is doing me no good. If things don't improve, I shall get another doctor.

I do not get any money from my son. He is in the army and his regiment is at present manuring on Salisbury plain.

Milk is wanted for my baby and the father is unable to supply it.

Re your dental enquiry. The teeth on top are alright but those on my bottom are hurting dreadfully.

I am very annoyed to find you have branded my son illiterate. This is a lie as I married his father a week before he was born.

I am sorry I omitted to put down all my children's names. This was due to contraceptional circumstances.

I wish to complain that my father hurt his ankle very badly when he put his foot in the hole in his back passage.

The lavatory is blocked. This is caused by the boys next door throwing balls on the roof.

This is to let you know there is a smell coming from the man next door.

The toilet seat is cracked – where do I stand?

! 📎 Lie Detector

Police in Radnor, Pennsylvania, interrogated a suspect by placing a metal colander on his head and connecting it with wires to a photocopy machine.

The message "He's lying" was placed in the copier, and police pressed the copy button each time they thought the suspect wasn't telling the truth.

Believing the "lie detector" was working, the suspect confessed.

! 🔟 News from Africa

🗑 The *Cape Times* (Cape Town):

"I have promised to keep his identity confidential," said Jack Maxim, a spokeswoman for the Sandton Sun Hotel, Johannesburg, "but I can confirm that he is no longer in our employment. We asked him to clean the lifts and he spent four days on the job. When I asked him why, he replied: 'Well, there are forty of them, two on each floor, and sometimes some of them aren't there.' Eventually, we realized that he thought each floor had a different lift, and he'd cleaned the same two twelve times. We had to let him go. It seemed best all round. I understand he is now working for Woolworths."

🗑 The *Star* (Johannesburg):

"The situation is absolutely under control," Transport Minister Ephraem Magagula told the Swaziland parliament in Mbabane. "Our nation's merchant navy is perfectly safe. We just don't know where it is, that's all." Replying to an MP's question, Minister Magagula admitted that the land-locked country had completely lost track of its only ship, the Swazimar: "We believe it is in a sea somewhere. At one time, we sent a team of men to look for it, but there was a problem with drink and they failed to find it, and so, technically, yes, we've lost it a bit. But I categorically reject all suggestions of incompetence on the part of this government. The Swazimar is a big ship painted in the sort of nice bright colours you can see at night. Mark my words, it will turn up. The right honourable gentleman opposite is a very naughty man, and he will laugh on the other side of his face when my ship comes in."

🗑 The *Standard* (Kenya):

"What is all the fuss about?" Weseka Sambu asked a hastily convened news conference at Jomo Kenyatta International Airport.

"A technical hitch like this could have happened anywhere in the world. You people are not patriots. You just want to cause trouble." Sambu, a spokesman for Kenya Airways, was speaking after the cancellation of a through flight from Kisumu, via Jomo Kenyatta, to Berlin.

"The forty-two passengers had boarded the plane ready for take-off, when the pilot noticed one of the tyres was flat. Kenya Airways did not possess a spare tyre, and unfortunately the airport nitrogen canister was empty. A passenger suggested taking the tyre to a petrol station for inflation, but unluckily the jack had gone missing so we couldn't get the wheel off. Our engineers tried heroically to reinflate the tyre with a bicycle pump, but had no luck, and the pilot even blew into the valve with his mouth, but he passed out. When I announced that the flight had to be abandoned, one of the passengers, Mr Mutu, suddenly struck me about the face with a life-jacket whistle and said we were a national disgrace. I told him he was being ridiculous, and that there was to be another flight in a fortnight. And, in the meantime, he would be able to enjoy the scenery around Kisumu, albeit at his own expense."

❗ 📎 Oh Bugger

From the *London Evening Standard*:

A drunk who claimed he had been raped by a dog was yesterday jailed for 12 months by a judge. Martin Hoyle, 45, was arrested by police after a passing motorist and his girlfriend found a Staffordshire bull terrier, called Badger, having sex with him at the side of a road in Highgate, North London.

Prosecutor Ben Crosland said the couple had stopped to help because they thought Hoyle was being attacked by the animal. But when they got closer they saw that he had his trousers round his ankles, was down on all fours and the dog was straddling him from behind.

"The defendant mumbled something about the dog having taken a liking to him," said Mr Crosland. "The couple were extremely offended and sickened by what they saw." Another passing motorist contacted the police and Hoyle was arrested as he walked with the dog down the road. Hoyle, of Finchley Road, Highgate, told police "I can't help it if the dog took a liking to me. He tried to rape me."

He repeated the rape allegation at the police station and added "The dog pulled my trousers down." Hoyle, who has had a long-standing alcohol problem, was jailed for 12 months after he admitted committing an act which outraged public decency. His barrister said Hoyle had no memory of the incident because of his drunken state, but was now very remorseful and incredibly embarrassed.

Jailing him, Judge Alistair McCallum told Hoyle "Never before in my time at the bar or on the bench have I ever had to deal with somebody who voluntarily allowed himself to be buggered by a dog on the public highway. Frankly it is beyond most of our comprehension. It is an absolutely disgusting thing for members of the public to have to witness."

! Performance Evaluations

THESE QUOTES WERE TAKEN FROM ACTUAL
PERFORMANCE EVALUATIONS:

1. "This associate is really not so much of a has-been, but more of a definitely won't be."
2. "This young lady has delusions of adequacy."

3. "When she opens her mouth, it seems that this is only to change whichever foot was previously in there."

THESE ARE ACTUAL LINES FROM MILITARY PERFORMANCE APPRAISALS:

1. Got into the gene pool while the lifeguard wasn't watching.
2. A room temperature IQ.
3. Got a full 6-pack, but lacks the plastic thingy to hold it all together.
4. A gross ignoramus – 144 times worse than an ordinary ignoramus.
5. A photographic memory but with the lens cover glued on.
6. As bright as Alaska in December.
7. Gates are down, the lights are flashing, but the train isn't coming.
8. He's so dense, light bends around him.
9. If he were any more stupid, he'd have to be watered twice a week.
10. It's hard to believe that he beat 1,000,000 other sperm.
11. Takes him 2 hours to watch 60 minutes.
12. Wheel is turning, but the hamster is dead.

Presidential Quiz

>> A – Bill Clinton   E – Lyndon B. Johnson
>> B – Warren G. Harding   F – John F. Kennedy
>> C – Andrew Jackson   G – Franklin D. Roosevelt
>> D – Thomas Jefferson   H – George Washington

1. Which president smoked marijuana with a nude playgirl while he joked about being too wasted to "push the button" in case of nuclear attack?
2. Which president allegedly had affairs with both a winner AND a finalist in the Miss America pageant?

3. Which president had sex with one of his secretaries stretched out atop a desk in the Oval Office?

4. Which president allegedly had an affair (as well as children) with a slave who was his wife's half sister?

5. Which president called his mistress "Pookie"?

6. Which president married a woman who hadn't yet divorced her first husband, and was branded an "adulterer" during his re-election campaign?

7. Which future president wrote love letters to his neighbour's wife while he was engaged to someone else?

8. Which president had a torrid affair with the first lady's personal secretary?

9. Which president had sex with a young woman in a White House coat closet – at one point, while a secret service agent prevented the hysterical first lady from attacking them?

10. Which president had sex in a closet while telling his partner about the "other" president who did the same in a closet? (The one from Question 9)

11. Which vice president was ticked off because he felt that HIS record of sexual conquests was much more "impressive" (i.e. numerous) than the president's?

12. Which future president, while a college student, enjoyed showing off his penis (which he named Jumbo)?

ANSWERS

>>	1. F	4. D	7. H, E	10. F
>>	2. A	5. A	8. G, F	11. E
>>	3. E	6. C	9. B	12. E

>>

>>

⚠ 📎 Questions of Paternity

The following are all replies on Child Support Agency forms in the section for listing father's details:

Regarding the identity of the father of my twins, child A was fathered by [name removed]. I am unsure as to the identity of the father of child B, but I believe that he was conceived on the same night.

I am unsure as to the identity of the father of my child as I was being sick out of a window when taken unexpectedly from behind. I can provide you with a list of names of men that I think were at the party if this helps.

I do not know the name of the father of my little girl. She was conceived at a party [address and date given] where I had unprotected sex with a man I met that night. I do remember that the sex was so good that I fainted. If you do manage to track down the father can you send me his phone number? Thanks.

....and more cow tales ....

```
>              (__)                        (o o)
>              (oo)                 (-----) \ /
>      /-------- VV                /  / \    o
>    / |        ||               *  | o |
>  *  ||----||                      -----
>     ^^      ^^
>
>  Cownt Dracula                 Phone Bull
```

I don't know the identity of the father of my daughter. He drives a BMW that now has a hole made by my stiletto in one of the door panels. Perhaps you can contact BMW service stations in this area and see if he's had it replaced.

I have never had sex with a man. I am awaiting a letter from the Pope confirming that my son's conception was immaculate and that he is Christ risen again.

I cannot tell you the name of child A's dad as he informs me that to do so would blow his cover and that would have cataclysmic implications for the British economy. I am torn between doing right by you and right by my country. Please advise.

I do not know who the father of my child was as all squaddies look the same to me. I can confirm that he was a Royal Green Jacket.

[Name given] is the father of child A. If you do catch up with him can you ask him what he did with my AC/DC CDs?

From the dates it seems that my daughter was conceived at Euro Disney, maybe it really is the Magic Kingdom.

So much about that night is a blur. The only thing that I remember for sure is Delia Smith did a programme about eggs earlier in the evening. If I'd have stayed in and watched more TV rather than going to the party at [address given] mine might have remained unfertilized.

! 📎 Smithsonian Letter

The story behind the letter below is that there is a person in Newport, Rhode Island named Scott Williams, who digs things out of his backyard and sends the stuff he finds to the Smithsonian Institute, labeling them with scientific names, insisting that they are actual archaeological finds.

This guy really exists and does this in his spare time!

Anyway ... here's the actual response from the Smithsonian Institute. Bear this in mind next time you think you are challenged in your duty to respond to a difficult situation in writing

----

Smithsonian Institute
207 Pennsylvania Avenue
Washington, DC 20078

Dear Mr Williams,

Thank you for your latest submission to the Institute, labelled "93211-D, layer seven, next to the clothesline post ... Hominid skull." We have given this specimen a careful and detailed examination, and regret to inform you that we disagree with your theory that it represents conclusive proof of the presence of Early Man in Charleston County two million years ago.

Rather, it appears that what you have found is the head of a Barbie doll, of the variety that one of our staff, who has small children, believes to be "Malibu Barbie". It is evident that you have given a great deal of thought to the analysis of this specimen, and you may be quite certain that those of us who are familiar with your prior work in the field were loathe to come to contradiction with your findings.

However, we do feel that there are a number of physical attributes of the specimen, which might have tipped you off to its modern origin:

1. The material is molded plastic. Ancient hominid remains are typically fossilized bone.

2. The cranial capacity of the specimen is approximately 9 cubic

centimeters, well below the threshold of even the earliest identified proto-hominids.

3. The dentition pattern evident on the skull is more consistent with the common domesticated dog than it is with the ravenous man-eating Pliocene clams you speculate roamed the wetlands during that time.

This latter finding is certainly one of the most intriguing hypotheses you have submitted in your history with this institution, but the evidence seems to weigh rather heavily against it. Without going into too much detail, let us say that:

A. The specimen looks like the head of a Barbie doll that a dog has chewed on.

B. Clams don't have teeth.

It is with feelings tinged with melancholy that we must deny your request to have the specimen carbon-dated. This is partially due to the heavy load our lab must bear in its normal operation, and partly due to carbon-dating's notorious inaccuracy in fossils of recent geologic record. To the best of our knowledge, no Barbie dolls were produced prior to 1956AD, and carbon-dating is likely to produce wildly inaccurate results.

Sadly, we must also deny your request that we approach the National Science Foundation Phylogeny Department with the concept of assigning your specimen the scientific name Australopithecus spiff-arino.

Speaking personally, I, for one, fought tenaciously for the acceptance of your proposed taxonomy, but was ultimately voted down because the species name you selected was hyphenated, and didn't really sound like it might be Latin. However, we gladly accept your generous donation of this fascinating specimen to the museum. While it is undoubtedly not a Hominid fossil, it is, nonetheless, yet another riveting example of the great body of work you seem to accumulate here so effortlessly. You should know that our Director has reserved a special shelf in his own office for the display of the specimens you have previously submitted to the Institution, and the entire staff speculates daily on what you will happen upon next in your digs at the site you have discovered in your Newport back yard.

We eagerly anticipate your trip to our nation's capital that you proposed in your last letter, and several of us are pressing the Director to pay for it. We are particularly interested in hearing you expand on your theories surrounding the trans-positating fillifitation of ferrous metal in a structural matrix that makes the excellent juvenile Tyrannosaurus rex femur you recently discovered take on the deceptive appearance of a rusty 9-mm Sears Craftsman automotive crescent wrench.

Yours in Science,

Harvey Rowe
Chief Curator – Antiquities

Strange News

From the *Gloucester Citizen*:
A sex line caller complained to Trading Standards. After dialling an 0891 number from an advertisement entitled "Hear Me Moan" the caller was played a tape of a woman nagging her husband for failing to do jobs around the house. Consumer Watchdogs in Dorset refused to look into the complaint, saying, "He got what he deserved."

From the *Guardian*:
After being charged £20 for a £10 overdraft, 30-year-old Michael Howard of Leeds changed his name by deed poll to "Yorkshire Bank Plc are Fascist Bastards". The Bank has now asked him to close his account, and

Mr Bastards has asked them to repay the 69p balance by cheque, made out in his new name.

Phreakers, or 'phone hackers, managed to break into the telephone system of Weight Watchers in Glasgow, and changed the outgoing message to "Hello, you fat bastard".

From the *Churchdown Parish Magazine*:
Would the Congregation please note that the bowl at the back of the Church, labelled "For The Sick", is for monetary donations only.

From the *Guardian* concerning a sign seen in a police canteen in Christchurch, New Zealand:

"Will the person who took a slice of cake from the Commissioner's Office return it immediately. It is needed as evidence in a poisoning case."

From *The Times*:
A young girl, who was blown out to sea on a set of inflatable teeth, was rescued by a man on an inflatable lobster. A coast-guard spokesman commented: "This sort of thing is all too common these days."

From the Scottish *Big Issue*:
In Sydney, 120 men named Henry attacked each other during a "My Name is Henry" convention. Henry Pantie of Canberra accused Henry Pap of Sydney of not being a Henry at all, but in fact an Angus. "It was a lie," explained Mr Pap. "I'm a Henry and always will be." Whereupon Henry Pap attacked Henry Pantie, whilst two other Henrys – Jones and Dyer – attempted to pull them apart. Several more Henrys – Smith, Calderwood and Andrews – became involved and soon the entire convention descended into a giant fist fight. The brawl was eventually broken up by riot police, led by a man named Shane.

From the *Daily Telegraph* in a piece headed "Brussels Pays 200,000 Pounds to Save Prostitutes":

" … the money will not be going directly into the prostitutes' pocket, but will be used to encourage them to lead a better life. We will be training them for new positions in hotels."

From the *Derby Abbey Community News*

"We apologize for the error in the last edition, in which we stated that 'Mr Fred Nicolme is a Defective in the Police Force.' This was a typographical error. We meant of course that Mr Nicolme is a Detective in the Police Farce."

From the *Manchester Evening News*:

Police called to arrest a naked man on the platform at Piccadilly Station released their suspect after he produced a valid rail ticket.

! The Deadly Substance

A student at Eagle Rock Junior High won first prize at the Greater Idaho Falls Science Fair, April 26. He was attempting to show how conditioned we have become to alarmists practising junk science and spreading fear of everything in our environment. In his project he urged people to sign a petition demanding strict control or total elimination of the chemical "dihydrogen monoxide". And for plenty of good reasons, since:

1. it can cause excessive sweating and vomiting
2. it is a major component in acid rain
3. it can cause severe burns in its gaseous state
4. accidental inhalation can kill you
5. it contributes to erosion
6. it decreases effectiveness of automobile brakes
7. it has been found in tumours of terminal cancer patients

He asked 50 people if they supported a ban of the chemical.

Forty-three (43) said yes.

Six (6) were undecided.

Only one (1) knew that the chemical was water.

The title of his prize-winning project was, "How Gullible Are We?"

He feels the conclusion is obvious.

The Edward Bulwer-Lytton Prize

The Edward Bulwer-Lytton prize is awarded every year to the author of the worst possible opening line of a book. This has been so successful that Penguin now publishes five books-worth of entries. Some recent winners:

"As a scientist, Throckmorton knew that if he were ever to break wind in the sound chamber he would never hear the end of it."

"Just beyond the Narrows the river widens."

"With a curvaceous figure that Venus would have envied, a tanned, unblemished, oval face framed with lustrous, thick, brown hair, deep azure-blue eyes fringed with long black lashes, perfect teeth that vied for competition and a small straight nose, Marilee had a beauty that defied description."

"Andre, a simple peasant, had only one thing on his mind as he crept along the east wall: 'Andre creep … Andre creep … Andre creep.'"

"Stanislaus Smedley, a man always on the cutting edge of narcissism, was about to give his body and soul to a back-alley sex-change surgeon – to become the woman he loved."

"Although Sarah had an abnormal fear of mice, it did not keep her from seeking out a living at a local pet store."

"Stanley looked quite bored and somewhat detached, but then penguins often do."

"Like an overripe beefsteak tomato rimmed with cottage cheese, the corpulent remains of Santa Claus lay dead on the hotel floor."

"Mike Hardware was the kind of private eye who didn't know the meaning of the word 'fear', a man who could laugh in the face of danger and spit in the eye of death – in short, a moron with suicidal tendencies."

AND THE BEST OF ALL:
"The sun oozed over the horizon, shoved aside darkness, crept along the greensward and, with sickly fingers, pushed through the castle window, revealing the pillaged princess, hand at throat, crown asunder, gaping in frenzied horror at the sated, sodden amphibian lying beside her, disbelieving the magnitude of the toad's deception, screaming madly, 'You lied!'"

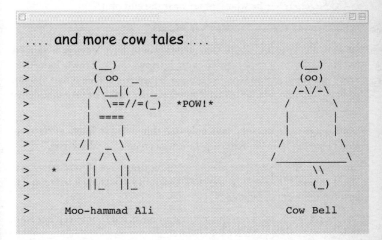

```
.... and more cow tales ....

>             (__)                              (__)
>            (  oo    _                         (oo)
>            /\__|( ) _                         /-\/-\
>           |   \==//=(_)   *POW!*             /        \
>           |   ====                          |          |
>           |     |                           |          |
>          /|   _  \                          /           \
>         /  /  / \ \                        /_____\
>    *    ||    ||                                \\
>         ||_   ||_                                (_)
>
>      Moo-hammad Ali                         Cow Bell
```

! 🔟 The Sweet Little Old Lady's Radio

Here's a heartwarming story. Someone who teaches at a Middle School in Safety Harbor, Florida forwarded the following letter. The letter was sent to the principal's office after the school had sponsored a luncheon for the elderly. This story is a credit to all human kind.

Dear Safety Harbor Middle School,

God blesses you for the beautiful radio I won at your recent senior citizens' luncheon. I am 84 years old and live at the Safety Harbor Assisted Home for the Aged. All of my family has passed away. It's nice to know that someone really thinks of me. God blesses you for your kindness to an old, forgotten lady.

My roommate is 95 and always had her own radio, but would never let me listen to it, even when she was napping. The other day her radio fell off the night stand and broke into a lot of pieces. It was awful and she was in tears.

She asked if she could listen to mine, and I said fuck you.

Sincerely,

Edna Johnston

>>
>>
>>
>>
>>
>>

! The Wgasa Monorail

Some years ago, the famous San Diego Zoo opened a second, larger branch called the San Diego Wild Animal Park. The Park is built around an enormous open-field enclosure where the animals roam free. To see the animals, visitors ride on a monorail called the Wgasa Bush Line which circles the enclosure. Here's the true story of how the Wgasa Bush Line got its name.

They wanted to give the monorail a jazzy, African-sounding name. So they sent out a memo to a bunch of zoo staffers saying, "What shall we call the monorail at the Wild Animal Park?" One of the memos came back with "WGASA" written on the bottom. The planners loved it and the rest is history.

What the planners didn't know was that the zoo staffer had not intended to suggest a name. He was using an acronym which was popular at the time. It stood for "Who Gives A Shit Anyhow?"

! Witless Witnesses, Airhead Attorneys

Now doctor, isn't it true that when a person dies in his sleep, he doesn't know about it until the next morning?

Were you present when your picture was taken?

Was it you or your younger brother who was killed in the war?

How far apart were the vehicles at the time of the collision?

You were there until the time you left, is that true?

How many times have you committed suicide?

Q: So the date of conception (of the baby) was August 8th?
A: Yes.
Q: And what were you doing at that time?

Q: You say the stairs went down to the basement?
A: Yes.
Q: And these stairs, did they go up also?

Q: How was your first marriage terminated?
A: By death.
Q: And by whose death was it terminated?

Q: Can you describe the individual?
A: He was about medium height and had a beard.
Q: Was this a male, or a female?

Q: Is your appearance here this morning pursuant to a deposition notice which I sent to your attorney?
A: No, this is how I dress when I go to work.

Q: Doctor, how many autopsies have you performed on dead people?
A: All my autopsies are performed on dead people.

Q: All your responses must be oral, OK? What school did you go to?
A: Oral.

Q: Do you recall the time that you examined the body?
A: The autopsy started around 8:30 p.m.
Q: And Mr Dennington was dead at the time?
A: No, he was sitting on the table wondering why I was doing an autopsy.

Q: You were not shot in the fracas?
A: No, I was shot midway between the fracas and the navel.

Q: Are you qualified to give a urine sample?
A: I have been since early childhood.

Q: Doctor, before you performed the autopsy, did you check for a pulse?
A: No.
Q: Did you check for blood pressure?
A: No.
Q: Did you check for breathing?
A: No.
Q: So, then it is possible that the patient was alive when you began the autopsy?
A: No.
Q: How can you be so sure, Doctor?
A: Because his brain was sitting on my desk in a jar.
Q: But could the patient have still been alive nevertheless?
A: It is possible that he could have been alive and practising law somewhere.

Q: What gear were you in at the moment of the impact?
A: Gucci sweats and Reeboks.

Q: This myasthenia gravis – does it affect your memory at all?
A: Yes.
Q: And in what ways does it affect your memory?
A: I forget.
Q: You forget. Can you give us an example of something that you've forgotten?

Q: How old is your son – the one living with you.
A: Thirty-eight or thirty-five, I can't remember which.
Q: How long has he lived with you?
A: Forty-five years.

Q: And where was the location of the accident?
A: Approximately milepost 499.
Q: And where is milepost 499?
A: Probably between milepost 498 and 500.

Q: Do you know if your daughter has ever been involved in the voodoo or occult?

A: We both do.

Q: Voodoo?

A: We do.

Q: You do?

A: Yes, voodoo.

Q: Trooper, when you stopped the defendant, were your red and blue lights flashing?

A: Yes.

Q: Did the defendant say anything when she got out of her car?

A: Yes, sir.

Q: What did she say?

A: What disco am I at?

Q: Did he kill you?

LAWYER: What did the tissue samples taken from the victim's vagina show?

WITNESS: There were traces of semen.

L: Male semen?

W: That's the only kind I know of.

LAWYER: Did you ever sleep with him in New York?

WITNESS: I refuse to answer that question.

L: Did you ever sleep with him in Chicago?

W: I refuse to answer that question.

L: Did you ever sleep with him in Miami?

W: No.

LAWYER: So, after the anaesthetic, when you came out of it, what did you observe with respect to your scalp?

WITNESS: I didn't see my scalp the whole time I was in the hospital.

L: It was covered?

W: Yes. Bandaged.

L: Then, later on, what did you see?

W: I had a skin graft. My whole buttocks and leg were removed and put on top of my head.

CLERK: Please repeat after me, "I swear by Almighty God ..."

WITNESS: "I swear by Almighty God."

C: "That the evidence that I give ..."

W: That's right.

C: Repeat it.

W: "Repeat it".

C: No! Repeat what I said.

W: What you said when?

C: "That the evidence that I give ..."

W: "That the evidence that I give."

C: "Shall be the truth and ..."

W: It will, and nothing but the truth!

C: Please, just repeat after me, "Shall be the truth and ..."

W: I'm not a scholar, you know.

C: We can appreciate that. Just repeat after me: "Shall be the truth and ..."

W: "Shall be the truth and."

C: Say, "Nothing ...".

W: Okay. (Witness remains silent.)

C: No! Don't say nothing. Say, "Nothing but the truth ..."

W: Yes.

C: Can't you say, "Nothing but the truth ..."?

W: Yes.

C: Well? Do so.

W: You're confusing me.

C: Just say: "Nothing but the truth ...".

W: Okay. I understand.

C: Then say it.

W: What?

C: "Nothing but the truth ..."

W: But I do! That's just it.

C: You must say: "Nothing but the truth ..."

W: I WILL say nothing but the truth!

C: Please, just repeat these four words: "Nothing", "But", "The", "Truth".

W: What? You mean, like, now?

C: Yes! Now. Please. Just say those four words.

W: "Nothing. But. The. Truth."

C: Thank you.

W: I'm just not a scholar.

LAWYER: On the morning of July 25th, did you walk from the farmhouse down the footpath to the cowshed?

WITNESS: I did.

L: And as a result, you passed within a few yards of the duck pond?

W: I did.

L: And did you observe anything?

W: I did. (Witness remains silent.)

L: Well, could you tell the Court what you saw?

W: I saw George.

L: You saw George *******, the defendant in this case?

W: Yes.

L: Can you tell the Court what George ******* was doing?

W: Yes. (Witness remains silent.)

L: Well, would you kindly do so?

W: He had his thing stuck into one of the ducks.

L: His "thing"?

W: You know ... His thing. His di ... I mean, his penis.

L: You passed close by the duck pond, the light was good, you were sober, you have good eyesight, and you saw this clearly?

W: Yes.

L: Did you say anything to him?

W: Of course I did!

L: What did you say to him?

W: "Morning, George."

! World Standard

The International Standards Organization (ISO) and the International Electrotechnical Commission (IEC) designated Oct. 14 as World Standards Day to recognize those volunteers who have worked hard to define international standards.

The United States celebrated World Standards Day on Oct. 11; Finland celebrated on Oct. 13; and Italy celebrated on Oct. 18.

Booze and Boozers

! 0 A Terrible Mistake

A drunk staggers into a church and sits down in a confessional and says nothing. The bewildered priest coughs to attract his attention, but still the man says nothing. The priest knocks on the wall three times in a final attempt to get the man to speak. The drunk replies, "No use knockin' mate, there's no paper in this one either!"

! 0 Double Martinis

A businessman enters a tavern, sits down at the bar, and orders a double martini on the rocks. After he finishes the drink, he peeks inside his shirt pocket, then he orders the bartender to prepare another double martini. After he finishes that one, he again peeks inside his shirt pocket and orders the bartender to bring another double martini.

The bartender says, "Look, buddy, I'll bring ya martinis all night long. But you gotta tell me why you look inside your shirt pocket before you order a refill."

The customer replies, "I'm peeking at a photo of my wife. When she starts to look good, then I know it's time to go home."

! 0 Drinking Contest

A Texan walks into O'Malley's pub in Ireland and clears his voice to the crowd of drinkers. He says, "I hear you Irish are a bunch of drinkin' motherfuckers. I'll give $500 American dollars to anybody in here who can drink 10 pints of Guinness back-to-back." The room is quiet and no one takes the Texan's offer. One man – an Irishman – even leaves.

30 minutes later the same gentleman who left shows back up and taps the Texan on the shoulder.

"Is your bet still good?" he asks. The Texan says yes and asks the bartender to line up 10 pints of Guinness. Immediately the Irishman tears into all 10 of the pint glasses, drinking them back-to-back. The other pub patrons cheer as the Texan sits in amazement.

The Texan gives the Irishman the $500 and says, "If ya don't mind me askin' where did you go for that 30 minutes you were gone?"

The Irishman replies, "To O'Halloran's pub down the street to see if I could do it."

! 🔟 Embarrassment

There are three guys drinking in a pub, when another man comes in and starts drinking at the bar. After a while he approaches the group of lads and, pointing at the one in the middle, shouts, "I've shagged your mum!" The three guys look bewildered as the man resumes his drinking at the bar.

Ten minutes later he comes back and yells at the middle guy again, "Your mum's sucked my cock!" And then goes back to his drink. The same thing happens.

Ten minutes later he's back again and announces "Oi! I've had your mum up the arse!" By now the young guys have had enough, and the one in the middle stands up and shouts,

"Look, Dad, this is really embarrassing. You're pissed, now just go home."

Giving It Up

An Irishman walks into a bar in Dublin, orders three pints of Guinness and sits in the back of the room, drinking a sip out of each one in turn. When he finishes them, he comes back to the bar and orders three more. The bartender asks him, "You know, a pint goes flat after I draw it; it would taste better if you bought one at a time." The Irishman replies, "Well, you see, I have two brothers. One is in America, the other in Australia and I'm here in Dublin. When we all left home, we promised that we'd drink this way to remember the days when we drank together." The bartender admits that this is a nice custom, and leaves it there.

The Irishman becomes a regular in the bar, and always drinks the same way: he orders three pints and drinks them in turn.

One day, he comes in and orders two pints. All the other regulars notice and fall silent.

When he comes back to the bar for the second round, the bartender says, "I don't want to intrude on your grief, but I wanted to offer my condolences on your great loss." The Irishman looks confused for a moment, then a light dawns in his eye and he laughs.

"Oh, no," he says, "everyone's fine. I've just quit drinking."

Increase Your Brain Power

A herd of buffalo can only move as fast as the slowest buffalo and when the herd is hunted, it is the slowest and weakest ones at the back that are killed first. This natural selection is good for the herd as a whole, because the general speed and health of the whole group keeps improving by the regular attrition of the weakest members.

In much the same way, the human brain can only operate as fast as the slowest brain cells. Excessive intake of alcohol, we all know, kills brain cells, but naturally it attacks the slowest and weakest brain cells first. In this way, regular consumption of beer eliminates the weaker brain cells, making the brain a faster and more efficient machine.

This is why you always feel smarter after a few beers!

The 5 Stages of Drunkenness

Stage 1: SMART

This is when you suddenly become an expert on every subject in the known Universe.

You know you know everything and want to pass on your knowledge to anyone who will listen.

At this stage you are always RIGHT.

And of course the person you are talking to is very WRONG.

This makes for an interesting argument when both parties are SMART.

Stage 2: GOOD LOOKING

This is when you realize that you are the BEST-LOOKING person in the entire bar and that people fancy you.

You can go up to a perfect stranger knowing they fancy you and really want to talk to you.

Bearing mind that you are still SMART, so you can talk to this person about any subject under the sun.

Stage 3: RICH

This is when you suddenly become the richest person in the world.

You can buy drinks for the entire bar because you have an armoured truck full of money parked behind the bar.

You can also make bets at this stage, because of course, you are still SMART, so naturally you win all your bets.

It doesn't matter how much you bet 'cause you are RICH.

You will also buy drinks for everyone that you fancy, because now you are the BEST-LOOKING person in the world.

Stage 4: BULLET PROOF

You are now ready to pick fights with anyone and everyone especially those with whom you have been betting or arguing.

This is because nothing can hurt you.

At this point you can also go up to the partners of the people who you fancy and challenge them to a battle of wits or money.

You have no fear of losing this battle because you are SMART, you are RICH and hell, you're BETTER-LOOKING than they are anyway!

Stage 5: INVISIBLE

This is the Final Stage of Drunkenness.

At this point you can do anything because NO ONE CAN SEE YOU.

You dance on a table to impress the people who you fancy because the rest of the people in the room cannot see you.

You are also invisible to the person who wants to fight you.

You can walk through the street singing at the top of your lungs because no one can see or hear you and because you're still SMART, you know all the words.

! 📖 The X-Files Drinking Game

Here's the deal: every time an event occurs, take the assigned amount of drinks from a beverage of your choice.

1 SIP

1. Every time Scully is examining internal organs of a corpse.
2. Every time Mulder or Scully gets a call on the cellular phone that ISN'T from their partner.
3. Every time a flashlight that is so bright it must require a car battery is used in a totally dark room.
4. If Mulder mentions that something could be paranormal and another character thinks he's joking.
5. If Mulder just happens to know some obscure case reference or fact that just happens to be similar to the case that they are working on.
6. Any time Mulder decides it would be fun to go into a dark place alone.
7. Any time Scully brings up some political/scientific fact.
8. Any time when Mulder and Scully split up and Scully goes somewhere on a wild goose chase, so that she misses the whole thing and doesn't believe Mulder when he tells her about it.

2 SIPS

1. Every time a mysterious character shows up at the end of an episode to keep Mulder from learning the truth/to save their lives.
2. Every time someone knows about Mulder's sister, but won't tell him about it.
3. If a computer does something computers don't do.
4. If you see the numbers 10/13, which correspond to the birthday of Chris Carter's wife.

5. Whenever Mulder is called by his first name.
6. Every time Cancer Man lights a cigarette.
7. Every time Mulder mentions his sister's abduction.
8. Whenever Mulder eats sunflower seeds.

3 SIPS

1. Whenever Mulder is called "Spooky Mulder."
2. Every time Deep Throat or Mr X is summoned.
3. If Mulder and Scully get into a fight.

4 SIPS

1. If a UFO appears in Scully's presence.
2. Whenever someone gets sick during an autopsy.
3. If Scully decides it would be fun to go into a dark place alone.

Events requiring special action:

1. Mulder and Scully get romantically involved: Drown yourself in your drink.
2. The case is completely solved with no unanswered questions and it ends up that the ghost haunting the house is a guy with a mask trying to decrease the property values and Scooby Doo and the gang end up helping out at the end: Same action.

Beer Drinking:
A Troubleshooting Guide

SYMPTOM: Feet cold and wet.
FAULT: Glass being held at incorrect angle.
ACTION: Rotate glass so that open end points toward ceiling.

S: Feet warm and wet.

F: Improper bladder control.
A: Stand next to nearest dog, complain about house training.

S: Beer unusually pale and tasteless.
F: Glass empty
A: Get someone to buy you another beer.

S: Opposite wall covered with fluorescent lights.
F: You have fallen over backward.
A: Have yourself leashed to bar.

S: Mouth contains cigarette butts.
F: You have fallen forward.
A: See above.

S: Beer tasteless, front of your shirt is wet.
F: Mouth not open, or glass applied to wrong part of face.
A: Retire to restroom, practice in mirror.

S: Floor blurred.
F: You are looking through bottom of empty glass.
A: Get someone to buy you another beer.

S: Floor moving.
F: You are being carried out.
A: Find out if you are being taken to another bar.

S: Room seems unusually dark.
F: Bar has closed.
A: Confirm home address with bartender.

S: Taxi suddenly takes on colourful aspect and textures.
F: Beer consumption has exceeded personal limitations.
A: Cover mouth.

S: Everyone looks up to you and smiles.

F: You are dancing on the table.
A: Fall on somebody cushy-looking.

S: Beer is crystal-clear.
F: It's water. Somebody is trying to sober you up.
A: Punch him.

S: Hands hurt, nose hurts, mind unusually clear.
F: You have been in a fight.
A: Apologize to everyone you see, just in case it was them.

S: Don't recognize anyone, or the room you're in.
F: You've wandered into the wrong party.
A: See if they have free beer.

S: Your singing sounds distorted.
F: The beer is too weak.
A: Have more beer until your voice improves.

S: Don't remember the words to the song.
F: Beer is just right.
A: Play air guitar.

Two Men in a Bar

Two men are drinking in a bar at the top of the Empire State Building. One turns to the other and says, "You know, last week I discovered that if you jump from the top of this building, by the time you fall to the 10th floor the winds around the building are so intense that they carry you around the building and back into the window."

The bartender just shakes his head in disapproval while wiping the bar. The second man says, "What, are you a nut? There is no way in hell that could happen."

The first man tells the second, "No, it's true. Let me prove it to you."

So he gets up from the bar, jumps over the balcony and careers toward the street below. When he passes the 10th floor, the high wind whips him around the building and back into the 10th floor window and he takes the elevator up to the bar.

The second man tells him, "You know, I saw that with my own eyes, but that must have been a one-time fluke."

The first man says, "No, I'll prove it again," and he jumps and hurtles toward the street where the 10th floor wind gently carries him around the building and into the window.

Once upstairs, he urges his fellow drinker to try it. The second man finally agrees.

"Well, what the hell, it works, I'll try it." So he jumps over the balcony, plunges downward, passes the 11th, 10th, 9th, 8th floors and hits the sidewalk with a splat.

Back upstairs the bartender turns to the other drinker, "You know, Superman, you're a real asshole when you're drunk."

Cerebrally Challenged Persons

A woman called the poison control center very upset because she caught her little daughter eating ants. The worker quickly reassured her that the ants are not harmful and there would be no need to take her daughter to the hospital. She calmed down, and at the end of the conversation happened to mention that she gave her daughter some ant poison to eat in order to kill the ants.

It seems that a year ago, some Boeing employees on the field decided to steal a life raft from one of the 747s. They were successful in getting it out of the plane and home. When they took it for a float on the river, they were quite surprised by a Coast Guard helicopter coming towards them. It turned out that the chopper was homing in on the emergency locator that is activated when the raft is inflated. They are no longer employed by Boeing.

A true story from San Francisco. A man, wanting to rob a downtown Bank of America, walked into the branch and wrote: "This iz a stikkup. Put allyour muny in this bag." While standing in line, waiting to give his note to the teller, he began to worry that someone had seen him write the note and might call the police before he reached the teller window. So he left the Bank of America and crossed the street to Wells Fargo. After waiting a few minutes in line, he handed his note to the Wells Fargo teller.

She read it and, surmising from his spelling errors that he wasn't the brightest light in the harbor, told him that she could not accept his stickup note because it was written on a Bank of America deposit slip and that he would either have to fill out a Wells Fargo deposit slip or go back to Bank of America. Looking somewhat defeated, the man said "OK" and left. The Wells Fargo teller then called the police, who arrested the man a few minutes later, as he was waiting in line back at Bank of America.

A motorist was unknowingly caught in an automated speed trap that measured his speed using radar and photographed his car. He later received in the mail a ticket for $40 and a photo of his car. Instead of payment, he sent the police department a photograph of $40. Several days later, he received a letter from the police that contained another picture – of handcuffs.

A woman was reporting her car as stolen, and mentioned that there was a car phone in it. The policeman taking the report called the phone and told the guy that answered that he had read the ad in the newspaper and wanted to buy the car. They arranged to meet, and the thief was arrested.

Drug possession defendant Christopher Jansen, on trial in March in Pontiac, Michigan, said he had been searched without a warrant. The prosecutor said the officer didn't need a warrant because a bulge in Christopher's jacket could have been a gun. Nonsense, said Christopher, who happened to be wearing the same jacket that day in court. He handed it over so the judge could see it. The judge discovered a packet of cocaine in the pocket and laughed so hard he required a five-minute recess to compose himself.

Oklahoma City: Dennis Newton was on trial for the armed robbery of a convenience store in a district court when he fired his lawyer. Assistant district attorney Larry Jones said Newton, 47, was doing a fair job of defending himself until the store manager testified that Newton was the robber. Newton jumped up, accused the woman of lying and then said, "I should have blown your (expletive) head off." The defendant paused, then quickly added, "If I'd been the one that was there." The jury took 20 minutes to convict Newton and recommended a 30-year sentence.

R.C. Gaitlan, 21, walked up to two patrol officers who were showing their squad car computer equipment to children in a Detroit neighborhood. When he asked how the system worked, the officer asked him for identification. Gaitlan gave them his driver's license, they entered it into the computer and moments later they arrested Gaitlan because information on the screen showed Gaitlan was wanted for a two-year-old armed robbery in St. Louis, Missouri.

A guy walked into a little corner store with a shotgun and demanded all the cash from the cash drawer. After the cashier put the cash in a bag, the robber saw a bottle of Scotch that he wanted behind the counter on the shelf. He told the cashier to put it in the bag as well. But the cashier refused, "Because I don't believe you are over 21." The robber said he was, but the clerk still refused to give it to him because he didn't believe him. At this point the robber took his driver's license out of his wallet and gave it to the clerk. The clerk looked it over, and agreed that the man was in fact over 21 and he put the Scotch in the bag. The robber then ran from the store with his loot. The cashier promptly called the police and gave the name and address of the robber that he got off the license. They arrested the robber two hours later.

A pair of Michigan robbers entered a record shop nervously waving revolvers. The first one shouted, "Nobody move!" When his partner moved, the startled first bandit shot him.

! Virus Alert – Irish-Style

>> Hi, I'm a virus from County Kerry.
>>
>> Please forward this e-mail to all the contacts in your personal
>> address book.
>>
>> Then delete all the files on your hard disk.
>>
>> That's great, thanks very much.

Christmas

! ⓜ Besht Cishmash Reshippy

The Best Ever Christmas Cake Ingredients:

>> 1 cup butter	1 teaspoon baking soda
>> 1 cup sugar	1 tablespoon lemon juice
>> 4 large eggs	1 cup brown sugar
>> 1 cup dried fruit	1 cup nuts
>> 1 teaspoon baking powder	1 or 2 quarts of aged whiskey

Before you start, sample the whiskey to check for quality. Good, ain't it?

Now go ahead. Select a large mixing bowl, measuring cup, etc. Check the whiskey again as it must be just right. To be sure the whiskey is of the highest quality, pour 1 level cup into a glass and drink it as fast as you can.

Repeat.

With an eclectic mixer, beat 1 cup of butter in a large fluffy bowl.

Add 1 teaspoon of sugar and beat the hell out of it again. Meanwhile, a this parsnicular point in time, wake sure that the whixey hasn't gon bad while you weren't lookin'. Open second quart if nestessary.

Add 2 large leggs, 2 cups fried druit an' beat 'til high. If druit gets shtucl in peaters, just pry the monsters loosh with a drewscriver.

Example the whikstey again, shecking confistancy, then shitf 2 cups o salt or destergent or whatever, like anyone gives a schit.

Chample the whitchey shum more.

Shitf in shum lemon zhoosh. Fold in chopped sputter and shrained nuts Add 100 babblespoons of brown booger or whushever's closhest and mi well.

Greash ubben and turn the cakey pan to 350 decrees. Now pour the whole mesh into the washin' machine and set on sinsh shycle.
Check dat whixney wunsh more and pash out.

! Christmas Disclaimer

Our Legal Department has approved the following Holiday Greeting:

Please accept with no obligation, implied or implicit, my best wishes for an environmentally conscious, socially responsible, low stress, non-addictive, gender neutral, celebration of the winter solstice holiday, practiced within the most enjoyable traditions of the religious persuasion of your choice, or secular practices of your choice, with respect for the religious/secular persuasions and/or traditions of others, or their choice not to practice religious or secular traditions at all . . . and a fiscally successful, personally fulfilling and medically uncomplicated recognition of the onset of the generally accepted calendar year 2000, but not without due respect for the calendars of choice of other cultures whose contributions to society have helped make America great (not to imply that America is necessarily greater than any other country or is the only "AMERICA" in the western hemisphere), and without regard to the race, creed, color, age, physical ability, religious faith, choice of computer platform or sexual orientation of the wishee.

By accepting this greeting, you are accepting these terms. This greeting is subject to clarification or withdrawal. It is freely transferable with no alteration to the original greeting. It implies no promise by the wisher to actually implement any of the wishes for her/himself or others, and is void where prohibited by law and is revocable at the sole discretion of the wisher.

This wish is warranted to perform as expected within the usual application of good tidings for a period of one year, or until the issuance of a subsequent holiday greeting, whichever comes first, and warranty is limited to replacement of this wish or issuance of a new wish at the sole discretion of the wisher.

Christmas Handicap

Riding the favourite at Cheltenham, a jockey was well ahead of the field. Suddenly he was hit on the head by a turkey and a string of sausages. He managed to keep control of his mount and pulled back into the lead, only to be struck by a box of Christmas crackers and a dozen mince pies as he went over the last fence. With great skill he managed to steer the horse to the front of the field once more when, on the run in, he was struck on the head by a bottle of sherry and a Christmas pudding. Thus distracted he succeeded in coming only second.

He immediately went to the stewards to complain that he had been seriously hampered.

The Christmas Angel

One particular Christmas a long time ago, Santa was getting ready for the annual trip ... but there were problems everywhere. Four of the elves were sick, and the trainee elves did not produce the toys fast enough to meet demands. Santa was beginning to feel stressed. Mrs Claus told him that her mother was coming for the holidays, and this stressed poor Santa even more. When he went to harness his reindeer, he found that 2 of them were about to give birth and 3 others were nowhere to be found. More stress. Then, while he was loading the sleigh, a floor board cracked under his weight and the toy bag fell to the ground and scattered the toys.

Frustrated, Santa went into the house for a cup of coffee and a shot of whisky, only to find that the sick elves' hot toddies had emptied the drinks cabinet. In his frustration, he dropped the coffee pot and it broke into hundreds of tiny pieces. He went to the broom closet and found that the mice had eaten the straw from the broom.

Just then the doorbell rang and Santa cussed on his way to the door. It was an angel with a tall beautiful evergreen. The angel said cheerfully, "Merry Christmas Santa! Isn't it a wonderful day? I've brought you a lovely Christmas tree to celebrate with. Where would you like me to stick it?"

Thus began the tradition of the little angel on top of the Christmas tree.

Clinton

A Monica Job

A guy walks into his local bordello and picks out a girl. They go back to her room and discuss prices.

She says, "It's $100 for a blow job, $200 for straight sex and $250 for a Monica."

"What's a Monica?" he asks.

She explains, "That's where I blow you now and screw you later."

A Trip to Oz

The last four US presidents are caught in a tornado, and off they spin to OZ. After threatening trials and tribulations, they finally make it to the Emerald City and come before the Great Wizard.

"WHAT BRINGS YOU BEFORE THE GREAT WIZARD OF OZ? WHAT DO YOU WANT?" Jimmy Carter steps forward timidly: "I had a terrible time with Iran, so I've come for some courage."

"NO PROBLEM" says the Wizard, "WHO IS NEXT?"

Ronald Reagan steps forward: "Well ..., Well ..., Well ..., I need a brain."

"DONE," says the Wizard. "WHO COMES NEXT BEFORE THE GREAT WIZARD?"

Up steps George Bush sadly: "I'm told by the American people that I need a heart."

"I'VE HEARD IT'S TRUE," says the Wizard. "CONSIDER IT DONE."

Then there is a great silence. Bill Clinton is just standing there, looking around, not saying a word. Irritated, the Wizard finally asks,

"WELL, WHAT BRINGS YOU TO THE EMERALD CITY?"

Bill says, "Is Dorothy around?"

All His Fault

Hillary Clinton goes to her doctor for a physical, only to find out that she's pregnant. She is furious! Here she is, about to run for Senator of New York and this has happened to her. She calls the White House, gets Bill on the phone, and immediately starts screaming:

"How could you have let this happen? With all that's going on right now, you go and get me pregnant! How could you???!!! I can't believe this! I just found out I am five weeks pregnant and it is all your fault!!! YOUR FAULT!!! Well, what have you got to say???"

There is nothing but dead silence on the end of the phone.

She screams again, "DID YOU HEAR ME???!!!"

Finally, she hears Bill's very, very quiet voice. In a barely audible whisper, he says,

"Who is this?"

Clinton Anagram

Clinton, President of the USA = To copulate, he finds interns.

Clinton and Saddam

Hussein and Bill Clinton meet up in Baghdad for the first round of talks in a new peace process. When Bill sits down, he notices three buttons on the side of Saddam's chair.

They begin talking. After about five minutes Saddam presses the first button. A boxing glove springs out of a box on the desk and punches Clinton in the face. Startled, Clinton carries on talking as Saddam laughs.

A few minutes later the second button is pressed. This time a big boot comes out and kicks Clinton in the shin. Again Saddam laughs, and again Clinton carries on talking, not wanting to put off the bigger issue of peace between the two countries.

But when the third button is pressed and another boot comes out and kicks Clinton in the privates, he's finally had enough, knowing that he's getting nowhere.

"I'm going back home!" he tells the Iraqi. "We'll finish these talks in two weeks!"

A fortnight passes and Saddam flies to the United States for talks. As the two men sit down, Hussein notices three buttons on Clinton's chair and prepares himself for the Yank's revenge.

They begin talking and Bill presses the first button. Saddam ducks, but nothing happens. Clinton snickers. A few seconds later he presses the second button. Saddam jumps up, but again nothing happens. Clinton roars with laughter. When the third button is pressed, Saddam jumps up again, and again nothing happens. Clinton falls on the floor in a fit of hysterics.

"Forget this," says Saddam. "I'm going back to Baghdad!"

Clinton says through tears of laughter, "What Baghdad?"

Clinton's Day in Heaven

President Clinton and the Pope died on the same day, and due to an administrative foul-up, Clinton was sent to heaven and the Pope was sent to hell.

The Pope explained the situation to the devil, who checked out the paperwork, and the error was acknowledged. The Pope was told, however, that it would take about 24 hours to fix the problem and correct the error.

The next day, the Pope was called in and the devil said his good-bye as he went off to heaven. On his way up, he met Clinton who was on his way down, and they stopped to chat.

Pope: Sorry about the mix up.
Clinton: No problem.
P: Well, I'm really excited about going to heaven.
C: Why's that?
P: All my life I've wanted to meet the Virgin Mary.

C: Um ... Sorry, you're a day late.

Cruising Altitude

The Rev. Ian Paisley was seated next to President Clinton on a recent flight to Ireland. Once the plane was airborne, the flight attendant came around for drink orders. The President asked for a whisky and soda which was brought and placed before him.

The attendant then asked the minister if he would also like a drink. The Rev. Paisley replied in disgust, "Madam, I'd rather be savagely raped by a brazen whore than let liquor touch these lips."

The President handed his drink back to the attendant and said, "I'm sorry, I didn't know there was a choice ..."

! 🔟 Hillary and the Hooker

Every morning Clinton takes a jog around D.C. Each day he passes a hooker on a particular street corner and, as he goes by, she shouts out, "Fifty dollars!" and he replies, "No, five dollars!"

This continues for several days. He runs by, she says, "Fifty dollars!" and he says, "No, five dollars!"

One day Hillary decides that she wants to go jogging with Bill. As they are approaching the now infamous street corner, Bill suddenly realizes that the hooker will bark out her $50 offer and that he will have some explaining to do with the First Lady.

As they turn the corner, Bill is still in a quandary as to what to do. Sure enough there is the hooker. She looks up as Bill and Hillary jog by and says to Bill,

"See what you get for five dollars?!"

! 🔟 Hillary Lets Rip

First Lady Hillary Clinton and Attorney General Janet Reno were having one of those girl-to-girl talks.

Hillary said to Janet, "You're lucky that you don't have to put up with men having sex with you. I have to put up with Bill, and there is no telling where he last had his pecker."

Janet responded, "Just because I am considered ugly, doesn't mean I don't have to fight off unwelcome sexual advances."

Hillary asked, "Well how do you deal with the problem?"

Janet: "Whenever I feel that a guy is getting ready to make a pass at me, I muster all my might and squeeze out the loudest, nastiest fart I can."

Well, that night, Bill was already in bed with the lights out when Hillary headed for bed. She could hear him start to stir, and knew that he would be wanting some action. She had been saving her farts all day, and was ready for him. She tensed up her butt cheeks and forced out the most disgusting-sounding fart you could imagine.

Bill rolled over and said, "Is that you, Janet?"

! 📎 It Depends What You Mean...

Someday, a long time from now, President Clinton finishes his time on earth and approaches the Pearly Gates of Heaven.

"And who might you be?" inquires St Peter.

"It's me, Bill Clinton, formerly the President of the United States and Leader of the Free World."

"Oh ... Mr President! What may I do for you?" asks St Peter.

"I'd like to come in," replies Clinton.

"Sure," says the Saint. "But first you have to confess your sins. What bad things have you done in your life?"

Clinton bites his lip and answers, "Well, I tried marijuana, but you can't call it dope-smoking, because I didn't inhale. There were inappropriate extramarital relationships, but you can't call it adultery, because I didn't have full sexual relations. And I made some statements that were misleading, but legally accurate, but you can't call it bearing false witness because, as far as I know, it didn't meet the legal standard of perjury."

With that St Peter consults the Book of Life briefly, and declares, "OK, here's the deal. We'll send you somewhere hot, but we won't call it hell. You'll be there indefinitely, but we won't call it eternity. And when you enter, you don't have to abandon all hope, just don't hold your breath waiting for it to freeze over."

! Now It Can Be Told

Some time ago Mr Clinton was hosting a state dinner when at the last minute his regular cook took ill and they had to get a replacement at short notice. The fellow arrived and turned out to be a very grubby-looking man named Jon. The President voiced his concerns to his chief of staff but was told that this was the best they could do at such short notice.

Just before the meal, the President noticed the cook sticking his fingers in the soup to taste it and again he complained to the chief of staff about the cook, but he was told that this man was supposed to be a very good chef.

The meal went okay but the President was sure that the soup tasted a little off, and by the time dessert came, he was starting to have stomach cramps and nausea.

It was getting worse and worse until finally he had to excuse himself from the state dinner to look for the bathroom. Passing through the kitchen, he caught sight of the cook, Jon, scratching his rear end and this made him feel even worse. By now he was desperately ill with violent cramps and was so disorientated that he couldn't remember which door led to the bathroom.

He was on the verge of passing out from the pain when he finally found a door that opened. As he undid his trousers and ran in, he realized to his horror that he had stumbled into Monica Lewinsky's office with his trousers around his knees. As he was just about to pass out, she bent over him and heard her president whisper in a barely audible voice,

"Sack my cook."

And that is how the whole misunderstanding occurred.

! The Moving Hand . . .

Bill Clinton steps out onto the White House lawn in the dead of winter. Right in front of him, on the White House lawn, he sees "The President Must Die" written in urine across the snow.

Well, old Bill is pretty ticked off. He storms into his security staff's HQ, and yells, "Somebody wrote a death threat in the snow on the front damn lawn! And they wrote it in urine! Son-of-a-bitch had to be standing right on the porch when he did it! Where were you guys?!"

The security guys stay silent and stare ashamedly at the floor. Bill hollers, "Well dammit, don't just sit there! Get out and FIND OUT WHO DID IT! I want an answer, and I want it TONIGHT!" The entire staff immediately jump up and race for the exits.

Later that evening, his chief security officer approaches him and says, "Well Mr President, we have some bad news and we have some really bad news. Which do you want first?"

Clinton says, "Oh hell, give me the bad news first."

The officer says, "Well, we took a sample of the urine and tested it. The results just came back, and it was Al Gore's urine."

Clinton says "Oh my god, I feel so … so … betrayed! My own vice president! Damn. … Well, what's the really bad news?"

The officer replies, "Well, it's Hillary's handwriting!"

Computery Stuff

! 🔗 11 Reasons Why E-mail is Like a Penis

- Those who have it would be devastated if it was ever cut off.
- Those who have it think those who do not are somehow inferior.
- Those who don't have it may agree it is neat, but think it is not worth the fuss that those who have it make about it.
- Many of those who don't have it would like to try, a phenomenon psychologists call "e-mail envy".
- It's more fun when it's up, but this makes it hard to get any real work done.
- In the distant past, its only purpose was to transmit information vital to the survival of the species. Some people think that is the only thing it should be used for, but most folks today use it only for fun.
- If you don't use proper precautions, it can spread viruses.
- If you use it too much, you'll find it becomes more and more difficult to think coherently.
- We attach an importance to it that is far greater than its actual size and influence warrant.
- If you are not careful what you do with it, it can get you in a lot of trouble.

> AND ... THE NUMBER ONE REASON IS ...

- If you play with it too much, you will go blind.

>>
>>
>>
>>

! Beyond Help

This is an allegedly true story from the WordPerfect helpline.

Actual dialogue of a former WordPerfect Customer Support employee:

"Ridge Hall, computer assistant; may I help you?"

"Yes, well, I'm having trouble with WordPerfect."

"What sort of trouble?"

"Well, I was just typing along, and all of a sudden the words went away."

"Went away?"

"They disappeared."

"Hmm. So what does your screen look like now?"

"Nothing."

"Nothing?"

"It's blank; it won't accept anything when I type."

"Are you still in WordPerfect, or did you get out?"

"How do I tell?"

"Can you see the C: prompt on the screen?"

"What's a sea-prompt?"

"Never mind. Can you move the cursor around on the screen?"

"There isn't any cursor: I told you, it won't accept anything I type."

"Does your monitor have a power indicator?"

"What's a monitor?"

"It's the thing with the screen on it that looks like a TV. Does it have a little light that tells you when it's on?"

"I don't know."

"Well, then look on the back of the monitor and find where the power cord goes into it. Can you see that?"

"Yes, I think so."

"Great. Follow the cord to the plug, and tell me if it's plugged into the wall."

" ... Yes, it is."

"When you were behind the monitor, did you notice that there were two cables plugged into the back of it, not just one?"

"No."

"Well, there are. I need you to look back there again and find the other cable."

" ... Okay, here it is."

"Follow it for me, and tell me if it's plugged securely into the back of your computer."

"I can't reach."

"Uh huh. Well, can you see if it is?"

"No."

"Even if you maybe put your knee on something and lean way over?"

"Oh, it's not because I don't have the right angle – it's because it's dark."

"Dark?"

"Yes – the office light is off, and the only light I have is coming in from the window."

"Well, turn on the office light then."

"I can't."

"No? Why not?"

"Because there's a power cut."

"A power ... A power cut? Aha, Okay, we've got it licked now. Do you still have the boxes and manuals and packing stuff your computer came in?"

"Well, yes, I keep them in the closet."

"Good. Go get them, and unplug your system and pack it up just like it was when you got it. Then take it back to the store you bought it from."

"Really? Is it that bad?"

"Yes, I'm afraid it is."

"Well, all right then, I suppose. What do I tell them?"

"Tell them you're too fucking stupid to own a computer."

⚠ 📎 Computer Acronyms

ISDN	It Still Does Nothing
APPLE	Arrogance Produces Profit-Losing Entity
SCSI	System Can't See It
DOS	Defective Operating System
BASIC	Bill's Attempt to Seize Industry Control
IBM	I Blame Microsoft
DEC	Do Expect Cuts
CD-ROM	Consumer Device, Rendered Obsolete Monthly
OS/2	Obsolete Soon Too
WWW	World Wide Wait
MACINTOSH	Most Applications Crash, If Not, The Operating System Hangs
PENTIUM	Produces Erroneous Numbers Through Incorrect Understanding of Maths
COBOL	Completely Obsolete Business Oriented Language
AMIGA	A Merely Insignificant Game Addiction
LISP	Let's Insert Some Parentheses
MIPS	Meaningless Indication of Processor Speed
WINDOWS	Will Install Needless Data On Whole System
MICROSOFT	Most Intelligent Customers Realize Our Software Only Fools Teenagers

! Computer Terms Explained

STATE-OF-THE-ART
Any computer you can't afford.

OBSOLETE
Any computer you own.

MICROSECOND
The time it takes for your state-of-the-art computer to become obsolete.

SYNTAX ERROR
Walking into a computer store and saying: "Hi, I want to buy a computer and money is no object."

HARD DRIVE
The sales technique employed by computer salesmen, especially after a Syntax Error.

GUI
What your computer becomes after spilling your coffee on it. (Pronounced "gooey".)

KEYBOARD
The standard way to generate computer errors.

MOUSE
An advanced input device to make computer errors easier to generate.

FLOPPY
The state of your wallet after purchasing a computer.

PORTABLE COMPUTER
A device invented to force businessmen to work at home, on vacation and on business trips.

DISK CRASH
A typical computer response to any critical deadline.

POWER USER
Anyone who can format a disk from DOS.

SYSTEM UPDATE
A quick method of trashing ALL your software.

386
The average IQ needed to understand a PC.

Computers in Movies

Have you noticed …

Word processors never display a cursor.

You never have to use the space-bar when typing long sentences.

All monitors display inch-high letters.

High-tech computers, such as those used by NASA, the CIA or some such governmental institution, will have easy-to-understand graphical interfaces. Those that don't have incredibly powerful text-based command shells that can correctly understand and execute commands typed in plain English.
Corollary: you can gain access to any information you want by simply typing "ACCESS ALL OF THE SECRET FILES" on any keyboard. Likewise, you can infect a computer with a destructive virus by simply typing "UPLOAD VIRUS" (see Fortress/ID4).

All computers are connected. You can access the information on the villain's desktop computer, even if it's turned off.

Powerful computers beep whenever you press a key or whenever the screen changes. Some computers also slow down the output on the screen so that it doesn't go faster than you can read.

The really advanced ones also emulate the sound of a dot-matrix printer (see *The Hunt For Red October* or *Alien*).

All computer panels have thousands of volts and flash pots just underneath the surface. Malfunctions are indicated by a bright flash, a puff of smoke, a shower of sparks and an explosion that forces you backwards.

Corollary: sending data to a modem/tape drive/printer faster than expected causes it to explode.

People typing away on a computer will turn it off without saving the data (see the opening credits for *The Hunt For Red October*).

A hacker can get into the most sensitive computer in the world before intermission and guess the secret password in two tries.

Any PERMISSION DENIED has an OVERRIDE function (see *Demolition Man* and countless others)

Complex calculations and loading of huge amounts of data will be accomplished in under three seconds. Movie modems usually appear to transmit data at the speed of two gigabytes per second.

When the power plant/missile-site/whatever overheats, all the control panels will explode, as will the entire building.

If a disk has got encrypted files, you are automatically asked for a password when you try to access it.

No matter what kind of computer disk it is, it'll be readable by any system you put it into. All application software is usable by all computer platforms.

The more high-tech the equipment, the more buttons it has (see *Aliens*). However, everyone must have been highly trained, because none of the buttons are labelled.

Most computers, no matter how small, have reality-defying three-dimensional, active animation, photo-realistic graphics capability.

Laptops, for some strange reason, always seem to have amazing real-time video phone capabilities and the performance of a CRAY Supercomputer.

Whenever a character looks at a VDU, the image is so bright that it projects itself onto his/her face (see *Alien*, *2001*, *Jurassic Park*).

Either a Jacob's Ladder or a Van Der Graaf Generator is absolutely necessary for the operation of new, experimental computers (especially when built by brilliant scientists), although in real life, these devices do absolutely nothing.

One can issue any complex set of commands in a few keystrokes (see *Star Trek*).

The Internet connects to everything in the movies. You can edit credit records, search hotel registries, look up police criminal files, search (and edit) driver's license databases, edit social security files and more just using the Internet! (see *The Net*).

Floppy Care

1. Never leave diskettes in the disk drive, as data can leak out of the disk and corrode the inner mechanics of the drive. Diskettes should be rolled up and stored in pencil holders.

2. Diskettes should be cleaned and waxed once a week. Microscopic metal particles can be removed by waving a powerful magnet over the surface of the disk. Any stubborn metallic shavings can be removed with scouring powder and soap. When waxing the diskettes, make sure the surface is even. This will allow the diskette to spin faster, resulting in better access time.

3. Do not fold diskettes unless they do not fit into the drive. "Big" diskettes may be folded and used in "little" disk drives.

4. Never insert a diskette into the drive upside down. The data can fall off the surface of the disk and jam the intricate mechanics of the drive.

5. Diskettes cannot be backed up by running them through the Xerox machine.

! 📎 Garbage in …

I worked with an individual who plugged her power strip back into itself and for the life of her could not understand why her system would not turn on.

A friend had a brilliant idea for saving disk space. He thought if he put all his Microsoft Word documents into a tiny font they'd take up less room in the hard drive. When he told me I was with another friend. She thought it was a good idea too.

Tech Support: How much free space do you have on your hard drive?
Individual: Well, my wife likes to get up there on that Internet, and she downloaded ten hours of free space. Is that enough?

Individual: Now what do I do?

Tech Support: What is the prompt on the screen?
Individual: It's asking for "Enter Your Last Name."
Tech Support: Okay, so type in your last name.
Individual: How do you spell that?

！ Haiku Error

Apparently Sony's new portable PC comes complete with Haiku error messages designed to be more soothing to the frustrated Windows user. For example:

> A file that big?
> It might be very useful.
> But now it is gone.

> You seek a Web site.
> It cannot be located.
> Countless more exist.

> Chaos reigns within.
> Stop, reflect and reboot.
> Order shall return.

> Aborted effort:
> Close all that you have worked on.
> You ask way too much.

> Yesterday it worked
> Today it is not working
> Windows is like that.

> First snow, then silence.
> This thousand dollar screen dies
> So beautifully.

With searching comes loss.
The presence of absence.
"June Sales.doc" not found.

The Tao that is seen
Is not the true Tao
Until you bring fresh toner.

Windows NT crashed.
The Blue Screen of Death.
No one hears your screams.

Stay the patient course.
Of little worth is your ire.
The network is down.

A crash reduces
Your expensive computer
To a simple stone.

Three things are certain:
Death, taxes and lost data.
Guess which has occurred.

You step in the stream
But the water has moved on.
Page not found.

Out of memory.
We wish to hold the whole sky,
But we never will.

Having been erased,
The document you are seeking
Must now be retyped.

Serious error.
All shortcuts have disappeared.
Screen. Mind. Both are blank.

! ◫ If Microsoft Built Cars

At a computer expo (COMDEX), Bill Gates reportedly compared the computer with the auto industry and stated:

"If GM had kept up with technology like the computer industry has, we would all be driving twenty-five dollar cars that got 1000 mi/gal."

General Motors addressed this comment by releasing the statement: "Yes, but would you want your car to crash twice a day?"

Every time they repainted the lines on the road, you would have to buy a new car.

Occasionally your car would die on the freeway for no reason and you would just accept this, restart and drive on.

Occasionally, executing a manoeuvre would cause your car to stop and fail and you would have to re-install the engine. For some strange reason, you would accept this too.

You could only have one person in the car at a time, unless you bought "Car95" or "CarNT". But then you would have to buy more seats.

Macintosh would make a car that was powered by the sun, was reliable, five times as fast, twice as easy to drive, but would only run on five per cent of the roads.

The Macintosh car owners would get expensive Microsoft upgrades to their cars, which would make their cars run much slower.

The oil, gas and alternator warning lights would be replaced by a single "general car default" warning light.

New seats would force everyone to have the same size butt.

The airbag system would say "are you sure?" before going off.

If you were involved in a crash, you would have no idea what happened.

! 📎 Major Technological Breakthrough

We have to share with you the news just received of a Major Technological Breakthrough:

"Announcing the new Built-in Orderly Organized Knowledge device (BOOK).

It's a revolutionary breakthrough in technology: no wires, no electric circuits, no batteries, nothing to be connected or switched on. It's so easy to use even a child can operate it. Just lift its cover. Simple and portable, it can be used anywhere – even sitting in an armchair by the fire – yet it is powerful enough to hold as much information as a CD-ROM disk.

Here's how it works:

BOOK is constructed of sequentially numbered sheets of paper (recyclable), each capable of holding thousands of bits of information. These pages are locked together with a custom-fit device called a binder which keeps the sheets in their correct sequence. By using both sides of each sheet, manufacturers are able to cut costs in half. Each sheet is scanned optically, registering information directly into your brain. A flick of the finger takes you to the next sheet.

BOOK may be taken up at any time and used by merely opening it.

The "browse" feature allows you to move instantly to any sheet and move forward or backward as you wish. Most come with an "index" feature, which pinpoints the exact location of any selected information for instant retrieval. An optional "BOOKmark" accessory allows you to open the BOOK at the exact place you left it in a previous session – even if the BOOK has been closed. BOOKmarks fit universal design standards; thus a single BOOKmark can be used in BOOKs by various manufacturers.

Compact, durable and affordable, the BOOK is the entertainment wave of the future, and many new titles are expected soon, due to the surge in popularity of its programming tool, the Portable Erasable-Nib Cryptic Intercommunication Language Stylus (referred to by the acronym PENCILS to those in the trade).

Aren't human beings just amazing and wonderful!
Have a good evening and enjoy your BOOKs!"

Microsoft Help

Three engineers are riding down the road in a car. Suddenly, the car begins to develop trouble. It's sputtering and it sounds like it's going to stall.

The first engineer is a chemical engineer. He says, "It could be something in the fuel line. Lets put an additive into the gas and maybe that will take care of the problem."

The second engineer is an electrical engineer. She says, "It could be something in the electrical system. Let's replace the wires and the distributor cap. Maybe that will take care of the problem."

The third engineer is a software engineer from Microsoft. He says, "It could be that we've too many windows open. Let's close all the windows, turn off the car, then restart the car and open all the windows again. Maybe that will take care of the problem."

⚠ 📎 Microsoft TV Dinner Instructions

You must first remove the plastic cover. By doing so you agree to accept and honor Microsoft rights to all TV dinners. You may not give anyone else a bite of your dinner (which would constitute an infringement of Microsoft's rights). You may, however, let others smell and look at your dinner and are encouraged to tell them how good it is.

If you have a PC microwave oven, insert the dinner into the oven.
Set the oven using these keystrokes: \mstv.dinn.//08.5min@@50%heat//

Then enter: ms//start.cook_dindin/yummy\|/yum~yum:)gohot#cookme.

If you have a Mac oven, insert the dinner and press start. The oven will set itself and cook the dinner.

If you have a Unix oven, insert the dinner, enter the ingredients of the dinner (found on the package label), the weight of the dinner and the desired level of cooking and press start. The oven will calculate the time and heat and cook the dinner exactly to your specification.

Be forewarned that Microsoft dinners may crash, in which case your oven must be restarted. This is a simple procedure. Remove the dinner from the oven and enter:
ms.nodamn.good/tryagain\again/again.crap.

This process may have to be repeated. Try unplugging the microwave and then doing a cold reboot. If this doesn't work, contact your hardware vendor.

Many users have reported that the dinner tray is far too big, larger than the dinner itself, having many useless compartments, most of which are empty. These are for future menu items. If the tray is too large to fit in your oven, you will need to upgrade your equipment.

Dinners are only available from registered outlets, and only the chicken variety is currently produced. If you want another variety, call Microsoft Help and they will explain that you really don't want another variety. Microsoft Chicken is all you really need.

Microsoft has disclosed plans to discontinue all smaller versions of their chicken dinners. Future releases will only be in the larger family size. Excess chicken may be stored for future use, but must be saved only in Microsoft-approved packaging.

Microsoft promises a dessert with every dinner after '98. However, that version has yet to be released. Users have permission to get thrilled in advance.

Microsoft dinners may be incompatible with other dinners in the freezer, causing your freezer to self-defrost. This is a feature, not a bug. Your freezer probably should have been defrosted anyway.

Tennis Elbow

One day Pete was complaining to his friend, "My elbow hurts. I'd better see a doctor." His friend said, "Don't do that. There's a computer in the drug store that can diagnose anything. It's quicker and cheaper than visiting a doctor. Simply put a urine sample in the machine and it will diagnose your problem and tell you what to do about it. It only costs $10.00."

Pete figured he had nothing to lose, so he filled a jar with a urine sample. He went to the drug store. Finding the computer, he poured in the sample and deposited $10.00. The computer started to make a weird nose and various lights began to flash. After a brief pause, a small slip of paper printed. It said:

You have tennis elbow.
Soak your arm in warm water, avoid heavy labor, it will be better in two weeks.

Later that evening, while thinking how amazing that computer was, Pete began to wonder if it could be fooled. He decided to give it a try.

He mixed some tap water, a stool sample from his dog, urine samples from his wife and daughter. To top it off, he masturbated into the concoction. He went back to the drug store, poured the sample into the machine and deposited $10.00. The machine again made the usual noise and printed out the following analysis:

Your water is hard, get a softener.
Your dog has worms, get him treated.
Your daughter's using cocaine, get her into a rehab clinic.
Your wife's pregnant, it's not yours, get a lawyer.

And if you don't stop jerking off, your tennis elbow will never get better!

☝ 📎 The Nerd and the Frog

A computer programmer was walking along the side of a lake when he came across a funny-looking frog. The guy picked up the frog, put it into his pocket and went on his way.

A couple of minutes of walking later, the man heard a cry from inside his pocket:

"Help, Help!" He took out the frog, looked at it, smiled and put it back into his pocket.

Again, "Help, Help me, a wicked witch has turned me into a frog, kiss me and I'll turn into a beautiful princess." Again the man took the frog out of his pocket, smiled at it and put it back again.

Moments later, "Help me, help me, a wicked witch has turned me into a frog, kiss me and I'll turn into a beautiful princess. I'll do anything if you help me, anything!" The man simply took the frog out of his pocket, smiled at it and put it back again.

The little green frog again screamed out, "Help, I'm the most beautiful princess, if you kiss me and help me I'll do anything, marry you, sleep with you, give you money, ANYTHING!!" The man took the frog out of his pocket, smiled and said, "I'm a computer programmer; I work too much so a girlfriend or wife is of no use to me.

"But a small talking green frog is cool."

Three Monkeys

A tourist walked into a pet shop and was looking at the animals on display. While he was there another customer walked in and said to the shopkeeper, "I'll have a C-monkey please."

The shopkeeper nodded, went to a cage at the side of the shop and took out a monkey. He fitted the monkey with a collar and a leash and handed it to the customer, saying, "That'll be £5,000." The customer paid and walked out with his monkey.

Startled, the tourist went over to the shopkeeper and said, "That was a very expensive monkey. Most of them are only a few hundred pounds. Why did it cost so much?" The shopkeeper answered, "Ah, that monkey can program in C. He's very fast, does tight code, no bugs, well worth the money."

The tourist looked at the monkey in another cage. It was wearing a price tag on its collar.

"That one's even more expensive! £10,000! What does it do?" The shopkeeper said, "Oh, that one's a C++ monkey; it can manage object-oriented programming, Visual C++, even some Java. All the really useful stuff."

The tourist looked around for a little longer and saw a third monkey in a cage of its own. The price tag around its neck read £50,000. He gasped to the shopkeeper, "That one costs more than all the others put together! What on earth does it do?"

The shopkeeper replied, "Well, I haven't actually seen it do anything, but it says it's a consultant."

From: laocoon@doomgloom.edu
To: Trojan Army Listserv <Trojans-L@troy.org>
Subject: WARNING!! BEWARE GREEKS BEARING GIFTS!

Hey Hector,

This was forwarded to me by Cassandra – it looks legit. Please distribute to Priam, Hecuba and your 99 siblings.

Thanks,

Laocoon.

>WARNING! WARNING! WARNING!

>IF YOU RECEIVE A GIFT IN THE SHAPE OF A LARGE
>WOODEN HORSE DO NOT DOWNLOAD IT!!!! It is EXTREMELY
>DESTRUCTIVE and will overwrite your ENTIRE CITY!

>The "gift" is disguised as a large wooden horse about two storeys
>tall. It tends to show up outside the city gates and appears to be
>abandoned. DO NOT let it through the gates! It contains hardware
>that is incompatible with Trojan programming, including a crowd of
>heavily armed Greek warriors that will destroy your army, sack your
>town and kill your women and children. If you have already
>received such a gift, DO NOT OPEN IT! Take it back out of the city
>unopened and set fire to it by the beach.

>FORWARD THIS MESSAGE TO EVERYONE YOU KNOW!

>Poseidon

From: hector@studmuffin.com
To: laocoon@doomgloom.edu
Subject: Re: WARNING!! BEWARE GREEKS BEARING GIFTS!

Laocoon,

> I hate to break this to you, but this is one of the oldest hoaxes there
> is. I've seen variants on this warning come through on other listservs,
> one involving some kind of fruit that was supposed to kill the people
> who ate it and one having to do with something called the "Midas
> Touch".
> Here are a few tipoffs that this is a hoax:

1) This "Forward this message to everyone you know" crap. If it were
really meant as a warning about the Greek army, why tell anyone to post
it to the Phoenicians, Sumerians and Cretans?

2) Use of exclamation points. Always a give-away.

3) It's signed "from Poseidon." Granted he's had his problems with
Odysseus but he's one of their guys, isn't he? Besides, the lack of a real
header with a detailed address makes me suspicious.

4) Technically speaking, there is no way for a horse to overwrite your
entire city. A horse is just an animal, after all.

> Next time you get a message like this, just delete it. I appreciate your
concern, but once you've been around the block a couple of times you'll
realize how annoying this kind of stuff is.
> Bye now,

> Hector

Differently Located Americans

1. One hand on wheel, one hand on horn: CHICAGO

2. One hand on wheel, one finger out window: NEW YORK

3. One hand on wheel, one finger out window, cutting across all lanes of traffic: NEW JERSEY

4. One hand on wheel, one hand on newspaper, foot solidly on accelerator: BOSTON

5. One hand on wheel, one hand on non-fat double decaf cappuccino, cradling cell phone, brick on accelerator, gun in lap: LOS ANGELES

6. Both hands on wheel, eyes shut, both feet on brake, quivering in terror: OHIO, but driving in California

7. Both hands in air, gesturing, both feet on accelerator, head turned to talk to someone in back seat: ITALY

8. One hand on 12 oz. double shot latte, one knee on wheel, cradling cell phone, foot on brake, mind on radio game, banging head on steering wheel while stuck in traffic: SEATTLE

9. One hand on wheel, one hand on hunting rifle, alternating between both feet being on the accelerator and both feet on brake, throwing McDonald's bag out the window: TEXAS

10. Four-wheel drive pick-up truck, shotgun mounted in rear window, beer cans on floor, squirrel tails attached to antenna: ALABAMA

11. Two hands gripping wheel, blue hair barely visible above windshield, driving 35 on the Interstate in the left lane with the left blinker on: FLORIDA

How Texan Drivers Die

The National Transportation Safety Board recently divulged their joint venture with the US auto makers for the past five years. The NTSB covertly funded a project whereby the auto makers were installing black boxes in four-wheel drive pickup trucks in an effort to determine, in fatal accidents, the circumstances in the last 15 seconds before the crash. They were surprised to find in 49 of the 50 states the last words of drivers in 61.2% of fatal crashes were, "Oh, shit!"

Only the state of Texas was different, where 89.3% of the final words were, "Hey y'all, hold my beer and watch this!"

Southern Charm

Two delicate flowers of Southern womanhood were conversing on the porch swing of a large white pillared mansion.

The first woman said, "When my first child was born, my husband built this beautiful mansion for me." The second woman commented, "Well, isn't that nice."

The first woman continued: "When my second child was born, my husband bought me that fine Cadillac automobile you see parked in the drive." Again, the second woman commented, "Well, isn't that nice."

The first woman boasted: "Then, when my third child was born, my husband bought me this exquisite diamond bracelet." Yet again, the second woman commented, "Well, isn't that nice."

The first woman then asked her companion, "What did your husband buy for you when you had your first child?" The second woman replied "My husband sent me to charm school."

"Charm school!" the first woman cried, "Land sakes, child, what on earth for?"

The second woman responded, "So that instead of saying 'who gives a shit', I learned to say, 'Well, isn't that nice ...'"

State Mottoes

ALABAMA	YES, WE HAVE ELECTRICITY
ALASKA	11,623 ESKIMOS CAN'T BE WRONG
ARIZONA	BUT IT'S A DRY HEAT
ARKANSAS	LITTERASY AIN'T EVERYTHANG
CALIFORNIA	OUR WOMEN HAVE MORE PLASTIC THAN YOUR HONDA
COLORADO	IF YOU DON'T SKI, DON'T BOTHER
CONNECTICUT	LIKE MASSACHUSETTS, ONLY THE KENNEDYS DON'T OWN IT YET
DELAWARE	WE REALLY DO LIKE THE CHEMICALS IN OUR WATER
FLORIDA	ASK US ABOUT OUR GRANDKIDS
GEORGIA	WE PUT THE FUN IN FUNDAMENTALIST EXTREMISM
HAWAII	HAKA TIKI MOU SHA'AMI LEEKI TORU (DEATH TO MAINLAND SCUM, BUT LEAVE YOUR MONEY)
IDAHO	MORE THAN JUST POTATOES ... WELL OK, WE'RE NOT, BUT THE POTATOES ARE REAL GOOD

ILLINOIS	PLEASE DON'T PRONOUNCE THE "S"
INDIANA	2 BILLION YEARS TIDAL WAVE FREE
IOWA	WE DO AMAZING THINGS WITH CORN
KANSAS	FIRST OF THE RECTANGLE STATES
KENTUCKY	FIVE MILLION PEOPLE, FIFTEEN LAST NAMES
LOUISIANA	WE'RE NOT ALL DRUNK CAJUN WACKOS, BUT THAT'S OUR TOURISM CAMPAIGN
MAINE	WE'RE REALLY COLD BUT WE HAVE CHEAP LOBSTER
MARYLAND	IF YOU CAN DREAM IT, WE CAN TAX IT
MASSACHUSETTS	OUR TAXES ARE LOWER THAN SWEDEN'S (FOR MOST TAX BRACKETS)
MICHIGAN	FIRST LINE OF DEFENSE FROM THE CANADIANS
MINNESOTA	10,000 LAKES AND 10,000,000 MOSQUITOS
MISSISSIPPI	COME FEEL BETTER ABOUT YOUR OWN STATE
MISSOURI	YOUR FEDERAL FLOOD RELIEF TAX DOLLARS AT WORK
MONTANA	LAND OF THE BIG SKY, THE UNABOMBER, RIGHT-WING CRAZIES, AND VERY LITTLE ELSE
NEBRASKA	ASK ABOUT OUR STATE MOTTO CONTEST
NEVADA	WHORES AND POKER
NEW HAMPSHIRE	GO AWAY AND LEAVE US ALONE
NEW JERSEY	YOU WANT A $##*&^ MOTTO? I GOT YOUR $##*&^ MOTTO RIGHT HERE
NEW MEXICO	LIZARDS MAKE EXCELLENT PETS
NEW YORK	YOU HAVE THE RIGHT TO REMAIN SILENT, YOU HAVE THE RIGHT TO AN ATTORNEY
NORTH CAROLINA	TOBACCO IS A VEGETABLE
NORTH DAKOTA	WE REALLY ARE ONE OF THE FIFTY STATES
OHIO	AT LEAST WE'RE NOT MICHIGAN
OKLAHOMA	LIKE THE PLAY, ONLY NO SINGING
OREGON	SPOTTED OWL ... IT'S WHAT'S FOR DINNER

PENNSYLVANIA	COOK WITH COAL
RHODE ISLAND	WE'RE NOT REALLY AN ISLAND
SOUTH CAROLINA	REMEMBER THE CIVIL WAR? WE DIDN'T ACTUALLY SURRENDER
SOUTH DAKOTA	CLOSER THAN NORTH DAKOTA
TENNESSEE	THE EDUCASHUN STATE
TEXAS	SI, HABLO INGLIS (YES, I SPEAK ENGLISH)
UTAH	OUR JESUS IS BETTER THAN YOUR JESUS
VERMONT	YEP
VIRGINIA	WHO SAYS GOVERNMENT STIFFS AND SLACKJAW YOKELS DON'T MIX?
WASHINGTON	HELP! WE'RE OVERRUN BY NERDS AND SLACKERS
WASHINGTON DC	HEY – WANNA BE MAYOR?
WEST VIRGINIA	ONE BIG HAPPY FAMILY … REALLY
WISCONSIN	COME CUT THE CHEESE
WYOMING	WHERE MEN ARE MEN … AND THE SHEEP ARE SCARED!

E-animals

! 📎 Animal Quickies

Q: How do you make a dog drink?
A: Put it in a liquidizer.

Q: What's got four legs and an arm?
A: A rottweiler.

Q: What do you call bears with no ears?
A: B.

Q: What's got two legs and bleeds?
A: Half a dog.

! 📎 Declan the Crab

Declan the humble crab and Kate the Lobster Princess were madly, deeply and passionately in love. For months they enjoyed an idyllic relationship until one day Kate scuttled over to Declan in tears.

"We can't see each other anymore," she sobbed.

"Why?" gasped Declan.

"Daddy says that crabs are too common," she wailed. "He claims you are a mere crab, and a poor one at that, and the lowest class of crustacean ... and that no daughter of his will marry someone who can only walk sideways." Declan was shattered, and scuttled sidewards away into the darkness and to drink himself into a filthy state of aquatic oblivion.

That night, the great lobster ball was taking place. Lobsters came from far and wide, dancing and merry-making, but the Lobster Princess refused to join in, choosing instead to sit by her father's side, inconsolable.

Suddenly the doors burst open, and Declan the crab strode in. The lobsters all stopped their dancing, the Princess gasped and the King Lobster rose from his throne.

Slowly, painstakingly, Declan the crab made his way across the floor ... and all could see that he was walking not sideways, but FORWARDS, one claw after another! Step by step he made his approach towards the throne until he finally looked King Lobster in the eye.

There was a deadly hush. Finally, Declan the crab spoke:

"Fuck, am I pissed."

! ▯ Dog Seeks Work

A local business was looking for office help. They put a sign in the window, stating the following: "HELP WANTED. Must be able to type, must be good with a computer and must be bilingual. We are an Equal Opportunity Employer."

A short time afterwards, a dog trotted up to the window, saw the sign and went inside. He looked at the receptionist and wagged his tail, then walked over to the sign, looked at it and whined. Getting the idea, the receptionist got the office manager. The office manager looked at the dog and was surprised, to say the least. However, the dog looked determined, so he led him into the office.

Inside, the dog jumped up on the chair and stared at the manager. The manager said, "I can't hire you. The sign says you have to be able to type." The dog jumped down, went to the typewriter and proceeded to type out a perfect letter. He took out the page and trotted over to the manager and gave it to him, then jumped back on the chair.

The manager was stunned, but then told the dog, "The sign says you have to be good with a computer." The dog jumped down again and went to the computer. The dog proceeded to enter and execute a perfect program, that worked flawlessly the first time.

By this time the manager was totally dumbfounded. He looked at the dog and said, "I realize that you are a very intelligent dog and have some interesting abilities. However, I still can't give you the job." The dog jumped down and went to a copy of the sign and put his paw on the sentences that told about being an Equal Opportunity Employer. The manager said, "Yes, but the sign also says that you have to be bilingual."

The dog looked at the manager calmly and said, "Meow."

! 📎 House Training

Jake got a 6-month-old dog at the dog pound and was having trouble getting it house broke. He decided to rub the dog's nose in it every time it wet on the floor and throw the dog out the window to teach the dog a lesson.

After about a week of faithfully doing it, Jake thought it was about time the dog figured it out. Sure enough, the next time the dog wet on the floor, he rubbed his own nose in it and jumped out the window.

! 📎 In The Shit

A little bird was flying south for the winter. It was so cold, the bird froze and fell to the ground in a large field. While it was lying there, a cow came by and dropped some dung on it. As the frozen bird lay there in the pile of cow dung, it began to realize how warm it was. The dung was actually thawing him out! He lay there all warm and happy, and soon began to sing for joy.

A passing cat heard the bird singing and came to investigate. Following the sound, the cat discovered the bird under the pile of cow dung, and promptly dug him out and ate him!

The morals of this story are:

1) Not everyone who drops shit on you is your enemy.
2) Not everyone who gets you out of shit is your friend.
3) And when you're in deep shit, keep your mouth shut.

The Vampire Bat

A vampire bat came flapping in from the night, face all covered in fresh blood and parked himself on the roof of the cave to get some sleep.

Pretty soon all the other bats smelt the blood and began hassling him about where he got it. He told them to piss off and let him get some sleep, but they persisted until he finally gave in.

"OK, follow me," he said and flew out of the cave with hundreds of bats behind him. Down through a valley they went, across a river and into a huge forest of trees. Finally he slowed down and all the other bats excitedly milled around him, tongues hanging out for blood.

"Do you see that large oak tree over there?" he asked.

"YES, YES, YES!!!!" the bats all screamed in a frenzy.

"Good!" said the first bat, "Because I fucking didn't."

Three Ducks

A guy walks into a quiet bar. He is carrying three ducks, one in each hand and one under his left arm. He places them on the bar. He has a few drinks and chats with the bartender. The bartender is experienced and has learned not to ask people about the animals that they bring into the bar, so he doesn't mention the ducks.

They chat for about 30 minutes before the guy with the ducks has to go to the restroom. The ducks are left on the bar. The bartender is alone with the ducks. There is an awkward silence. The bartender decides to try to make some conversation.

"What's your name?" he says to the first duck.

"Huey," said the first duck.

"How's your day been, Huey?"

"Great. Lovely day. Had a ball. Been in and out of puddles all day."

"Oh. That's nice," says the bartender. Then he says to the second duck "Hi. And what's your name?"

"Dewey," came the answer.

"So how's your day been, Dewey?"

"Great. Lovely day. Had a ball. Been in and out of puddles all day. If I had the chance another day I would do the same again." So the bartender turns to the third duck and says, "So, you must be Louie."

"No," growls the third duck. "My name is Puddles. And don't ask about my fucking day."

Facts and Factoids

>> Include Your Children When Baking Cookies
>> Something Went Wrong in Jet Crash, Experts Say
>> Police Begin Campaign to Run Down Jaywalkers
>> Drunks Get Nine Months in Violin Case
>> Iraqi Head Seeks Arms
>> Is There a Ring of Debris around Uranus?
>> Prostitutes Appeal to Pope
>> Panda Mating Fails; Veterinarian Takes Over
>> British Left Waffles on Falkland Islands
>> Teacher Strikes Idle Kids
>> Clinton Wins Budget; More Lies Ahead
>> Plane Too Close to Ground, Crash Probe Told
>> Miners Refuse to Work After Death
>> Juvenile Court to Try Shooting Defendant
>> Stolen Painting Found by Tree
>> Two Sisters Reunited after 18 Years in Checkout Counter
>> War Dims Hope for Peace
>> If Strike Isn't Settled Quickly, It May Last a While
>> Couple Slain; Police Suspect Homicide
>> Man Struck by Lightning Faces Battery Charge
>> New Study of Obesity Looks for Larger Test Group
>> Astronaut Takes Blame for Gas in Space
>> Kids Make Nutritious Snacks
>> Local High School Dropouts Cut in Half
>> Typhoon Rips through Cemetery; Hundreds Dead

! How Did They Verify These?

Things You Won't Find In *The Guinness Book Of Records...*

MOST SEMEN SWALLOWED
Michelle Monahan had 1.7 pints of semen pumped out of her stomach in Los Angeles in July 1991.

LONGEST PUBES
Maoni Vi of Cape Town has hair measuring 32 inches from the armpits and 28 inches from her vagina.

MOST CAVERNOUS CROTCH
Linda Manning of Los Angeles could, without preparation, completely insert a lubricated American football into her vagina.

ZIT POPPING
In July 1987, Carl Chadwick of Rugby, England, squeezed a zit and projected a detectable amount of yellow pus a distance of 7 feet 1 inch.

WORST DRINK
The most horrible drink to be considered a beverage and safely drunk is Khoona. It is drunk by Afghani tribesmen on their wedding night and consists of a small amount of still-warm, very recently obtained bull semen. It is believed to be a potent aphrodisiac.

MOST OFFENSIVE COCKTAIL
This is available from a few select bars in New York. It contains tomato juice, a double shot of vodka, a spoonful of French mustard and a dash of lime. It is not mixed, but served with a tampon (unused) instead of a cocktail umbrella and is known as a 'Cunt Pump'.

GREATEST DISTANCE ATTAINED FOR A JET OF SEMEN
Horst Schultz achieved 18 feet 9 inches with a 'substantial' amount of

seminal fluid. He also hold the records for the greatest height (12 feet 4 inches) and the greatest speed of ejaculation, or muzzle velocity, with 42.7 mph.

LONGEST TURD
The longest dump ever verified was produced by an American, who produced a 'staggering turd' over a period of 2 hours 12 minutes which was officially measured at 12 feet 2 inches. The offender is banned from 134 washrooms in his state.

MOST PROLONGED FART
Bernard Clemmens of London managed to sustain a fart for an officially recorded time of 2 minutes 42 seconds.

Rude Place Names

Nobber (Donegal, Ireland)
Arsoli (Lazio, Italy)
Muff (Northern Ireland)
Bastard (Norway)
Twatt (Shetland, UK)
Twatt (Orkney, UK)
Dildo (Newfoundland, Canada)
Wankie (Zimbabwe)
Climax (Colorado, USA)
Lickey End (West Midlands, UK)
Shafter (California, USA)
Dongo (Democratic Republic of Congo)
Dong Rack (Thailand–Cambodia border)
Donk (Belgium)
Intercourse (Pennsylvania, USA)
Brown Willy (every schoolboy's favourite, Cornwall, UK)

Lord Berkeley's Knob (Sutherland, Scotland)
Shitlingthorpe (Yorkshire, UK)
Stains (Near Paris, France)
Seymen (Turkey)
Turdo (Romania)
Fukum (Yemen)
Fukue (Honshu, Japan)
Fukui (Honshu, Japan)
Fuku (Shensi, China)
Wankie Colliery (Zimbabwe)
Wanks River (Nicaragua)
Wankendorf (Schleswig-Holstein, Germany)
Wankener (India)
Shag Island (Indian Ocean)
Sexmoan (Luzon, Philippines)
Hold With Hope (Greenland)
Beaver (Oklahoma, USA)
Beaver Head (Idaho, USA)
Wet Beaver Creek (Australia)
Pis Pis River (Nicaragua)
Tittybong (Australia)
Dikshit (India)
Middle Intercourse Island (Australia)
Chinaman's Knob (Australia)

40 Interesting Things
You Probably Never Knew

1. The average chocolate bar has 8 insects' legs in it.
2. The average human eats 8 spiders in their lifetime at night.

3. A rhinoceros horn is made of compacted hair.

4. The shortest war in history was between Zanzibar and Britain in 1896. Zanzibar surrendered after 38 minutes.

5. A polar bear's skin is black. Its fur is not white, but clear.

6. Elvis had a twin brother named Garon, who died at birth, which is why Elvis' middle name was spelled Aron, in honor of his brother.

7. Dueling is legal in Paraguay as long as both parties are registered blood donors.

8. Donald Duck comics were banned in Finland because he doesn't wear pants.

9. More people are killed by donkeys annually than are killed in plane crashes.

10. 'Stewardesses' is the longest word typed with only the left hand.

11. Shakespeare invented the words 'assassination' and 'bump'.

12. Marilyn Monroe had six toes on one of her feet.

13. If you keep a goldfish in the dark room, it will eventually turn white.

14. Women blink nearly twice as much as men.

15. Right-handed people live, on average, nine years longer than left-handed people.

16. The sentence, 'The quick brown fox jumps over the lazy dog' uses every letter in the English language.

17. The names of all the continents end with the same letter that they start with.

18. The word "lethologica" describes the state of not being able to remember the word you want.

19. 'Typewriter' is the longest word that can be made using the letters on only one row of the keyboard.

20. If the population of China walked past you in single file, the line would never end because of the rate of reproduction.

21. The words 'racecar' and 'kayak' are the same whether they are read left to right or right to left.

22. A snail can sleep for three years.
23. American Airlines saved $40,000 in 1987 by eliminating one olive from each salad served in first class.
24. China has more English speakers than the United States.
25. The electric chair was invented by a dentist.
26. Did you know you share your birthday with at least nine million other people in the world?
27. 'I am' is the shortest complete sentence in the English language. Not quite. 'Be' is a complete sentence; in an imperative statement, the subject 'you' is understood.
28. The longest word in the English language is 1909 letters long and refers to a distinct part of DNA.
29. Cats have over one hundred vocal sounds, dogs only have about ten.
30. Our eyes are always the same size from birth, but our nose and ears never stop growing.
31. In every episode of Seinfeld there is a Superman somewhere.
32. If Barbie were life-size her measurements would be 39-23-33. She would stand seven feet, two inches tall and have a neck twice the length of a normal human's neck.
33. February 1865 is the only month in recorded history not to have a full moon.
34. The flea can jump 350 times its body length. It's like a human jumping the length of a football field.
35. No word in English rhymes with 'month', 'orange', 'silver' or 'purple'.
36. The cruise liner *Queen Elizabeth II* moves only six inches for each gallon of diesel that it burns.
37. There are two credit cards for every person in the United States.
38. Cat's urine glows under a black light.
39. Leonardo Da Vinci invented scissors.
40. In the last 4000 years, no new animals have been domesticated.

Gender Wars

A language instructor was explaining to her class that French nouns, unlike their English counterparts, are grammatically designated as masculine or feminine. Things like 'chalk' or 'pencil', she described, would have a gender association, although in English these words are neutral.

Puzzled, one student raised his hand and asked: "What gender is a computer?" The teacher didn't know and subsequently divided the class into two groups and asked them to decide if a computer should be masculine or feminine.

One group was composed of the women in the class, and the other of the men. Both groups were asked to give four reasons for their recommendation.

The group of women concluded that computers should be referred to in the masculine gender because:
1. In order to get their attention, you have to turn them on.
2. They have a lot of data but are still clueless.
3. They are supposed to help you solve your problems, but half the time they ARE the problem.
4. As soon as you commit to one, you realize that, if you had waited a little longer, you could have had a better model.

The men, on the other hand, decided that computers should definitely be referred to in the feminine gender because:
1. No-one but their creator understands their internal logic.
2. The native language they use to communicate with other computers is incomprehensible to everyone else.
3. Even your smallest mistakes are stored in long-term memory for later retrieval.

4. As soon as you make a commitment to one, you find yourself spending half your paycheck on accessories for it.

! 🔟 Her Story, His Story

Girl and boy have been in a relationship for about four months now. One Friday night they meet at a bar after work. They stay for a few, then go on to get some food at a local restaurant near their respective houses. They eat, then go back to his house and she stays over.

HER STORY...

Well, Ed was in an odd mood when I got to the bar, I thought it might have been because I was a bit late but he didn't say anything much about it, but the conversation was quite slow going so I thought we should go off somewhere more intimate so we could talk more privately.

So we go to this restaurant and he's still a bit funny and I'm trying to cheer him up and start to wonder whether it's me or something, so I ask him and he says no but you know I'm not really sure, so anyway, in the cab back to his house I say that I love him and he just puts his arm around me and I don't know what the hell that means because you know he doesn't say it back or anything.

So when we get back to his I'm wondering if he's going off me and so I try to ask him about it but he just switches on the TV and so I say I'm going to go to sleep and then after about ten minutes he joins me and we have sex, but he seemed really distracted and so afterwards I just want to leave and I dunno I just don't know what he thinks anymore, I mean, do you think he's met someone else???

HIS STORY...

Shit day at work. Great shag later.

! 🗐 La Différence

NICKNAMES
If Laura, Suzanne, Debra and Rose go out for lunch, they will call each other Laura, Suzanne, Debra and Rose. But if Mike, Charlie, Bob and John go out for a pint, they will affectionately refer to each other as Fat Boy, Godzilla, Peanut-Head and Useless.

EATING OUT
When the bill arrives, Mike, Charlie, Bob and John will each throw in $20, even though it's only for $22.50. None of them will have anything smaller, and none will actually admit they want change back. When the girls get their bill, out come the pocket calculators.

MONEY
A man will pay $2 for a $1 item he wants. A woman will pay $1 for a $2 item that she doesn't want.

BATHROOMS
A man has six items in his bathroom: a toothbrush, shaving cream, razor, a bar of soap and a towel from the Holiday Inn. The average number of items in the typical woman's bathroom is 337. A man would not be able to identify most of these items.

ARGUMENTS
A woman has the last word in any argument. Anything a man says after that is the beginning of a new argument.

FUTURE
A woman worries about the future until she gets a husband. A man never worries about the future until he gets a wife.

SUCCESS
A successful man is one who makes more money than his wife can spend.

A successful woman is one who can find such a man.

MARRIAGE
A woman marries a man expecting he will change, but he doesn't. A man marries a woman expecting that she won't change and she does.

DRESSING UP
A woman will dress up to go shopping, water the plants, empty the garbage, answer the phone, read a book, get the mail. A man will dress up for weddings and funerals.

NATURAL
Men wake up as good-looking as they went to bed. Women somehow deteriorate during the night.

OFFSPRING
Ah, children. A woman knows all about her children. She knows about dentist appointments and romances, best friends and favourite foods and secret fears and hopes and dreams. A man is vaguely aware of some short people living in the house.

Mind Your Language

HOW TO SPEAK ABOUT WOMEN AND BE POLITICALLY CORRECT:

She is not a BABE or a CHICK – She is a BREASTED PERSON.

She is not a SCREAMER or MOANER – She is VOCALLY APPRECIATIVE.

She is not EASY – She is HORIZONTALLY ACCESSIBLE.

She does not TEASE or FLIRT – She engages in ARTIFICIAL STIMULATION.

She is not DUMB – She is a DETOUR OFF THE INFORMATION SUPER-HIGHWAY.

She has not BEEN AROUND – She is a PREVIOUSLY ENJOYED COMPANION.

She does not GET YOU EXCITED – She causes TEMPORARY BLOOD DISPLACEMENT.

She is not KINKY – She is a CREATIVE CARETAKER.

She does not have a KILLER BODY – She is TERMINALLY ATTRACTIVE.

She is not an AIRHEAD – She is REALITY IMPAIRED.

She does not get DRUNK or TIPSY – She gets CHEMICALLY INCONVENIENCED.

She is not HORNY – She is SEXUALLY FOCUSED.

She does not have BREAST IMPLANTS – She is MEDICALLY ENHANCED.

She does not NAG YOU – She becomes VERBALLY REPETITIVE.

She is not a SLUT – She is SEXUALLY EXTROVERTED.

She does not have MAJOR LEAGUE HOOTERS – She is PECTORALLY SUPERIOR.

She is not a TWO-BIT WHORE – She is a LOW COST PROVIDER.

HOW TO SPEAK ABOUT MEN AND BE POLITICALLY CORRECT:

He does not have a BEER GUT – He has developed a LIQUID GRAIN STORAGE FACILITY.

He is not a BAD DANCER – He is OVERLY CAUCASIAN.

He does not GET LOST ALL THE TIME – He INVESTIGATES ALTERNATIVE DESTINATIONS.

He is not BALDING – He is in FOLLICLE REGRESSION.

He is not a CRADLE ROBBER – He prefers GENERATIONALLY DIFFERENTIAL RELATIONSHIPS.

He does not get FALLING-DOWN DRUNK – He becomes ACCIDENTALLY HORIZONTAL.

He does not act like a TOTAL ASS – He develops a case of RECTAL-CRANIAL INVERSION.

He is not a SEX MACHINE – He is ROMANTICALLY AUTOMATED.

He is not a MALE CHAUVINIST PIG – He has SWINE EMPATHY.

He is not afraid of COMMITMENT – He is MONOGAMOUSLY CHALLENGED.

He does not UNDRESS YOU WITH HIS EYES – He has an INTROSPECTIVE GRAPHIC MOMENT.

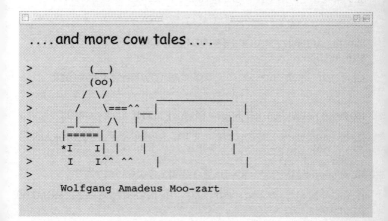

```
....and more cow tales ....

>          (__)
>          (oo)
>         / \/
>        /    \===^^___|
>       _|___ /\  |_____|
>      |=====| |   |                |
>      *I   I| |   |                |
>      I    I^^ ^^ |                |
>
>      Wolfgang Amadeus Moo-zart
```

! Reading the Personals

It's Wednesday, and you're looking for a date in the "Personals" for this weekend. We decided to present this information as a public service:

>> IF A WOMAN SAYS	SHE MEANS
>> 40-ish	49
>> Adventurous	Nymphomaniac
>> Artistic	Depressive
>> Athletic	Flat-chested
>> Average looking	Plain
>> Beautiful	Pathological liar
>> Bubbly	Never shuts up
>> Contagious smile	Bring your penicillin
>> Educated	Opinionated
>> Emotionally secure	Medicated
>> Feisty	Offensive
>> Feminist	Fat, hairy ball-buster
>> Free spirit	Substance user
>> Friendly	Homely and/or promiscuous
>> Friendship first	Trying to live down reputation as a slut
>> Fun	Annoying
>> Gentle	Comatose
>> Good listener	Borderline autistic
>> Gregarious	Drunk and/or promiscuous
>> New-Age	All body hair, all the time
>> Old-fashioned	Lights out, missionary position only
>> Open-minded	Ugly and/or desperate
>> Outgoing	Loud
>> Passionate	Loud and manic
>> Professional	Real witch

>> Rubensesque	Grossly fat
>> Romantic	Looks better by candlelight
>> Voluptuous	Very fat
>> Wants soulmate	Borderline stalker
>> Young at heart	Old

IF A MAN SAYS	HE MEANS
>> 40-ish	55 and looking for a 25 year old
>> Artistic	Unwashed
>> Athletic	Sits on the couch and watches sports
>> Average looking	Unusual hair growth on ears, nose and back
>> Bon viveur	Drunk
>> Creative	Broke
>> Dependable	Boring
>> Educated	Will always treat you like an idiot
>> Free spirit	Serial philanderer
>> Friendship first	Tightfisted and/or ugly
>> Fun	Good with a remote and a six pack
>> Good looking	Arrogant
>> Honest	Pathological liar
>> House-trained	Lifts seat before splashing floor
>> Huggable	Overweight, more body hair than a bear
>> Intellectual	Arrogant, boring, bearded and/or bald
>> Like to cuddle	Insecure, overly dependent
>> Loyal	Desperate
>> Mature	Old
>> Open-minded	Wants to sleep with your sister as well
>> Physically fit	Spends a lot of time admiring himself
>> Poet	Has written on a bathroom stall
>> Rugged	Raddled
>> Spiritual	Once went to church with his grandmother

>> Stable   Occasional stalker, but never arrested
>> Successful   Sad
>> Thoughtful   Says "please" when demanding a beer

! 📎 The Perfect Day

FOR HER

08:15   Wake up to hugs and kisses
08:30   Weigh in 2kg lighter than yesterday
8:45   Breakfast in bed: freshly squeezed orange juice and croissants;
        open presents – expensive jewellery chosen by thoughtful partner
09:15   Soothing hot bath with frangipani oil
10:00   Light workout at club with handsome, funny personal trainer
10:30   Facial, manicure, shampoo, condition, blow dry
12:00   Lunch with best friend at fashionable outdoor cafe
12:45   Catch sight of husband's/boyfriend's ex and notice that she has
        gained 7 kg
13:00   Shopping with friends; unlimited credit
15:00   Nap
16:00   3 dozen red roses delivered by florist from a secret admirer
16:15   Light workout at club followed by massage from strong but gentle
        hunk who says that he rarely gets to work on such a perfect body
17:30   Choose outfit from expensive, designer wardrobe; parade in front
        of full-length mirror
19:30   Candlelit dinner for two followed by dancing, with compliments
        received from other diners/dancers
22:00   Hot shower (alone)
22:50   Carried to bed; freshly ironed, crisp, new white linen
23:00   Pillow talk, light touching and cuddling
23:15   Fall asleep in his big, strong arms

FOR HIM

10:00 Alarm
10:01 Blow job
10:15 Massive, satisfying dump while reading the sports pages
10:30 Breakfast: rump steak and eggs, coffee and toast, all cooked by naked buxom wench
11:00 Limo arrives
11:15 Several whiskies en route to airport
11:30 Flight in personal Lear jet
12:00 Limo to St Andrew's golf club (blow job en route)
13:00 Play front nine (2 under)
13:15 Lunch: pie, chips and gravy, 3 lagers and a bottle of Dom Perignon
13:30 Blow job
14:30 Play back nine (4 under)
14:45 Limo back to airport (several whiskies)
15:00 Fly to Monte Carlo
16:00 Late afternoon fishing excursion with all-female crew (all nude)
16:30 Land world record marlin (1234lb) – on light tackle
17:00 Fly home; massage and hand job by Elle McPherson
18:45 Shit, shower and shave
19:00 Watch news: Brad Pitt assassinated; marijuana and porn legalized
19:45 Dinner: lobster appetizers; Dom Perignon (1953); big juicy fillet steak followed by ice cream served on a big pair of tits
21:00 Napoleon brandy and Cohiba cigar in front of wall-sized TV, showing International Match of the Day – England 11, Germany 0
22:45 Sex with three bisexual women
23:30 Massage and jacuzzi with tasty pizza snacks and a cleansing ale
00:15 Nightcap and blow job
00:30 In bed alone
00:35 A 12-second fart which changes note 4 times and forces the dog to leave the room

Giggles for Girls

⚡ 30 Harsh Things a Woman
📎 Can Say to a Naked Man

>> 1. I've smoked fatter joints than that.
>> 2. Ahhhh, it's cute.
>> 3. Why don't we just cuddle?
>> 4. You know they have surgery to fix that.
>> 5. Make it dance.
>> 6. Can I paint a smiley face on it?
>> 7. Wow, and your feet are so big.
>> 8. It's OK, we'll work around it.
>> 9. Will it squeak if I squeeze it?
>> 10. Oh no ... a flash headache.
>> 11. (giggle and point)
>> 12. Can I be honest with you?
>> 13. How sweet, you brought incense.
>> 14. This explains your car.
>> 15. Maybe if we water it, it'll grow.
>> 16. Why is God punishing me?
>> 17. At least this won't take long.
>> 18. I never saw one like that before.
>> 19. But it still works, right?
>> 20. It looks so unused.
>> 21. Maybe it looks better in natural light.
>> 22. Why don't we skip right to the cigarettes?
>> 23. Are you cold?
>> 24. If you get me real drunk first.

>> 25. Is that an optical illusion?
>> 26. What is that?
>> 27. It's a good thing you have so many other talents.
>> 28. Does it come with an air pump?
>> 29. So this is why you're supposed to judge people on personality.
>> 30. I guess this makes me the early bird.

Courses for Men

1. Introduction to Common Household Objects I: The Mop
2. Introduction to Common Household Objects II: The Sponge
3. Dressing Up: Beyond Weddings and Funerals
4. Refrigerator Forensics: Identifying and Removing the Dead
5. Design Pattern or Splatter Stain on the Linoleum?: You CAN Tell the Difference!
6. If It's Empty, You Can Throw It Away: Accepting Loss I
7. If the Milk Expired Three Weeks Ago, Keeping It In the Refrigerator Won't Bring It Back: Accepting Loss II
8. Going to the Supermarket: It's Not Just for Women Anymore!
9. Recycling Skills I: Boxes that the Electronics Came In
10. Recycling Skills II: Styrofoam that Came in the Boxes that the Electronics Came In
11. Bathroom Etiquette I: How to Remove Beard Clippings from the Sink
12. Bathroom Etiquette II: Let's Wash Those Towels!
13. Bathroom Etiquette III: Five Easy Ways to Tell When You're About to Run Out of Toilet Paper!
14. Giving Back to the Community: How to Donate 15-Year-Old Levis to the Charity Shop
15. Retro? Or Just Hideous?: Re-examining Your 1970s Polyester Shirts
16. No, The Dishes Won't Wash Themselves: Knowing the Limitations of Your Kitchenware

17. Romance: More Than a Cable Channel!
18. Strange But True!: She Really May NOT Care What "Fourth Down and Ten" Means
19. Going Out to Dinner: Beyond the Pizza Hut
20. Expand Your Entertainment Options: Renting Movies That Don't Fall under the "Action/Adventure" Category
21. Yours, Mine and Ours: Sharing the Remote
22. Directions: It's Okay to Ask for Them
23. Adventures in Housekeeping I: Let's Clean the Closet
24. Adventures in Housekeeping II: Let's Clean Under the Bed
25. "I Don't Know": Be the First Man to Say It!
26. The Gas Gauge in Your Car: Sometimes Empty MEANS Empty
27. Accepting Your Limitations: Just Because You Have Power Tools Doesn't Mean You Can Fix It.

! Creation of Man

Seems that the Bible got creation all wrong ... it was actually Eve that God created first.

After three weeks in the garden, God came to visit. "How's it going, Eve?" he asked.

"It is all so beautiful, God, the sunrises and sunsets are breathtaking, the smells, the grandeur ... just so wonderful, but I have this problem with these three breasts of mine. The middle one pushes out the other two and I am constantly knocking them with my arms and catching them on branches and it is basically a nuisance!" reported Eve.

God replied, "Well, that's a good point, but hey, it was my first shot at this, you know. I gave the animals what, six? So I just figured halve it, but I see that you are right. I'll fix that up right away!" So God reached down and ripped that middle breast right out of there and tossed it into the bushes.

Three weeks passed and God once again visited Eve in the garden. "Well, how is my favourite creation?" he asked.

"Just fantastic!" she replied. "But for one small oversight on your part. You see, all the animals are paired off. The ewe has her ram and the cow has her bull; all the animals have a mate except for me and I feel very alone here."

"Oh my! You're so right! How could I have overlooked this! You do need a mate and I will immediately create Man from a part of you! Now let's see ...Where did I leave that useless tit?"

The Desert Island

An ambitious and financially successful guy finally decided to take a vacation. He booked himself on a tropical sea cruise and proceeded to have the time of his life – until the boat sank. The man found himself swept up on the shore of an island with no other people. No supplies, nothing, only bananas and coconuts.

After about four months surviving frugally, he was lying on the beach one day when the most gorgeous woman he had ever seen rowed up to him. In disbelief, he asked her: "Where did you come from? How did you get here?"

"I rowed from the other side of the island," she said. "I landed here when my cruise ship sank."

"Amazing," he replied. "You were really lucky to have a rowboat wash up with you."

"Oh, this?" answered the woman. "I made the rowboat out of raw material that I found on the island; the oars were whittled from gum tree branches; I wove the bottom from palm branches; and the sides and stern came from a Eucalyptus tree."

"But ... but, that's impossible," he stuttered, "You had no tools or hardware. How did you manage?"

"Oh, that was no problem," replied the woman. "On the south side of the island, there is a very unusual strata of alluvial rock exposed. I found that if I fired it to a certain temperature in my kiln, it melted into forgeable ductile iron. I used that for tools and used the tools to make the hardware."

The guy was stunned. So the woman said: "Let's row over to my place."

After a few minutes of rowing, she docked the boat at a small wharf. As the man looked onshore, he nearly fell out of the boat. Before him was a stone walkway leading to an exquisite bungalow.

While the woman tied up the rowboat with an expertly woven hemp rope, the man could only stare ahead, dumbstruck. As they walked into the house, she said casually, "It's not much, but I call it home. Sit down please; would you like to have a drink?"

"No, no thank you," he replied, still dazed. "I can't take any more coconut juice."

"It's not juice," the woman answered. "I have a still. How about a Pina Colada?" Trying to hide his continued amazement, the man accepted, and they sit down on her couch to talk.

After they have exchanged their stories, the woman announced, "I'm going to slip into something more comfortable. Would you like to take a shower and shave? There is a razor upstairs in the cabinet in the bathroom."

No longer questioning anything, the man went into the bathroom. There, in the cabinet, was a razor made from a bone handle. Two shells honed to a hollow ground edge are fastened on to its end, inside of a swivel mechanism. "This woman is amazing," he mused. "What next?"

When he returned, she greeted him wearing nothing but vines strategically positioned – and smelling faintly of gardenias. She beckoned him to sit down next to her.

"Tell me," she began, suggestively, slithering closer to him, "We've been here a very long time. You've been lonely. So have I. There must be something you really miss. Something you'd really like to do?"

He couldn't believe what he was hearing.

"You mean – ?" he swallowed excitedly, "I can check my e-mail from here?"

Golf

A couple met at Hilton Head and fell in love. They were discussing how they would continue the relationship after their vacations were over.

"It's only fair to warn you, Jody," he said. "I'm a golf nut. I live, eat, sleep and breathe golf."

"Well, since you're being honest, so will I," Jody said. "I'm a hooker."

"I see," he said. Then brightening, he smiled. "It's probably because you're not keeping your wrists straight when you hit the ball."

Guide to Men

What do ceramic tile and men have in common? If you lay them right the first time, you can walk on them for life!

How many men does it take to change a roll of toilet paper? Nobody knows. It has never happened.

Why do men have a hole in their penis? So oxygen can get to their brains.

What is the insensitive bit at the base of the penis called? The man.

My boyfriend said that for his physical, the doctor needed a urine specimen, a stool sample and a semen specimen. I told him, "Just give them your underwear."

What do men and beer bottles have in common? They are both empty from the neck up.

Why do men think women have no brains? Because they don't have any testicles to put them in.

What do you call a man with 99% of his brain missing? Castrated.

Why don't men get haemorrhoids? Because they are all perfect assholes.

What's a man's idea of helping with the housework? Lifting his legs so you can vacuum.

Why is psychoanalysis quicker for men than for women? When it's time to go back to childhood, he's half-way there.

What is the best way to get a man to do sit-ups? Put the remote control between his toes.

How do men exercise at the beach? By sucking in their stomachs every time they see a bikini.

Why is it good that we now have female astronauts? When the crew gets lost in space, at least the woman will ask for directions.

What does a man consider to be a seven-course meal? A hotdog and a six pack.

What do a clitoris, an anniversary and a toilet have in common? Men always miss them.

What do you call a woman without an asshole? Divorced.

How do you keep a man from wanting sex? You marry him.

What do most men think Mutual Orgasm is? An insurance company.

How to Shower Like a Man

1. Take off clothes while sitting on the edge of the bed and leave them in a pile.

2. Walk naked to the bathroom. If you see your girlfriend/wife along the way, flash her making the "woo" sound.

3. Look at your manly physique in the mirror and suck in your gut to

see if you have pecs (no). Admire the size of your penis in the mirror, scratch your balls and smell your fingers for one last whiff.

4. Get in the shower.

5. Don't bother to look for a washcloth (you don't use one).

6. Wash your face.

7. Wash your armpits.

8. Crack up at how loud your fart sounds in the shower.

9. Wash your privates and surrounding area.

10. Wash your ass, leaving hair on the soap bar.

11. Shampoo your hair (do not use conditioner).

12. Make a shampoo Mohawk.

13. Pull back shower curtain and look at yourself in the mirror.

14. Pee (in the shower).

15. Rinse off and get out of the shower. Fail to notice water on the floor because you left the curtain hanging out of the tub the whole time.

16. Partial dry off.

17. Look at yourself in the mirror, flex muscles. Admire dick size.

18. Leave shower curtain open and wet bath mat on the floor.

19. Leave bathroom and fan light on.

20. Return to the bedroom with towel around your waist. If you pass your girlfriend/wife, pull off the towel, grab your penis, go "Yeah baby" and thrust your pelvis at her.

21. Throw wet towel on the bed. Take two minutes to get dressed.

! ◎ If Men Had Vaginas

The top ten things MEN would do if they woke up and had a vagina:

10. Immediately go shopping for zucchini and cucumbers.
9. Squat over a hand-held mirror for an hour and a half.
8. See if they could finally do the splits.
7. See if it's truly possible to launch a ping pong ball 20 feet.
6. Cross their legs without rearranging their crotch.
5. Get picked up in a bar in less than 10 minutes ... BEFORE closing.
4. Have consecutive multiple orgasms and still be ready for more without sleeping first.
3. Go to the gynaecologist for a pelvic examination and ask to have it recorded on video.
2. Sit on the edge of the bed and pray for breasts too.

AND the NUMBER ONE thing men would do if they woke up with a vagina:

1. Finally, find that damned G-spot!

! ◎ I'm a Wife

Two guys and a gal were sitting at a bar talking about their professions. The one guy says, "I'm a YUPPIE, you know, Young, Urban, Professional."

The second guys says, "I'm a DINK, you know, Double Income No Kids."

They turn around and ask the woman, "What are you?"

She replies, "I'm a WIFE, you know, Wash, Iron, Fuck, Etc."

! Love is Blind

After a quarrel, a husband said to his wife, "You know, I was a fool when I married you."

She replied, "Yes, dear, but I was in love and didn't notice."

! Men Are Like . . .

Men are like . . . Coffee.
The best ones are rich, warm, full-bodied and can keep you up all night long.

Men are like . . . Cement.
After getting laid, they take a long time to get hard.

Men are like . . . Chocolate bars.
Sweet, smooth and they usually head right for your hips.

Men are like . . . Blenders.
You need one, but you're not quite sure why.

Men are like . . . Coolers.
Load them with beer and you can take them anywhere.

Men are like . . . Copiers.
You need them for reproduction, but that's about it.

Men are like . . . Curling irons.
They're always hot, and they're always in your hair.

Men are like . . . Government bonds.
They take so long to mature.

Men are like . . . High heels.
They're easy to walk on once you get the hang of it.

Men are like ... Horoscopes.
They always tell you what to do and are usually wrong.

Men are like ... Lawn mowers.
If you're not pushing one around, then you're riding it.

Men are like ... Lava lamps.
Fun to look at, but not all that bright.

Men are like ... Laxatives.
They irritate the shit out of you.

Men are like ... Mascara.
They usually run at the first sign of emotion.

Men are like ... Mini skirts.
If you're not careful, they'll creep up your legs.

Men are like ... Noodles.
They're always in hot water, they lack taste and they need dough.

Men are like ... Plungers.
They spend most of their lives in a hardware store or the bathroom.

Men are like ... Popcorn.
They satisfy you, but only for a little while.

Men are like ... Placemats.
They only show up when there's food on the table.

Men are like ... Snowstorms.
You never know when he's coming, how many inches you'll get or how long he will last.

Men are like ... Used cars.
Both are easy-to-get, cheap and unreliable.

Men are like ... Vacations.
They never seem to be long enough.

Men are like ... Weather.
Nothing can be done to change either one of them.

! 📎 Men's English

"I'm hungry." = *I'm hungry.*

"I'm sleepy." = *I'm sleepy.*

"I'm tired." = *I'm tired.*

"Do you want to go to a movie?" = *I'd eventually like to have sex with you.*

"Can I take you out to dinner?" = *I'd eventually like to have sex with you.*

"Can I call you sometime?" = *I'd eventually like to have sex with you.*

"May I have this dance?" = *I'd eventually like to have sex with you.*

"Nice dress!" = *Nice cleavage!*

"You look tense, let me give you a massage." = *I want to fondle you.*

"What's wrong?" = *I don't see why you are making such a big deal out of this.*

"What's wrong?" = *What meaningless self-inflicted psychological trauma are you going through this time?*

"What's wrong?" = *I guess sex tonight is out of the question.*

"I'm bored." = *Do you want to have sex?*

"I love you." = *Let's have sex now.*

"I love you, too." = *Okay, I said it ... we'd better have sex now!*

"Let's talk." = *I am trying to impress you by showing that I am a deep person and maybe this will make you have sex with me.*

"Will you marry me?" = *I want to make it illegal for you to have sex with other guys.*

"I don't think that blouse and that skirt go well together." = *I am gay.*

New Barbie

Introducing WHITE TRASH BARBIE: She's larger and meaner than them other prissy, stuck-up, think-they're-better'n-you Barbies! Now every girl can live the fantasy of ignorance and poverty with her special trailer-park friend.

Every WHITE TRASH BARBIE comes complete with:

• Two packs of Marlboro Lights for Barbie's smoking pleasure!

• A six-pack of Pabst Blue Ribbon beer (it's on sale!) to refresh Barbie during her busy day of bitching and watching TV.

• Stylish, every occasion Spandex pants, halter top and sandals.

• Hot pants or blue jean cut-offs may be substituted on dolls shipped to Alabama. Waffle House uniform sold separately.

• Platinum blonde hair and black roots showing.

• Miracle-o'-procreation button! Press button on Barbie's back and she's pregnant ... again!

• Action bitch pull string! Barbie can say 11 phrases including,
"I tol' jew #$%&@* kids to git the hell outa my yard!"
"Git me anuther beer, baybee."
"Whur's my #$%&@* cigarettes?" – and more!

ALSO AVAILABLE:

1. Barbie double-wide dream trailer: Mobile home comes complete with stained carpet, broken steps and TV set. Barbie's wormy pet cat Rufus also included. Trailer disassembles for use with the Tornado Action Playset (sold separately).

2. Barbie dream car: 1982 Camaro in mix-'n'-match colors, smokin' chokin' exhaust* and coat hanger radio antenna. Holds two white Trash Barbies or fifteen MexMigrant Barbies (sold separately).
*Smoke non-toxic, unless breathed.

3. Abusive boyfriend Ken with Asskickin' leg action and BitchSlap backhand. With cowboy boots and MD 20/20 bottle. Curses and mumbles when string is pulled.

4. Married life Ken with Beer-bustin' expanding waist*. Molded to recliner, with TV remote, beer and chips. Says "Shut up, woman," and "Git me a beer."
*Waist cannot be reduced once expanded.

Road Test

Three women were talking about their love lives.

The first said, "My husband is like a Rolls-Royce; smooth and sophisticated."

The second said, "Mine is like a Porsche; fast and powerful."

The third said, "Mine is like an old Chevy. It needs a hand start and I have to jump on while it's still going."

! 📎 The Female Stress Diet

This is a specially formulated diet, designed to help you cope with the stress that builds up during the day:

BREAKFAST
1 grapefruit
1 slice wholewheat toast
1 cup skimmed milk

LUNCH
Small portion lean, steamed chicken with a cup of spinach
1 cup herbal tea
1 biscuit

AFTERNOON TEA
The rest of the biscuits in the packet
1 tub of Rocky Road Ice Cream with Choc-Ice Topping
1 jar Nutella

DINNER
4 bottles of red wine
2 loaves garlic bread
1 family size supreme pizza
3 Snickers bars

LATE NIGHT SNACK
Whole frozen Sarah Lee cheesecake (eaten directly from the freezer)

DIET RULES
1. If no-one sees you eat something, it has no calories;
2. When drinking a diet Coke with a chocolate bar, the fat in the chocolate bar is cancelled out by the diet Coke;
3. When you eat with someone else, calories don't count if you do not ea

more than they do;

4. Food used for medical purposes does NOT count (for example: hot chocolate, cheesecake and vodka);

5. If you fatten up the people around you, you will look thinner;

6. Cinema-related foods have a zero calorie count as they are part of the entertainment package and not counted as food intake (this includes popcorn, Minties, Maltesers, Jaffas and frozen Cokes);

7. Biscuit pieces have no calories because breaking the biscuits up causes calorie leakage;

8. Food licked from knives and spoons has no fat if you are in the process of cooking something;

9. Foods that are the same colour have the same amount of fat. Examples are: spinach and peppermint ice-cream; apples and red jelly snakes;

10. Chocolate is like a food-colour wildcard and may be substituted for any other colour;

11. Anything eaten while standing has no calories due to gravity and the density of the calorie mass;

12. Food consumed from someone else's plate has no fat as it rightfully belongs to the other person and will cling to his/her plate (oh, how fat likes to cling!).

And remember: STRESSED SPELLED BACKWARDS IS DESSERTS.

! 📎 The Male Stages of Life

	AGE	DRINK
>>	17	beer
>>	25	vodka
>>	35	scotch
>>	48	double scotch
>>	66	cod liver oil

>>	AGE	SEDUCTION LINE
>>	17	My parents are away for the weekend.
>>	25	My girlfriend is away for the weekend.
>>	35	My fiancée is away for the weekend.
>>	48	My wife is away for the weekend.
>>	66	My wife is dead.

>>	AGE	FAVORITE SPORT
>>	17	sex
>>	25	sex
>>	35	sex
>>	48	channel surfing
>>	66	napping

>>	AGE	DEFINITION OF A SUCCESSFUL DATE
>>	17	"Tongue"
>>	25	"Breakfast"
>>	35	"She didn't set back my therapy."
>>	48	"I didn't have to meet her kids."
>>	66	"Got home alive."

>>	AGE	FAVORITE FANTASY
>>	17	a winning goal after the whistle
>>	25	sex in an aeroplane
>>	35	ménage à trois
>>	48	taking over the company
>>	66	Swiss maid/Nazi love slave

>>	AGE	WHAT'S THE IDEAL AGE TO GET MARRIED?
>>	17	25
>>	25	35
>>	35	48

```
>>    48    66
>>    66    17
```

	AGE	IDEAL DATE
>>	17	Triple horror special feature at a drive-in
>>	25	"Split the cheque before we go back to my place."
>>	35	"Just come over."
>>	48	"Just come over and cook."
>>	66	Sex in the company jet on the way to Las Vegas

! 📎 The Wonderful Wife

Sam and Becky are celebrating their 50th wedding anniversary. Sam says to Becky, "Becky, I was wondering – have you ever cheated on me?" Becky replies, "Oh Sam, why would you ask such a question now? You don't want to ask that question ..."

"Yes, Becky, I really want to know. Please ..."

"Well, all right. Yes, 3 times ..."

"Three? Well, when were they?" he asked.

"Well, Sam, remember when you were 35 years old and you really wanted to start the business on your own and no bank would give you a loan? Remember, then one day the bank president himself came over to the house and signed the loan papers, no questions asked?"

"Oh, Becky, you did that for me! I respect you even more than ever, to do such a thing for me. So, when was number two?"

"Well, Sam, remember when you had that last heart attack and you were needing that very tricky operation, and no surgeon would touch you? Then remember how Dr DeBakey came all the way up here, to do the surgery himself, and then you were in good shape again?"

"I can't believe it! Becky, you should do such a thing for me, to save my life. I couldn't have a more wonderful wife. To do such a thing, you must really love me darling. I couldn't be more moved. So, all right then, when was number three?"

"Well, Sam, remember a few years ago, when you really wanted to be president of the golf club and you were 17 votes short ...?"

! Why Do Men ...

Why do men like love at first sight?
It saves them a lot of time.

A woman of 35 thinks of having children. What does a man of 35 think of?
Dating children.

How can you tell soap operas are fictional?
In real life, men aren't affectionate out of bed.

What should you give a man who has everything?
A woman to show him how to work it.

Why don't men have mid-life crises?
They stay stuck in adolescence.

How was Colonel Sanders a typical male?
All he cared about were legs, breasts and thighs.

How is being at a singles bar different from going to the circus?
At the circus the clowns don't talk.

Why do men chase women they have no intention of marrying?
For the same reason dogs chase cars they have no intention of driving.

What's the difference between a new husband and a new dog?
A. A dog is always happy to see you.
B. A dog only takes a couple of months to train.

Why is sleeping with a man like a soap opera?
Just when it's getting interesting, they're finished until next time.

Why are blonde girl jokes so short?
So men can remember them.

Husband: Want a quickie?
Wife: As opposed to what?

What do you have when you have two little balls in your hand?
A man's undivided attention.

Why Men Stand to Pee

Seems God was just about done creating the universe, but he had two extra things left in his bag of creations, so he decided to split them between Adam and Eve. He told the couple that one of the things he had to give away was the ability to stand up while urinating. "It's a very handy thing," God told the couple, who he found under an apple tree. "I was wondering if either one of you wanted the ability."

Adam jumped up and blurted, "Oh, give that to me! I'd love to be able to do that! It seems a sort of thing a man should do. Oh please, oh please, oh please, let me have that ability, it'd be so great! When I'm working in the garden or naming the animals, I could just stand there and let it fly. It'd be so cool, I could write my name in the sand. Oh please God, let it be me who you give that gift to, let me stand and pee, oh please ..."

On and on he went. Eve just smiled and told God that if Adam really wanted that so badly, then he should have it. It seemed to be the sort of thing that would make him happy and she really wouldn't mind if Adam were the one given this ability.

And so Adam was given the ability to control the direction of his misdirection while in a vertical position. And so, he was happy and did celebrate by wetting down the bark on the tree nearest him, laughing with delight all the while. And it was good.

"Fine," God said, looking back into his bag of leftover gifts. "What's left here? Oh yes, multiple orgasms ..."

Why Women Marry

Just think, if it weren't for marriage, men would go through life thinking they had no faults at all.

Grave Matters

Dorothy is very upset as her husband Albert has just passed away. She goes to the mortuary to look at her dearly departed and the instant she sees him she starts wailing and crying. One of the attendants rushes up to comfort her. Through her tears she explains that she is upset because Albert is wearing a black suit and that it was his dying wish to be buried in a blue suit.

"I can't afford to buy one for him," she sobs, "and I feel I've let him down." The attendant apologizes and explains that they always put the bodies in black suits as a matter of course.

"I can't promise anything," he says, "but call in tomorrow, and I'll see what I can do."

The next day Dorothy returns to the mortuary to have one last moment with Albert before his funeral the following day.

When the attendant pulls back the curtain, Dorothy manages to smile through her tears as Albert is now wearing a smart blue suit. She asks the attendant, "How did you manage to get hold of that beautiful blue suit? It's so very kind of you to have gone to all that trouble."

"No, really," says the attendant, "it was no trouble at all. You see, yesterday afternoon after you left, a man about your husband's size and build was brought in and he was wearing a blue suit. His wife explained that she was very upset as he had always wanted to be buried in a black suit.

"After that it was simply a matter of swapping the heads round."

! The Perfect Solution

Paparelli was hung like a horse. He died with an erection, and with rigor mortis, well, the funeral home staff had quite a job ahead of them! They tried strapping it to his body, but it pulled him up into a standing position. They tied it to his leg, but his leg sprang up in the air!

The funeral director called Mrs. Paparelli as to what to do, and she told them to cut it off and shove it up his ass. The undertaker wondered why he hadn't thought of that himself.

At the funeral, the widow noticed that there was a pained expression on the dead man's face. There was even a tear in the corner of his eye. She leaned over and whispered, "See, you bastard, I told you it hurts!"

....and more cow tales....

```
>                 ()  ()                                          (___)
>                  ()()                                  _____|  oo  |
>                  (oo)                                 /            |
>          /-------UU                                  /             |
>         /  |        | |                              /_____      |
>      *   | |w---| |                                     ^ ^        ^ ^
>           ^ ^       ^ ^
>      Eh, What's up Doc?                         Cow dressed up
>                                               as Halloween ghost
```

Guffaws for Guys

⚠ ⓤ Anything for $100

A man was sitting at a bar enjoying an after-work cocktail when an exceptionally gorgeous and sexy young woman entered. She was so striking that the man could not take his eyes away from her. The young woman noticed his overly attentive stare and walked directly toward him.

Before he could offer his apologies for being so rude, the young woman said to him, "I'll do anything, absolutely anything, that you want me to do, no matter how kinky, for $100 on one condition." Flabbergasted, the man asked what the condition was. The young woman replied, "You have to tell me what you want me to do in just three words."

The man considered her proposition for a moment, withdrew his wallet from his pocket and slowly counted out five $20 bills, which he pressed into the young woman's hand.

He looked deeply into her eyes and said, slowly and meaningfully, "Paint my house."

⚠ ⓤ Beer Hormone Test

Scientists had a theory that beer contains small traces of female hormones.

To test their theory, they fed 100 men 12 pints of beer, and observed that 100% of them gained weight, talked excessively loudly without making sense, became emotional and couldn't drive. No further testing was found to be necessary.

! 📎 Boom-boom!

Why do men fart more than women?
Because women won't shut up long enough to build up pressure.

What's the difference between your paycheck and your dick?
You don't have to beg a woman to blow your paycheck.

How is a woman like a laxative?
They both irritate the shit out of you.

Why did God give women nipples?
To make suckers out of men.

What's worse than a male chauvinist pig?
A woman who won't do as she's told.

What's the difference between a woman with PMS and a pitbull?
Lipstick.

How can you tell a macho woman?
She rolls her own tampons.

How many men does it take to fix the vacuum cleaner?
Why the hell should we fix it, we don't use the damn thing!

Why do women skydivers wear tampons?
So they don't whistle on the way down.

How many male chauvinists does it take to change a light bulb?
None. They let the bitch do it when she's finished the dishes.

Why did God create women?
Because dogs can't get beer out the fridge.

What's the difference between a woman from Wigan and a walrus?
One's got a moustache and smells of fish and the other lives in the sea.

What have women and condoms got in common?
If they're not on your dick they're in your wallet.

What's the difference between PMT and BSE?
One's mad cow disease and the other's an agricultural problem.

What do you do if your boiler explodes?
Buy her some flowers.

How can you tell if your wife is dead?
The sex is the same but the dishes pile up.

Courses for Women

Training courses are now available for all women on the following subjects:

1. Silence, the Final Frontier: Where No Woman Has Gone Before
2. The Undiscovered Side of Banking: Making Deposits
3. Parties: Going Without New Outfits
4. Man Management: Minor Household Chores Can Wait
   Till After The Game
5. Bathroom Etiquette I: Men Need Space in the Bathroom Cabinet Too
6. Bathroom Etiquette II: His Razor is His
7. Communication Skills I: Tears – The Last Resort, Not the First
8. Communication Skills II : Thinking Before Speaking
9. Communication Skills III: Getting What You Want Without Nagging
10. Driving a Car Safely: A Skill You CAN Acquire
11. Telephone Skills: How to Hang Up
12. Introduction to Parking

! ◍ Drive-thru Cashpoint Instructions

Please note that with the arrival of the new "Drive-thru" cash point machines customers will be able to withdraw cash without leaving their vehicles.

To enable customers to use this new facility, the following procedures have been drawn up. Please read the procedure that applies to your own circumstances (i.e. MALE or FEMALE) and remember them for when you use the machine for the first time.

MALE PROCEDURE
1. Drive up to the cash machine.
2. Wind down your car window.
3. Insert card into machine and enter PIN.
4. Enter amount of cash required and withdraw.
5. Retrieve card, cash and receipt.
6. Wind up window.
7. Drive off.

FEMALE PROCEDURE

1. Drive up to cash machine.
2. Reverse back the required amount to align car window to machine.
3. Re-start the stalled engine.
4. Wind down the window.
5. Find handbag, remove all contents on to passenger seat to locate card.
6. Locate make-up bag and check make-up in rear view mirror.
7. Attempt to insert card into machine.
8. Open car door to allow easier access to machine due to its excessive distance from the car.
9. Insert card.
10. Re-insert card the right way up.
11. Re-enter handbag to find diary with your PIN written on the inside back page.
12. Enter PIN.
13. Press cancel and re-enter correct PIN.
14. Enter amount of cash required.
15. Re-check make-up in rear view mirror.
16. Retrieve cash and receipt.
17. Empty handbag again to locate purse and place cash inside.
18. Place receipt in back of cheque book.
19. Check eyelashes in mirror.
20. Drive forwards 2 metres.
21. Reverse back to cash machine.
22. Retrieve card.
23. Re-empty handbag, locate card holder and place card into the slot provided.
24. Restart stalled engine and pull off.
25. Drive for three to four miles.
26. Release hand brake.

! 🔟 Feel Like a Woman

In a transatlantic flight, a plane passes through a severe storm. The turbulence is awful, and things go from bad to worse when one wing is struck by lightning.

One woman in particular loses it. Screaming, she stands up in the front of the plane. "I'm too young to die!" she wails. Then she yells, "Well, if I'm going to die, I want my last minutes to be memorable! I've had plenty of sex in my life, but no-one has ever made me really feel like a woman! Well, I've had it! Is there ANYONE on this plane who can make me feel like a WOMAN??"

For a moment there is silence. Everyone has forgotten their own peril, and they all stare, riveted, at the desperate woman in the front of the plane. Then, a man stands up in the rear of the plane. "I can make you feel like a woman," he says.

He's gorgeous. Tall, built, with long, flowing black hair and jet black eyes, he starts to walk slowly up the aisle, unbuttoning his shirt one button at a time. No one moves. The woman is breathing heavily in anticipation as the stranger approaches.

He removes his shirt. Muscles ripple across his chest as he reaches her and extends the arm holding his shirt to the trembling woman, and whispers: "Iron this."

! 🔟 How to Shower Like a Woman

1. Take off clothing and place it in sectioned laundry hamper according to lights and darks.

2. Walk to bathroom wearing long dressing gown. If you see your boyfriend/husband along the way, cover up any exposed flesh and rush

to bathroom.

3. Look at your womanly physique in the mirror and stick out your gut so that you can complain and whine even more about how you're getting fat.

4. Get in the shower. Look for facecloth, armcloth, legcloth, long loofah, wide loofah and pumice stone.

5. Wash your hair once with Cucumber and Lamfrey shampoo with 83 added vitamins.

6. Wash your hair again with Cucumber and Lamfrey shampoo with 83 added vitamins.

7. Condition your hair with Cucumber and Lamfrey conditioner enhanced with natural crocus oil. Leave on hair for fifteen minutes.

8. Wash your face with crushed apricot facial scrub for ten minutes until red raw.

9. Wash entire rest of body with Ginger Nut and Jaffa Cake body wash.

10. Rinse conditioner off hair (this takes at least fifteen minutes as you must make sure that it has all come off).

11. Shave armpits and legs. Consider shaving bikini area but decide to get it waxed instead.

12. Scream loudly when your boyfriend/husband flushes the toilet and you lose the water pressure.

13. Turn off shower.

14. Squeegee off all wet surfaces in shower. Spray mould spots with Tilex.

15. Get out of shower. Dry with towel the size of a small African country. Wrap hair in super-absorbent second towel.

16. Check entire body for the remotest sign of a zit. Attack with nails/tweezers if found.

17. Return to bedroom wearing long dressing gown and towel on head.

18. If you see your boyfriend/husband along the way, cover up any exposed flesh and then rush to bedroom to spend an hour and a half getting dressed.

! New Drugs for Women

With the introduction of Viagra to fix a perennial male problem, a famous British pharmaceutical company is working to redress the balance:

MIRRORCILLIN
A 5cc dose enables a woman to walk past mirrors for up to four hours without pausing once.

STOPPANAGGIN
Gives women a vague feeling of contentment towards their spouse/boyfriend.

COSMOPOLIRA
Doubles female intelligence, allowing 'facts' in trash lifestyle magazines to be disputed.

LOGICON
Trials showed that females taking this were able to follow a proposition through to its logical conclusion, and argue effectively without being diverted into non-relevant postulates such as "You don't love me any more."

PARKATRON

72% of women taking this were able to safely reverse park a Ford Fiesta into a space only 12 metres long; 54% achieved this in under 15 minutes.

MAGNATACK

Uniquely distorts the cornea, making certain shapes appear much larger than in reality – no practical use for this drug has yet been found.

WARDROBIA

Clinical trials show that almost 23% of women taking this drug can safely walk past a sale notice, and an amazing 42% stayed within their credit limit.

BEERINTULIN

Engenders a female desire to bring her spouse/boyfriend alcoholic beverages and snacks during televized sports.

Snails

A wife and her husband were having a dinner party for some important guests. The wife was very excited about this and wanted everything to be perfect.

At the very last minute, she realized that she didn't have any snails for the dinner party, so she asked her husband to run down to the beach with the bucket to gather some snails. Very grudgingly he agreed. He took the bucket, walked out the door, down the steps and out to the beach.

As he was collecting the snails, he noticed a beautiful woman strolling alongside the water just a little further down the beach. He kept thinking to himself, "Wouldn't it be great if she would just come down and talk to me?"

He went back to gathering the snails. All of a sudden he looked up, and the beautiful woman was standing right next to him. They started talking and she invited him back to her place.

They ended up spending the night together. At seven o'clock the next morning he woke up and exclaimed, "Oh no!!! My wife's dinner party!!!"

He gathered all his clothes, put them on real fast, grabbed his bucket and ran out the door. He ran down the beach all the way to his apartment. He ran up the stairs of his apartment.

He was in such a hurry that when he got to the top of the stairs, he dropped the bucket of snails. There were snails all down the stairs. The door opened just then, with a very angry wife standing in the doorway wondering where he's been all this time.

He looked at the snails all down the steps, then he looked at her then back at the snails and said . . .

"Come on guys, we're almost there!"

Ten Things Women Seldom Say

10. Do you think this dress makes me look too slim?
9. You take me out too much, can't we just stay in?
8. A fake one will do.
7. You look stressed out, let me give you a blow job.
6. Have a night out with your mates, you deserve it.
5. That Pamela Anderson has a lovely body.
4. My mother is a real old bitch.
3. No, no, you buy me too much already.
2. Give it to me hard up the butt, big boy, you know I love it.
1. What headache?

The Ages of Women

13 – 18, she is like Africa, virgin and unexplored.
19 – 35, she is like Asia, hot and exotic.

36 – 45, she is like America, fully explored.

46 – 55, she is like Europe, exhausted but still with points of interest.

56+, she is like Australia, everyone knows it's down there but no-one could give a damn.

! The Explanation

A wife arrived home from a shopping trip and was shocked to find her husband in bed with a lovely young woman. Just as she was about to storm out of the house, her husband called out, "Perhaps you should hear how all this came about . . ."

"I was driving home on the highway when I saw this young woman looking tired and bedraggled. I brought her home and made her a meal from the roast beef you had forgotten about in the fridge. She was bare-footed so I gave her your good sandals which you had discarded because they had gone out of style. She was cold so I gave her the sweater which I bought for you for your birthday but you never wore because the colour didn't suit you. Her pants were torn, so I gave her a pair of your jeans, which were perfectly good, but too small for you now.

"Then just as she was about to leave, she asked, 'Is there anything else your wife doesn't use any more?'"

! The Female Stages of Life

>>	AGE	DRINK
>>	17	Wine coolers
>>	25	White wine
>>	35	Red wine
>>	48	Dom Perignon
>>	66	Shot of Jack Daniels with a Napkin chaser

	AGE	EXCUSES FOR REFUSING DATES
>>	17	Need to wash my hair
>>	25	Need to wash and condition my hair
>>	35	Need to colour my hair
>>	48	Need to have Stefan colour my hair
>>	66	Need to have Stefan colour my wig

	AGE	FAVORITE SPORT
>>	17	shopping
>>	25	shopping
>>	35	shopping
>>	48	shopping
>>	66	shopping

	AGE	DEFINITION OF A SUCCESSFUL DATE
>>	17	"McDonalds"
>>	25	"Free meal"
>>	35	"A diamond"
>>	48	"A bigger diamond"
>>	66	"Home Alone"

	AGE	FAVORITE FANTASY
>>	17	tall, dark and handsome
>>	25	tall, dark and handsome with money
>>	35	tall, dark and handsome with money and a brain
>>	48	a man with hair
>>	66	a man

	AGE	WHAT'S THE IDEAL AGE TO GET MARRIED
>>	17	17
>>	25	25

```
>>      35      35
>>      48      48
>>      66      66
```

	AGE	IDEAL DATE
>>	17	He offers to pay
>>	25	He pays
>>	35	He cooks breakfast the next morning
>>	48	He cooks breakfast the next morning for the kids
>>	66	He can chew breakfast

! 📎 The Game of Love

In the world of romance, one single rule applies:

Make the woman happy. Do something she likes, and you get points. Do something she dislikes and points are subtracted. Do something she expects, and you don't get any points. Sorry, that's the way the game is played.

Here is a guide to the point system:

SIMPLE DUTIES:

You make the bed	+1
You make the bed, but forget to add the decorative pillows	0
You throw the bedspread over rumpled sheets	-1
You leave the toilet seat up	-5
You replace the toilet paper roll when it is empty	0
When the toilet paper roll is barren, you resort to Kleenex	-1
When the Kleenex runs out you use the next bathroom	-2
You go out to buy her extra-light panty liners with wings	+5
In the snow	+8

But return with beer .... -5
You check out a suspicious noise at night 0
You check out a suspicious noise and it is nothing 0
You check out a suspicious noise and it is something .... +5
You pummel it with a six iron .... +10
It's her pet .... -10

SOCIAL ENGAGEMENTS
You stay by her side the entire party 0
You stay by her side for a while, then leave to chat with a
   college drinking buddy .... -2
Named Tiffany .... -4
Tiffany is a dancer .... -6
Tiffany has implants .... -8

HER BIRTHDAY:
You take her out to dinner 0
You take her out to dinner and its not a sports bar .... +1
Okay, it is a sports bar .... -2
And it's all-you-can-eat night .... -3
It's a sports bar, it's all-you-can-eat night and your face is
   painted the colours of your favourite team .... -10

A NIGHT OUT WITH THE BOYS:
Go with a pal .... -5
The pal is happily married .... -4
Or frighteningly single .... -7
And he drives a Mustang .... -10
With a personalised license plate (GR8 N BED) .... -15

A NIGHT OUT:
You take her to a movie .... +2
You take her to a movie she likes .... +4
You take her to a movie you hate .... +6

You take her to a movie you like .... -2
It's called DeathCop 3 .... -3
Which features cyborgs that eat humans .... -9
You lied and said it was a foreign film about orphans .... -15

YOUR PHYSIQUE:
You develop a noticeable potbelly .... -15
You develop a noticeable potbelly and exercise to get rid of it. ...... +10
You develop a noticeable potbelly and resort to loose jeans and
   baggy Hawaiian shirts .... -30
You say, "It doesn't matter, you have one too." .... -800

THE BIG QUESTION:
She asks, "Do I look fat?"
You hesitate in responding .... -10
You reply, "Where?" .... -35
Any other response .... -20

COMMUNICATION:
When she wants to talk about a problem:
You listen, displaying what looks like a concerned expression 0
You listen, for over 30 minutes .... +5
You listen for more than 30 minutes without looking at the TV .... +100
She realizes this is because you have fallen asleep .... -200

POINT ACCUMULATION
• Positive points balance out bad points but a positive balance of points
  will evaporate.
• Positive points have a half-life of about 2 weeks.
• Negative points are forever.
• Reaching and maintaining a positive balance of 100 points is required
  for any sex at all.
• Reaching a negative balance of 1000 points will mean divorce.

! 🗐 Those Were the Days

This is an actual extract from a Home Economics textbook, printed in the early 1960s.

Absolutely unbelievable.

Men love it.

Women can't believe it actually existed.

THE GOOD WIVES' GUIDE

Have dinner ready. Plan ahead, even the night before, to have a delicious meal ready on time for his return home from work. This is a way of letting him know that you have been thinking about him and are concerned about his needs.

Most men are hungry when they come home and the prospect of a good meal (especially his favourite dish) is part of the warm welcome needed. Prepare yourself. Take 15 minutes to rest so you will be refreshed when he arrives. Touch up your make-up, put a ribbon in your hair and be fresh looking.

He has just been with a lot of work-weary people. Be a little gay and a little more interesting for him. His boring day may need a lift and one of your duties is to provide it.

Clear away the clutter. Make one last trip through the main part of the house just before your husband arrives. Gather up schoolbooks, toys, papers, etc. and then run a dust cloth over the tables.

Over the cooler months of the year you should prepare and light a fire for him to unwind by. Your husband will feel he has reached a haven o rest and order and it will give you a lift too. After all, catering for his comfort will provide you with immense personal satisfaction.

Minimize all noise. At the time of his arrival, eliminate all noise of the washer, dryer or vacuum. Try to encourage the children to be quiet. Be happy to see him. Greet him with a warm smile and show sincerity in your desire to please him.

Listen to him. You may have a dozen important things to tell him, but the moment of his arrival is not the time. Let him talk first; remember, his topics of conversation are more important than yours.

Make the evening his. Never complain if he comes home late, or goes out to dinner or to other places of entertainment without you. Instead, try to understand his world of strain and his very real need to be at home and relax.

Your goal: Try to make sure your home is a place of peace, order and tranquillity where your husband can renew himself in body and spirit. Don't greet him with complaints and problems.

Don't complain if he's late home for dinner, or even stays out all night. Count this as minor compared to what he might have gone through that day.

Make him comfortable. Have him lean back in a comfortable chair or have him lie down in the bedroom. Have a cool or warm drink ready for him. Arrange the pillow and offer to take off his shoes.

Speak in a low, soothing and pleasant voice.

Don't ask him questions about his actions or question his judgement or integrity. Remember, he is the master of the house and as such will always exercise his will with fairness and truthfulness.

! 📎 Tittyspotting

The Breast Identification Chart

>>	(o)(o)	Perfect breasts
>>	(*)(*)	High nipple breasts
>>	(@)(@)	Big nipple breasts
>>	(o)(o)	A cups
>>	(O)(O)	DD cups
>>	(oYo)	Wonderbra breasts
>>	(o)(O)	Lopsided breasts
>>	(^)(^)	Cold breasts
>>	(O)(Q)	Pierced breasts
>>	(p)(p)	Breasts with hanging tassles
>>	(:o)(o)	Bitten by a vampire breasts
>>	(-)(-)	Flat against the shower breasts
>>	\./\./	Grandma's breasts
>>	(%)(o)	Extra nipple breasts
>>	($)($)	Jenny McCarthy's breasts
>>	(o Y o)	Poses for Playboy magazine

⚠ 📎 True Man Quiz

1. In the company of feminists, coitus should be referred to as:
(a) Lovemaking
(b) Screwing
(c) The pigskin bus pulling into tuna town

2. You should make love to a woman for the first time only after you've both shared:
(a) Your views about what you expect from a sexual relationship
(b) Your blood-test results
(c) Five tequila slammers

3. You time your orgasm so that:
(a) Your partner climaxes first
(b) You both climax simultaneously
(c) You don't miss the big game

4. Passionate, spontaneous sex on the kitchen floor is:
(a) Healthy, creative love-play
(b) Not the sort of thing your wife/girlfriend would ever agree to
(c) Not the sort of thing your wife/girlfriend need ever find out about

5. Spending the whole night cuddling a woman you've just had sex with is:
(a) The best part of the experience
(b) The second best part of the experience
(c) $100 extra

6. Your girlfriend says she's gained five pounds in weight in the last month. You tell her that it is:
(a) No concern of yours
(b) Not a problem – she can join your gym
(c) A conservative estimate

7. You think today's sensitive, caring man is:
(a) A myth
(b) An oxymoron
(c) A moron

8. Foreplay is to sex as:
(a) Appetizer is to entree
(b) Priming is to painting
(c) A queue is to an amusement park ride

9. Which of the following are you most likely to find yourself saying at the end of a relationship?
(a) "I hope we can still be friends."
(b) "I'm not in right now. Please leave a message after the tone ..."
(c) "Welcome to Dumpsville. Population: You."

10. A woman who is uncomfortable watching you masturbate:
(a) Probably needs a little more time before she can cope with that sort of intimacy
(b) Is uptight and a waste of time
(c) Shouldn't have sat next to you on the bus in the first place

If you answered 'A' more than 7 times:
Check your pants to make sure you really are a man.

If you answered 'B' more than 7 times:
Check into therapy, you're still a little confused.

If you answered 'C' more than 7 times:
Give me a call and let's go on the piss!!

! When You're Caught Looking

A personal guide to what men should say when caught looking at another woman by their wife or girlfriend.

I can't believe that outfit she is wearing. (Said disdainfully)

Look at that guy ... over there ... behind the woman.

I think that's a man dressed as a woman. (Incredulous)

Isn't that the actress from the movie 'Delicatessen'? (Chances are she hasn't seen that movie and neither have you, but you will get Brownie points naming a foreign film, and it will be just obtuse enough to distract her.)

I think that's the girl I knew from high school who eventually joined a convent (or was committed to an asylum) and turned out to be a real nut case.

Help me, I got something in my eye ... can't see a thing!

I was staring off into space because I was about to have an epiphany about the direction of my life and the nature of my love for you, but it's gone now, thank you very much!

Hey that's the loser I dumped in order to go out with you. Boy am I glad I ever got away from her. What a moron.

I know you're probably thinking I was staring at a beautiful woman, but to me she is like one of those fancy bakery cakes that looks good, but then you have a bite and it is so sweet that it makes you sick. She makes me sick. (It helps if you convulse a little at the end here ... maybe it will camouflage your drool.)

I was just thinking how I felt sorry for her since she can never hold a candle to you. (This one might only get you punched, but it's worth a try.)

Do you think she's prettier than me? (Give her a taste of her own medicine.)

! Why Men Can't Win

If you work too hard, there is never any time for her.
If you don't work enough, you're a good-for-nothing bum.

If she has a boring repetitive job with low pay, it's exploitation.
If you have a boring repetitive job with low pay, you should get off your butt and find something better.

If you get a promotion ahead of her, it's favouritism.
If she gets a job ahead of you, it's equal opportunity.

If you mention how nice she looks, it's sexual harassment.
If you keep quiet, it's male indifference

If you cry, you're a wimp.
If you don't, you're insensitive.

If you make a decision without consulting her, you're a chauvinist.
If she makes a decision without consulting you, she's a liberated woman.

If you ask her to do something she doesn't enjoy, that's domination.
If she asks you, it's a favour.

If you try to keep yourself in shape, you're vain.
If you don't, you're a slob.

If you buy her flowers, you're after something.
If you don't, you're not thoughtful.

⚠ 📎 Women's English

"Yes" = *No*

"No" = *Yes*

"Maybe" = *No*

"I'm sorry" = *You'll be sorry.*

"We need" = *I want*

"It's your decision" = *The correct decision should be obvious by now.*

"Do what you want" = *You'll pay for this later.*

"We need to talk" = *I need to complain.*

"Sure . . . go ahead" = *I don't want you to.*

"I'm not upset" = *Of course I'm upset, you moron!*

"You're so . . . manly" = *You need a shave and you sweat a lot.*

"You're certainly attentive tonight" = *Is sex all you ever think about?*

"Be romantic, turn out the lights" = *I have flabby thighs.*

"This kitchen is so inconvenient" = *I want a new house.*

"I want new curtains" = *and carpeting, and furniture, and wallpaper . . .*

"Hang the picture there" = *NO, I mean hang it there!*

"I heard a noise" = *I noticed you were almost asleep.*

"Do you love me?" = *I'm going to ask for something expensive.*

"How much do you love me?" = *I did something today you're really not going to like.*

"I'll be ready in a minute" = *Kick off your shoes and find a good game on TV.*

"Is my butt fat?" = *Tell me I'm beautiful.*

"You have to learn to communicate" = *Just agree with me.*

"Are you listening to me!?" = *[Too late, you're dead.]*

"Was that the baby?" = *Why don't you get out of bed and walk until he goes to sleep.*

"I'm not yelling!" = *Yes I am yelling because I think this is important.*

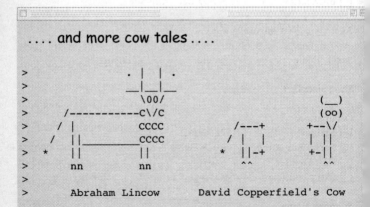

```
.... and more cow tales ....

>                      .  |   |  .
>                     __|__|__
>                       \oo/                        (__)
>      /-----------c\/c                             (oo)
>    /  |           cccc         /---+        +--\/
>   /   ||_____cccc          /  |   |       |  ||
>  *    ||          ||        *  ||-+        +-||
>       nn          nn           ^^            ^^
>
>       Abraham Lincow       David Copperfield's Cow
```

Hicks, Rednecks and Lowlife

⚠ 📎 Alabama Driver's License Application

Last Name: _____

First Name: (Check appropriate box)
[_] Billy-Bob   [_] Bobby-Sue
[_] Bobby-Lee   [_] Jim Bob IV
[_] Billy-Ray   [_] Bobby-Ann
[_] Billy-Sue   [_] Bobby-Lee
[_] Billy-Mae   [_] Bobby-Ellen
[_] Billy-Jack   [_] Bobby-Beth Ann Sue

Age: _____ (if unsure, guess)

Sex: [_]Male   [_]Female   [_]Unsure

Shoe Size: Left_____   Right_____

Occupation:
[_] Farmer   [_] Mechanic   [_] Nail Tech
[_] Postal Employee   [_] Truck Driver   [_] Professional Wrassler
[_] Hair Dresser   [_] Waitress   [_] Pizza deliverer
[_] Dirty Politician   [_] Massage Therapist   [_] Unemployed

Spouse's Name: _____

2nd Spouse's Name: _____

3rd Spouse's Name: _____

Lover's Name: _____

2nd Lover's Name: _____

Relationship to current spouse:
[_] Sister [_] Brother [_] Aunt [_] Uncle [_] Cousin
[_] Mother [_] Father [_] Son [_] Daughter [_] Pet

Number of children living in household:_____

Number of children living in shed:_____

Number that are yours (if known):_____

Mother's Name: _____

Father's Name: _____ (If not sure, leave blank)

Education:
(Circle highest grade completed) 1 2 3 4

Do you [_] own or [_] rent your mobile home?

____ Total number of vehicles that you own

____ Number of vehicles that still crank

____ Number of vehicles in front yard

___ Number of vehicles in back yard

___ Number of vehicles on cement blocks

Model and year of your pickup: _____ 194___

Color of your pickup: [_]Dirt [_]Rust [_]Unsure

Where your firearms are kept:
[_]truck [_]kitchen [_]bedroom [_]bathroom [_]shed

Do you have a gun rack? [_] Yes [_] No
If no, please explain: _____

Newspapers/magazines you subscribe to:
[_] Can't read
[_] National Enquirer   [_] The Globe
[_] TV Guide   [_] Soap Opera Digest
[_] The Star   [_] Rifle and Shotgun

___ Number of times you've seen a UFO
___ Number of times you've seen Elvis
___ Number of times you've seen Elvis in a UFO

How often do you bathe: [_]Weekly [_]Monthly [_]Not applicable

Color of teeth:
[_]Yellow [_]Brown [_]Brownish-Yellow [_]Black [_]N/A
How many? _____

Brand of chewing tobacco you prefer:
[_]Red-Man

Tattoos:

[_] Left Arm	[_] Back	[_] Chest
[_] Right Arm	[_] Neck	[_] Forehead
[_] Left Leg	[_] Right Leg	[_] Private Parts
[_] All of the above	If none, explain:_____	

Memberships:
[_] KKK
[_] NRA
[_] CFAFA (Citizens for a Free America)
[_] AMWF (American Mud Wrestling Federation)
[_] NASCAR Fan Club
[_] Dale Earnhardt Fan Club

Have you ever been arrested?
[_] Yes

How many DWIs in past 12 months?
[_] 1–5
[_] 5–10
[_] More than 10
[_] Can't remember

Criminal Conviction History:
[_] 1–5 Felony Convictions
[_] 6–10 Felony Convictions
[_] 10+ Felony Convictions
[_] Currently in Pen

How far is your home from a paved road?
[_] 5 miles
[_] 10 miles
[_] Don't know

Do you have a mailbox? [_] No [_] Yes

If you do have a mailbox, how many bulletholes are in it?
[_] More than 25

Thank you for your time in applying for an Alabama driver's license.

Please sign the line below to certify the above information is true and correct.

(place "x" here)

```
  ....and more cow tales....

>          (__)              (__)                 (__)
>          (OO)              (@@)                 (xx)
>      /------\/         /--------\/          /------\/
>     / |    ||         / |      ||          / |    ||
>   * ||----||      *  ||------||       *  ||----||
>     ^^    ^^         ^^    ^^            ^^    ^^
>
>   Cow who drank      Cow who ate        Cow who drank
>    Red Bull          psychedelic        Red Bull to wash down
>                      mushrooms          psychedelic mushrooms
```

❗ 📎 Birth Control

After having their eleventh child, a redneck couple decided that that was enough. They could not afford a larger double-wide. So, the husband went to his doctor, who also treated mules, and told him that he and his wife/cousin didn't want to have any more children.

The doctor told him that there was a procedure called a vasectomy that could fix the problem. The doctor instructed him to go home, get a cherry bomb, light it, put it in a beer can, then hold the can up to his ear and count to ten. The redneck said to the doctor, "I may not be the smartest man, but I don't see how putting a cherry bomb in a beer can next to my ear is going to help me."

So the couple drove to get a second opinion. The second doctor was just about to tell them about the medical procedure for a vasectomy when he realized how truly backwards these people were. This doctor instead told the man to go home and get a cherry bomb, light it, place it in a beer can, hold it to his ear and count to ten.

Figuring that BOTH learned physicians couldn't be wrong, the man went home, lit a cherry bomb and put it in a beer can. He held the can up to his ear and began to count. "1, 2, 3, 4, 5 …", at which point he paused, placed the beer can between his legs and resumed counting on his other hand.

❗ 📎 Bubba's Bar

An Irishman, an Italian and a Redneck are in a bar. They are having a good time and all agree that the bar is a nice place.

Then the Irishman says, "Aye, this is a nice bar, but where I come from, back in Dublin, there's a better one. At MacDougal's, you buy a drink, you buy another drink and MacDougal himself will buy your third drink!" The others agree that sounds like a nice place.

Then the Italian says, "Yeah, that's a nice bar, but where I come from, there's a better one. Over in Brooklyn, there's this place, Vinny's. At Vinny's, you buy a drink, Vinny buys you a drink. You buy anudda drink, Vinny buys you anudda drink." Everyone agrees that sounds like a great bar.

Then the Redneck says, "You think that's great? Where I come from, there's this place, Bubba's. At Bubba's, they buy you your first drink, they buy you your second drink, they buy you your third drink, and then, they take you in the back and get you laid!"

"Wow!" said the other two. "That's fantastic! Did that actually happen to you?"

"No," replied the Redneck, "but it happened to my sister!"

Redneck Etiquette

GOING OUT:
1. Never take a beer to a job interview.
2. Always identify people in your yard before shooting at them.
3. It's considered tacky to take a cooler to church.
4. If you have to vacuum the bed, it is time to change the sheets.
5. Even if you're certain that you are included in the will, it is still considered tacky to drive a U-Haul to the funeral home.

DINING OUT:
1. When decanting wine, make sure that you tilt the paper cup, and pour slowly so as not to "bruise" the fruit of the vine.
2. If drinking directly from the bottle, always hold it with your fingers covering the label.

ENTERTAINING IN YOUR HOME:
1. A centerpiece for the table should never be anything prepared by a taxidermist.

2. Do not allow the dog to eat at the table ... no matter how good his manners are.

PERSONAL HYGIENE:
1. While ears need to be cleaned regularly, this is a job that should be done in private using one's OWN truck keys.
2. Proper use of toiletries can forestall bathing for several days. However, if you live alone, deodorant is a waste of good money.
3. Dirt and grease under the fingernails is a social no-no, as they tend to detract from a woman's jewelry and alter the taste of finger foods.

DATING (Outside the Family):
1. Always offer to bait your date's hook, especially on the first date.
2. Be aggressive. Let her know you're interested: "I've been wanting to go out with you since I read that stuff on the bathroom wall two years ago."
3. Establish, with her parents, what time she is expected back. Some will say 10:00pm; others might say "Monday." If the latter is the answer, it is the man's responsibility to get her to school on time.

THEATER ETIQUETTE:
1. Crying babies should be taken to the lobby and picked up immediately after the movie has ended.
2. Refrain from talking to characters on the screen. Tests have proven they can't hear you.

WEDDINGS:
1. Livestock is usually a poor choice for a wedding gift.
2. Kissing the bride for more than five seconds may get you shot.
3. For the groom, at least, rent a tux. A leisure suit with a cummerbund and a clean bowling shirt can create a tacky appearance.
4. Though uncomfortable, say "yes" to socks and shoes for this special occasion.

DRIVING ETIQUETTE:

1. Dim your headlights for approaching vehicles, even if the gun is loaded, and the deer is in sight.
2. When approaching a four-way stop, the vehicle with the largest tires always has the right of way.
3. Never tow another car using panty hose and duct tape.
4. When sending your wife down the road with a gas can, it is impolite to ask her to bring back beer.
5. Do not lay rubber while traveling in a funeral procession.

Redneck Q & A

Q: Did you hear about the redneck who passed away and left his entire estate in trust for his beloved widow?
A: She can't touch it till she's fourteen.

Q: What's the difference between a good ol' boy and a redneck?
A: The good ol' boy raises livestock. The redneck gets emotionally involved.

Q: What's the most popular pick-up line in Arkansas?
A: Nice tooth!

Q: How do you know when you're staying in an Arkansas hotel?
A: When you call the front desk and say, "I've gotta leak in my sink," and the person at the front desk says, "Go ahead."

Q: What is a redneck's defense in court?
A: "Honest, your Honor, I was just helping the sheep over the fence."

Q: Did you hear that they have raised the minimum drinking age in West Virginia to 32?
A: It seems they want to keep alcohol out of the high schools!

Q: How many rednecks does it take eat a possum?
A: Two. One to eat, and one to watch for cars.

Telling Them Apart

A pregnant woman walked into a doctor's office to have an ultrasound. The doctor told her that she was going to have a little girl. He then asked her what she would name her daughter.

She said, "Helen."

He asked her, "Do you have any other children?"

She said, "Five other daughters, and their names are also Helen."

At that point the doctor asked, "How do you call them all home for dinner?"

She replied, "That's easy. I just yell, 'Helen, supper!' and they all come home."

He then asked, "What if you're going somewhere?"

She said, "That's easy too, I just say, 'Helen lets go!' and they all come running."

He questioned her again, "What if you only want to speak with one of them?"

"Well, then I just call them by their last name."

It's Education, Stupid

Quotes from British exam scripts. Every effort has been made to reproduce these gems verbatim.

"I've said goodbye to my boyhood, now I'm looking forward to my adultery."

"Monotony means being married to the same person for all your life."

"I always know when it's time to get up when I hear my mother sharpening the toast."

"A sexually transmitted disease is gonorrhea, the penis becomes inflammable."

"A major disease associated with smoking is premature death."

"The equator is a menagerie lion running around the earth through Africa."

"Artificial insemination is when the farmer does it to the cow instead of the bull."

"Cows produce large amounts of methane, so the problem could be solved by fitting them with catalytic converters."

"The process of flirtation makes water safe to drink because it removes large pollutants like grit, sand, dead sheep and canoeists."

"An important difference between the male and female reproductive systems is that a tube joins the testis to the exterior called the vast difference."

"Water is composed of two gins, Oxygin and Hydrogin. Oxygin is pure gin. Hydrogin is gin and water."

"When you breathe, you inspire. When you do not breathe, you expire."

"H_2O is hot water, and CO_2 is cold water."

"To collect fumes of sulphur, hold down a deacon over a flame in a test tube."

"When you smell an odourless gas, it is probably carbon monoxide."

"Nitrogen is not found in Ireland because it is not found in a free state."

"Three kinds of blood vessels are arteries, vanes and caterpillars."

"Blood flows down one leg and up the other."

"A super-saturated solution is one that holds more than it can hold."

"Mushrooms always grow in damp places and so they look like umbrellas."

"The body consists of three parts: the brainium, the borax and the abominable cavity. The brainium contains the brain, the borax contains the heart and lungs and the abominable cavity contains the bowels, of which there are five: a, e, i, o and u."

"For fainting: Rub the person's chest or, if a lady, rub her arm above the hand instead. Or put the head between the knees of the nearest medical doctor."

"To prevent contraception: wear a condominium."

"A permanent set of teeth consists of eight canines, eight cuspids, two molars and eight cuspidors."

"The tides are a fight between the earth and moon. All water tends towards the moon, because there is no water in the moon, and nature abhors a vacuum. I forget where the sun joins in this fight."

"A fossil is an extinct animal. The older it is, the more extinct it is."

"Red, pink, orange and blue are the colours of the rectum."

"Christians go on pilgrimage to Lord's."

"Ration is composed of two acts – first inspiration and then expectoration."

"The moon is a planet just like the earth, only deader."

"Dew is formed on leaves when the sun shines down on them and makes them perspire."

"Momentum – what you give a person when they are going away."

"Planet – a body of earth surrounded by sky."

"To remove dust from the eye pull the eye down over the nose."

"For a nosebleed put the nose much lower than the body until the heart stops."

"For drowning climb on top of the person and move up and down to make artificial perspiration."

"For dog bite put the dog away for several days. If the dog hasn't recovered, kill it."

"For a cold use an agonizer to spray the nose until it drops into your throat."

"To keep milk from turning sour keep it in the cow."

"The pistol of a flower is its only defence against insects."

"The alimentary canal is located in the northern part of Indiana."

"The skeleton is what is left after the insides have been taken out and the outsides have been taken off. The purpose of the skeleton is something to hitch meat to."

! Progress in Mathematics

TEACHING MATHS IN 1950 ...
A logger sells a truckload of lumber for $100.
His cost of production is 4/5 of the price.
What is his profit?

TEACHING MATHS IN 1960 ...
A logger sells a truckload of lumber for $100.
His cost of production is 4/5 of the price, or $80.
What is his profit?

TEACHING MATHS IN 1970 ...
A logger exchanges a set -L- of lumber for a set -M- of money.
The cardinality of set -M- is 100.
Each element is worth one dollar.
Make 100 dots representing the elements of the set -M-.
The set -C-, the cost of production, contains 20 fewer points than set -M-.
Represent the set -C- as a subset of set -M- and answer the following
    question:
What is the cardinality of the set -P- for profits?

TEACHING MATHS IN 1980 ...
A logger sells a truckload of lumber for $100.
Her cost of production is $80 and her profit is $20.
Your assignment: Underline the number 20.

TEACHING MATHS IN 1990 ...
By cutting down beautiful forest trees, the logger makes $20.
What do you think of this way of making a living?
Topic for class participation after answering the question:
How did the forest birds and squirrels feel as the logger cut down the trees?
There are no wrong answers.

TEACHING MATHS IN 1996 ...

By laying off 40% of its loggers, a company improves its stock price from
$80 to 100.

How much capital gain, per share, does the CEO make, by exercising his
stock options at 80?

Assume capital gains are no longer taxed, because this encourages
investment.

TEACHING MATHS IN 1997 ...

A company outsources all of its loggers.

The contracted logger charges $50 an hour.

The firm saves on benefits, and when demand for its product is down,
the logging work force can easily be cut back.

Prior to outsourcing loggers, the average logger employed by the
company used to earn $50,000 a year, had three weeks vacation, a nice
retirement plan and medical insurance.

Was outsourcing a good move?

TEACHING MATHS IN 1998 ...

A laid-off logger with four kids at home and a ridiculous alimony from
his first failed marriage comes into the logging company corporate
offices and goes postal, mowing down 16 executives and a couple of
secretaries, and gets lucky when he nails a politician on the premises
collecting his kickback.

Was outsourcing the loggers a good move for the company?

TEACHING MATHS IN 1999 ...

A laid-off logger serving time in prison for blowing away several people
at the logging company corporate offices is being trained computer
science in order to work on SAP projects.

What is the probability that the automatic cell doors will open on their
own as of 00:01, 01/01/00?

Kids' Stuff

❗📎 A Boy and His Frog

A little boy about twelve years old was walking down the sidewalk pulling a wagon and dragging a flattened frog on a string behind it, when he came up to the doorstep of a house of ill repute.

He knocked on the door, and the madam came to answer it, saw him and asked what he wanted. He said he wanted what she was selling inside, had the money to buy it and wasn't leaving until he got it. She thought she would have some fun with him, so she told him to come in.

Once he got in, she told him to pick one of the girls he liked; he asked her if any of the girls had any diseases, and of course the madam said no. But he said he'd heard that all the men were talking about having to go to the hospital and get shots after making love with Mabel, and THAT was the girl he wanted, and that he had the money to pay for it. The madam told him to go upstairs and go to the first room on the right.

So he headed down the hall dragging the frog behind him. Ten minutes later he came back down still dragging the frog. He paid the madam, and picked up his wagon and headed out the door, at which time the madam stopped him and asked him just why he picked the only girl she had in the place with a disease, instead of one of the others.

He said: "Well, if you must know, tonight when I get home, my parents are going out to a restaurant to eat, leaving me at home with a baby-sitter. When they leave, I'm going to screw the baby-sitter, who happens to be very fond of cute little boys, and give her the disease that I just caught. When mom and dad get back, dad will take the baby-sitter home, and on the way, he'll jump her bones, and he'll catch it. When dad gets home, he and mom will go to bed, they'll make love and mom will catch it. In the morning when Dad goes to work, the milkman will deliver the milk, and he'll have a quickie with mom, and he'll catch it, and HE'S the son-of-a-bitch that ran over my FROG . . ."

A Fact of Life

A father picked up his nine-year-old daughter after school to take her home. On the way home, the little girl looked out the window and saw two dogs, male and female, doing what dogs do.

"Daddy," she asked, "what are those dogs doing?"

Not wanting to get into a discussion about the facts of life with his daughter at her tender age, the father replied, "Well, honey, the little dog on top must have hurt his feet on the hot cement, so the doggie undeneath is just helping out by giving him a ride home. Okay?"

The little girl glanced back at the dogs and sighed, "Isn't that just the way it always is . . .

"you try to help someone out and they fuck you in the arse."

Are You Ready to Have Children?

THE MESS TEST:
Smear peanut butter on the sofa and curtains. Now rub your hands in the wet flower bed and rub on the walls. Cover the stains with crayons. Place a fish stick behind the couch and leave it there all summer.

THE TOY TEST:
Obtain a 55-gallon box of Lego. (If Lego is not available, you may substitute roofing tacks or broken bottles.) Have a friend spread it all over the house. Put on a blindfold. Try to walk to the bathroom or kitchen. Do not scream. (This could wake a child at night.)

THE GROCERY STORE TEST:
Borrow one or two small animals (goats are best) and take them with you as you shop at the grocery store. Always keep them in sight and pay for anything they eat or damage.

THE DRESSING TEST:
Obtain one large, unhappy, live octopus. Stuff into a small net bag, making sure that all arms stay inside.

THE FEEDING TEST:
Obtain a large plastic milk jug. Fill halfway with water. Suspend from the ceiling with a stout cord. Start the jug swinging. Try to insert spoonfuls of soggy cereal into the mouth of the jug, while pretending to be an airplane. When finished, dump the contents of the jug on the floor.

THE NIGHT TEST:
Prepare by obtaining a small cloth bag and fill it with 8–12 pounds of sand. Soak it thoroughly in water. At 8:00 p.m. begin to waltz and hum with the bag until 9:00 p.m. Lay down your bag and set your alarm for 10:00 p.m. Get up, pick up your bag and sing every song you have ever heard. Make up about a dozen more and sing these too until 4:00 a.m. Set alarm for 5:00 a.m. Get up and make breakfast. Keep this up for five years. Look cheerful.

THE PHYSICAL TEST (WOMEN):
Obtain a large beanbag chair and attach it to the front of your clothes. Leave it there for nine months. Now remove ten of the beans.

THE PHYSICAL TEST (MEN):
Go to the nearest drugstore. Set your wallet on the counter. Ask the clerk to help himself. Now proceed to the nearest food store. Go to the head office and arrange for your paycheck to be directly deposited to the store. Purchase a newspaper. Go home and read it quietly for the last time.

THE FINAL ASSIGNMENT:

Find a couple who already have a small child. Lecture them on how they can improve their discipline, patience, tolerance, toilet training and child's table manners. Suggest many ways they can improve, Emphasize to them that they should never allow their children to run riot. Enjoy this experience. It will be the last time you will have all the answers.

Bad

Q: How do the little boys at Michael Jackson's ranch know when it is bedtime?
A: When the big hand touches the little hand ...

Q: What's somewhat brown and often found in children's underpants?
A: Michael Jackson's hand.

Q: What is blonde, has six legs and roams Michael Jackson's dreams every night?
A: Hanson.

Children's Books That Didn't Make It

> 1 You are Different and That's Bad
> 2 The Boy Who Died From Eating All His Vegetables
> 3 Dad's New Wife Timothy
> 4 Fun Four-letter Words to Know and Share
> 5 Hammers, Screwdrivers and Scissors: An I-Can-Do-It Book
> 6 The Kids' Guide to Hitchhiking
> 7 Kathy Was So Bad Her Mom Stopped Loving Her
> 8 Curious George and the High-Voltage Fence
> 9 All Dogs Go to Hell
> 10 The Little Sissy Who Snitched

Great Little Truths That Children Have Learned

No matter how hard you try, you can't baptize cats.

When your Mom is mad at your Dad, don't let her brush your hair.

If your sister hits you, don't hit her back. They always catch the second person.

Never ask a three-year old to hold a tomato.

You can't trust dogs to watch your food.

Don't sneeze when someone is cutting your hair.

Puppies still have bad breath even after eating a tic-tac.

Never hold a dustbuster and a cat at the same time.

School lunches stick to the wall.

You can't hide a piece of broccoli in a glass of milk.

Don't wear polka-dot underwear under white shorts.

Hollywood Family Values

Two little girls were sitting in the lunchroom of the Beverly Hills Elementary School.

"Guess what?" one said. "Mommy's getting married again and I'll have a new Daddy."

"Really?" said the other girl. "Who is she marrying?"

"Winston James, the famous Director."

The second girl smiled. "Oh, you'll like him. He was my Daddy last year."

! 📎 Playing Doctor

After discovering her young daughter playing doctor with the neighbor boy, the angry mother grabbed the boy by the ear and dragged him to his house and confronted his mother.

"It's only natural for young boys and girls to explore their sexuality by playing doctor at their age," the neighbor said.

"Sexuality?!" the mother yelled. "He took out her appendix!"

! 📎 Playing Trains

There once was a five-year-old boy who enjoyed playing with his train set. One afternoon, his mother happened to be standing by the door listening to the boy play. She was shocked when she heard him saying,

"All right, all of you son of bitches who want to get on the train, get on train. And all of you son of bitches who want to get off the train, get off the train. And all of you son of bitches who want to change seats, change seats now 'cause the trains getting ready to leave. Whoo whooooo."

The mother was just devastated, so she scolded her son and said him, "Now son, I want you to go upstairs and take your nap, and when you get up, you can't play with your train set for two hours."

So the boy took his nap and didn't even mention his train set for two hours. After the two hours were up, the boy asked his mom if he could play with his train set again. She said yes, and asked him if he understood why he was punished. He nodded his head yes, and off he went.

The mother stood by door to listen to what her son would say. The boy sat down to his train set and calmly said,

"Whoo whooooooo. All of you ladies and gentlemen who want to get on the train, get on the train. All of you ladies and gentlemen who want to get off the train, get off the train.

"And all you son of bitches who are pissed 'cause the train is two hours late, go talk to the bitch in the kitchen."

Polysyllabic Johnny

The first grade teacher was starting a new lesson on multi-syllable words and thought it would be a good idea to ask a few of the children examples of words with more than one syllable.

"Jane, Do you know any multi-syllable words?" After some thought Jane proudly replied with Monday.

"Great Jane, that has two syllables, Mon – day. Does anyone know another word?"

"I do, I do, me, me, me," replied Johnny. Knowing Johnny's more mature sense of humor she picks Mike instead.

"OK Mike, what is your word."

"Saturday," says Mike.

"Great, that has three syllables."

Not wanting to be outdone, Johnny says "I know a four syllable word, pick me!"

Not thinking he can do any harm with a word that large the teacher reluctantly says, "O.K. Johnny what is your four syllable word?" Johnny proudly says, "Mas – tur – ba – tion."

Shocked, the teacher, trying to retain her composure says, "Wow, Johnny, four syllables, that certainly is a mouthful."

"No Ma'am, you're thinking of blow job, and that's only two syllables."

! Talented Dad

Three little boys were sitting on the porch, when one little boy says, "My Daddy smokes, and he can blow smoke rings."

The second little boy pipes up, "Well, my Dad smokes, too, and can blow smoke out of his eyes."

The third little boy, not to be outdone, responds, "My Dad can blow smoke out of his butt."

"Really, have you seen it?" reply the boys.

The third boy responds, "No, but I've seen the tobacco stains on his underwear..."

! Teenyboppers

Q: What's got 500 legs and no pubic hair?
A: The front row at a Boyzone concert.

! The View from the Balcony

Bill and Marla decided that the only way to pull off a Sunday afternoon quickie with their ten-year-old son in the apartment was to send him out on the balcony and order him to report on all the neighborhood activities.

The boy began his commentary as his parents put their plan into operation.

"There's a car being towed from the parking lot," he said.

"An ambulance just drove by."

A few moments passed.

"Looks like the Andersons have company," he called out, "Matt's riding a new bike and the Coopers are having sex."

Mom and Dad shot up in bed. "How do you know that?" the startled father asked.

"Their kid is standing out on the balcony too," his son replied.

Lavatorial Matters

! 🔗 Bathroom Graffiti

>> Here I sit,
>> All broken hearted
>> came to shit,
>> but only farted.
>> Then one day I took a chance;
>> went to fart, and shit my pants!
>>
>>
>> Here I sit, I'm at a loss
>> trying to shit out taco sauce.
>> When it comes, I hope and pray,
>> I don't blow my ass away.
>>
>>
>> Here I lie in stinky vapor,
>> Because some bastard stole the toilet paper,
>> Shall I lie, or shall I linger,
>> Or shall I be forced to use my finger.
>>
>>
>> Some come here to sit and think,
>> Some come here to shit and stink,
>> But I come here to scratch my balls,
>> And read the bullshit on the walls ...
>>

✪ ◍ Cough Syrup

John was a clerk in a small drugstore but he was not much of a salesman. He could never find the item the customer wanted. Bob, the owner, had had about enough and warned John that the next sale he missed would be his last.

Just then a man came in coughing, and he asked John for their best cough syrup. Try as he might, John could not find the cough syrup. Remembering Bob's warning, he instead sold the man a box of Ex-Lax and told him to take it all at once. The customer did as John said immediately, and then walked outside and leaned against a lamp post. Bob had seen the whole thing and came over to ask John what had transpired.

"He wanted something for his cough but I couldn't find the cough syrup. I substituted Ex-Lax and told him to take it all at once," John explained.

"But, Ex-Lax won't cure a cough!" Bob shouted angrily.

"Sure it will," John said, pointing at the man leaning on the lamp post.

"Look at him. He's afraid to cough."

✪ ◍ These You Have Shat

THE GHOST SHIT
The kind where you feel shit come out, see shit on the toilet paper, but there's no shit in the bowl.

THE CLEAN SHIT
The kind where you feel shit come out, see shit in the bowl, but there's no shit on the toilet paper.

THE WET SHIT
You wipe your ass fifty times and it still feels unwiped. So you end up putting toilet paper between your ass and your underwear so you don't ruin them with those dreadful skid marks.

THE SECOND WAVE SHIT
This shit happens when you've finished, your pants are up to your knees, and you suddenly realize you have to shit some more.

THE BRAIN HEMORRHAGE THROUGH YOUR NOSE SHIT
Also known as the "Pop a Vein in your Forehead" Shit. You have to strain so much to get it out that you turn purple and practically have a stroke.

THE CORN SHIT
No explanation necessary.

THE LINCOLN LOG SHIT
The kind of shit that's so enormous you're afraid to flush it down without first breaking it up into little pieces with the toilet brush.

THE NOTORIOUS DRINKER SHIT
The kind of shit you have the morning after a long night of drinking. Its most noticeable trait is the skid mark left on the bottom of the toilet bowl after you flush.

THE "GEE, I REALLY WISH I COULD SHIT" SHIT
The kind where you want to shit, but even after straining your guts out, all you can do is sit on the toilet, cramped and farting.

THE WET CHEEKS SHIT
Also known as the "Power Dump". That's the kind that comes out of your ass so fast that your butt cheeks get splashed with the toilet water.

THE LIQUID SHIT
That's the kind where yellowish-brown liquid shoots out of your butt, splashes all over the side of the toilet bowl and, at the same time, chronically

burns your tender poop-chute.

THE CROWD PLEASER

This shit is so intriguing in size and/or appearance that you have to show it to someone before flushing.

THE CRACK FLAPPER SHIT

This shit seems to create its own weather system. Your butt cheeks feel like they're flapping in the wind when this shit comes out.

THE MOOD ENHANCER

This shit occurs after a lengthy period of constipation, thereby allowing you to be your old self again.

THE "ON THE CLOCK" SHIT

This is any shit that you take while you are punched in at work. Lunch hour and coffee break shits do not qualify.

THE "BEST NICKEL I EVER SPENT" SHIT

This is any shit that you take in a "pay" bathroom. Thankfully, there aren't too many of these left. If you're ever in a Mexican border town, be sure to try one!

THE RITUAL

This shit occurs at the same time each day and is accomplished with the aid of a newspaper.

THE GUINESS BOOK OF RECORDS SHIT

A shit so noteworthy it should be recorded for future generations.

THE AFTERSHOCK SHIT

This shit has an odour so powerful than anyone entering the vicinity within the next seven hours is affected.

THE "HONEYMOON'S OVER" SHIT

This is any shit created in the presence of another person.

THE GROANER
A shit so huge it cannot exit without vocal assistance.

THE FLOATER
Characterized by its floatability, this shit has been known to resurface after many flushings.

THE RANGER
A shit which refuses to let go. It is usually necessary to engage in a rocking or bouncing motion, but quite often the only solution is to push it away with a small piece of toilet paper.

THE PHANTOM SHIT
This appears in the toilet mysteriously and no one will admit to putting it there.

THE PEEK-A-BOO SHIT
Now you see it, now you don't. This shit is playing games with you. Requires patience and muscle control.

THE BOMBSHELL
A shit that comes as a complete surprise at a time that is either inappropriate to shit (i.e. during lovemaking or a root canal) or you are nowhere near shitting facilities.

THE SNAKE CHARMER
A long skinny shit which has managed to coil itself into a frightening position – usually harmless.

THE OLYMPIC SHIT
This shit occurs exactly one hour prior to the start of any competitive event in which you are entered and bears a close resemblance to the Drinker's Shit.

THE BACK-TO-NATURE SHIT
This shit may be of any variety but is always deposited either in the

woods or while hiding behind the passenger side of your car.

THE PEBBLES-FROM-HEAVEN SHIT
An adorable collection of small turds in a cluster, often a gift from God when you actually CAN'T shit.

PREMEDITATED SHIT
Laxative induced. Doesn't count.

SHITZOPHRENIA
Fear of shitting – can be fatal!

ENERGIZER vs DURACELL SHIT
Also known as a "Still Going" shit.

THE ROCKET SHIT
The kind that comes out so fast, you barely get your pants down when you're done.

THE LIQUID PLUMBER SHIT
This kind of shit is so big it plugs up the toilet and it overflows all over the floor. (You should have followed the advice from the Lincoln Log Shit.)

THE SPINAL TAP SHIT
The kind of shit that hurts so much coming out, you'd swear it's got to be coming out sideways.

THE "I THINK I'M GIVING BIRTH THROUGH MY ASSHOLE" SHIT
Similar to the Lincoln Log and The Spinal Tap Shits. The shape and size of the turd resembles a tall boy beer can. Vacuous air space remains in the rectum for some time afterwards.

THE PORRIDGE SHIT
The type that comes out like toothpaste, and just keeps on coming. You have two choices: (a) flush and keep going, or (b) risk it piling up to your butt while you sit there helpless.

THE "I'M GOING TO CHEW MY FOOD BETTER" SHIT
When the bag of Doritos you ate last night lacerates the insides of your rectum on the way out in the morning.

THE "I THINK I'M TURNING INTO A BUNNY" SHIT
When you drop lots of cute, little round ones that look like marbles and make tiny splashing sounds when they hit the water.

THE "WHAT THE HELL DIED IN HERE?" SHIT
Also sometimes referred to as The Toxic Dump. Of course you don't warn anyone of the poisonous bathroom odour. Instead, you stand innocently near the door and enjoy the show as they run out gagging and gasping for air.

THE "I JUST KNOW THERE'S A TURD STILL DANGLING THERE" SHIT
Where you just sit there patiently and wait for the last cling-on to drop off because if you wipe now, it's going to smear all over the place.

THE PERFECT SHIT
Every once in a while, each of us experiences a perfect shit; it's rare, but a thing of beauty in all respects. You sit down expecting the worst, but what you get is a smooth sliding, fartless masterpiece that breaks the water with the splashless grace of an expert diver. But that's not the end of it. You use some toilet tissue only to find that it was totally unnecessary. It makes you feel that all is right with the world and you are in perfect harmony with it.

Militaria

Discharge Emission

"Well," snarled the tough old sergeant to the bewildered private. "I suppose after you get discharged from the Army, you'll just be waiting for me to die so you can come and spit on my grave."

"Not me, Sarge!" the private replied. "Once I get out of the Army, I'm never going to stand in line again!"

Expertise

The new Ensign was assigned to subs, where he'd dreamed of working since a young boy. He was trying to impress the Master Chief with his expertise learned in Sub School.

The Master Chief cut him off quickly and said, "Listen, 'sir', it's real simple. Add the number of times we dive to the number of times we surface. Divide that number by two. If the result doesn't come out even, don't open the hatch."

Naval Intelligence

This is the transcript of the ACTUAL radio conversation of a US Naval ship and the Canadian Coastguard, off the coast of Newfoundland, October 1995. Radio conversation released by the Chief of Naval Operations 10-10-95.

COASTGUARD: Please divert your course 15 degrees to the South, to avoid a collision.

AMERICANS: Recommend you divert your course 15 degrees to the North, to avoid a collision.

C: Negative. You will have to divert your course 15 degrees to the South to avoid a collision.

A: This is the Captain of a US Navy ship. I say again, divert YOUR course.

C: Negative. I say again, you will have to divert your course.

A: THIS IS THE AIRCRAFT CARRIER US LINCOLN, THE SECOND LARGEST SHIP IN THE UNITED STATES ATLANTIC FLEET. WE ARE ACCOMPANIED BY THREE DESTROYERS, THREE CRUISERS AND NUMEROUS SUPPORT VESSELS. I DEMAND THAT YOU CHANGE YOUR COURSE 15 DEGREES NORTH, I SAY AGAIN, THAT'S 15 DEGREES NORTH, OR COUNTERMEASURES WILL BE UNDERTAKEN TO ENSURE THE SAFETY OF THIS SHIP.

C: We're a lighthouse. Your call.

Mostly for the Brits

Acorn Computers	Crap to consumer
Actors	Scrota
A Decimal Point	I'm a Dot in Place
An Intel Pentium Processor	Customer nipple not arisen
Arnold Schwarzenegger	He's grown large 'n' crazed
Benson and Hedges	NHS been a godsend
Boddingtons, the cream of Manchester	Boddington's stomach ache fermenter
Chris Rea	Rich arse
Christians	Rich saints
Dame Agatha Christie	I am a right death case
David Ginola	Vagina dildo
David Mellor	Dildo marvel
Desperation	A Rope Ends It
Diego Maradona	O dear, I'm a gonad
Eastenders	Needs a rest
Eldorado	Real dodo
Eleven plus two	Twelve plus one
Evangelist	Evil's Agent
Gabriela Sabatini	Insatiable airbag
Gloria Estefan	Large fat noise
Home and Away	Aha … yawn mode
Irritable Bowel Syndrome	O my terrible drains below
Kylie Minogue	I like 'em young
Madonna, the material girl	Real dim man-eating harlot

Martina Navratilova	Variant rival to a man
Marti Pellow	Ill tapeworm
Mel Gibson	Big melons
Michael Heseltine	Elect him, he's alien
Mother-in-law	Woman Hitler
Ossie Ardiles	Arse is soiled
Pentium Processor	Computerizes porn
Performance-related pay	Mere end of year claptrap
Peter Ustinov	Eruptive snot
Rita Hayworth	Hot hairy wart
Robert DeNiro	Error on bidet
Selina Scott	Elastic snot
Semolina	Is No Meal
Sir Alec Guinness	Clearing sinuses
Stella Artois, reassuringly expensive	Pint o' lager virtually erases sexiness
Teddy Sheringham	Teddy Minge rash
The Houses of Parliament	Loonies far up the Thames
The Metropolitan Police Force	I'm fellatio, the erect porno cop
The Morse Code	Here Come Dots
Tony Blair PM	I'm Tory Plan B
Virginia Bottomley	I'm an evil Tory bigot

And a final one ...

Motorway Service Station	I eat coronary vomit stews.

! 🚫 Becks' Mental Training

Alex Ferguson pays a visit to Arsenal, to see if he can pick up any tips on continental training methods. He asks Arsène Wenger how he keeps the players mentally sharp.

"Simple," says Arsène. "I ask them riddles. Let me show you." Just then, Dennis Bergkamp is walking by.

"Dennis, I have a question for you," says Arsène. "He is not your brother, but he is your father's son. Who is he?"

"That is easy," says Dennis. "It is me."

Fergie goes back to Manchester, and the next day at training he calls David Beckham over. "David, I have a question for you. He is not your brother, but he is your father's son. Who is he?"

"Bleedin' 'ell, boss, I dunno. Why are you asking me?" Fergie explains that it's continental coaching, and gives Becks a couple of hours to think about it.

Becks decides to go and talk to Jaap Stam, since he knows about these continental coaching methods. "Jaap, do you know the answer to this? He is not your brother, but he is your father's son. Who is he?"

"That's easy Becks. It is me."

Becks goes back to see Fergie, full of confidence.

"I know the answer now, boss."

"Go on then, son. He is not your brother, but he is you father's son. Who is he?"

"It's Jaap Stam!"

Fergie rolls his eyes skywards. "No, you stupid bastard! It's Dennis Bergkamp!"

Home Colonials

A South African, an Aussie and a Londoner were sitting in a pub having a pint of beer. The South African grabs his beer, downs it, tosses his glass into the air, draws a handgun and shoots the glass in mid-air. He grins to the other two, puts the gun down on the bar and says, "In Suff Ifrika we haf so many glasses we never drink out of the same glass twice."

The Aussie then downs his beer throws his glass into the air, grabs the gun off the bar, shoots the glass, puts the gun back on the bar and proclaims: "Yeah mate, in Oz we have so much sand which makes glass really cheap so we too never drink out of the same glass twice."

The Londoner looks at the two of them, finishes his beer, puts the glass down on the bar, picks up the gun, shoots both the Aussie and the South African and says:

"In London we have so many South Africans and Aussies that we never have to drink with the same one twice."

! 🔘 Jigsaw

Alex Ferguson is sitting at home watching TV one day when he receives a phone call.

"Hello, boss, it's David Beckham."

"Yes, David, what can I do for you?"

"Well, boss, Posh has gone out and bought me a jigsaw to do. The problem is, though, none of the pieces fit together – it's impossible."

"What's it supposed to be?"

"The picture on the box is of a tiger, but like I said it's impossible. It's really doing my head in now. If I don't get finished by Saturday I don't think that I'll be able to concentrate on the game."

Fergie starts to panic now.

"I tell you what, David, bring it round here and we'll both have a go."

"Cheers, boss, that's brilliant!"

About half an hour later Beckham turns up at Ferguson's house with his jigsaw under his arm. They walk into the kitchen, and Beckham tips the pieces on to the table. Ferguson looks down at the table and then at Beckham.

"David, put the Frosties back in the box."

Maths Test for Secondary Schools in the North

NAME _____

NICKNAME _____

GANG NAME _____

1. Deco has 0.5 kilos of cocaine. If he sells an 8 ball to Vinno for £300 and 90 grams to Tomo for £90 a gram, what is the street value of the rest of his hold?

2. Anto pimps 3 brassers. If the price is £40 a royde, how many roydes per day must each brasser perform to support Vinno's £500 a day crack habit?

3. Whacker wants to cut the kilo of cocaine he bought for £7000 to make a 20% profit. How many grams of strychnine will he need?

4. Christy got 6 years for murder. He also got £350,000 for the hit. If his common-law wife spends £33,100 per month, how much money will be left when he gets out?

5. Extra Credit Bonus: How much more time will Christy get for killing the slapper who spent his money?

6. If an average can of spray paint covers 22 square metres and the average letter is 1 square metre, how many letters can be sprayed with eight fluid ounce cans of spray paint with 20% extra paint free?

7. Liamo steals Eamo's skateboard. As Liamo skates away at a speed of 35mph, Eamo loads his brother's Armalite. If it takes Eamo 20 seconds to load the gun, how far will Liamo have travelled when he gets whacked?

! Maths Test for Secondary Schools
in the South

NAME _____

_____
(if longer, please continue on separate sheet)
SCHOOL _____
DADDY'S COMPANY _____

1. Julian smashes up the old man's car, causing x amount of damage and killing three people. The old man asks his local MP to intervene in the court system, then forges his insurance claim and receives a payment of y. The difference between x and y is three times the life insurance settlement for the three dead people. What kind of car is Julian driving now?

2. Chloe's personal shopper decides to substitute generic and own-brand products for the designer goods favoured by her employer. In the course of a month she saves the price of a return ticket to Fiji, and Chloe doesn't even notice the difference. Is she thick or what?

3. Roly fancies the arse off a certain number of tarts, but he only has enough Rohypnol left to render 33.3% unconscious. If he has 14 Rohypnol, how is he ever going to shag the other two-thirds?

4. If Savannah throws up four times a day for a week she can fit a size 8 Versace. If she only throws up three times a day for two weeks, she has to make do with a size 10 Dolce et Gabbana. How much does liposuction cost?

5. Alexander is unsure about his sexuality. Three days a week he fancies women. On the other days he fancies men, ducks and vacuum cleaners. However he only has access to the Hoover every third week. When does his Independent on Sunday column start?

The Pope and Manchester United

A very holy young boy is going to the Vatican with his mum to see the Pope. The boy is a bit worried about whether or not they will see the Pope amongst the thousands of people. His mum says, "Don't worry son, the Pope is a big football fan, so I'll buy you a QPR strip, the Pope will see the famous hooped strip and he'll talk to you."

So they buy the strip and the boy has it on while they are standing in the crowd as the Pope goes along in his Popemobile. Next thing John Paul stops the Popemobile and gets out to talk to a different little boy wearing a Manchester United top. Then he gets back into the Popemobile and it drives right past the QPR fan. The little boy is very upset and is in tears.

"Don't worry," says his mum. "I'll buy you a Man. Utd. strip, we'll come back tomorrow and then the Pope is guaranteed to stop and talk to you."

So the boy is back the next day now wearing the Man. Utd. shirt. The Popemobile comes along and the boy is all excited. The Popemobile stops and John Paul gets out, bends down to talk to the little boy, and says:

"I thought I told you to fuck off yesterday!"

Yorkshire Clubbers

Clubbers in Yorkshire have taken to using dental syringes to inject ecstasy directly into their mouths.

This dangerous practice is known as 'E by gum'.

Office Life

! 📎 A Manager in a Balloon

A man is flying in a hot air balloon and realizes he is lost. He reduces height and spots a man down below. He lowers the balloon further and shouts, "Excuse me. Can you help me? I promised my friend I would meet him half an hour ago, but I don't know where I am."

The man below says, "You are in a hot air balloon, hovering approximately 30 feet above this field. You are between 40 and 42 degrees N. latitude, and between 58 and 60 degrees W. longitude."

"You must be an engineer", says the balloonist.

"I am, how did you know?"

"Well, everything you have told me is technically correct, but I have no idea what to make of your information, and the fact is I am still lost."

"You must be a manager."

"I am, but how did you know?"

"Well, you don't know where you are, or where you are going. You have made a promise which you have no idea how to keep, and you expect me to solve your problem. The fact is you are in exactly the same position you were in before we met, but now it is somehow my fault."

! 📎 Administratium

SCIENTISTS DISCOVER NEW ELEMENT

The heaviest element known to science was recently discovered by university physicists. The element, tentatively named Administratium, has no protons or electrons and thus has an atomic number of 0

However, it does have one neutron, 15 assistant neutrons, 70 vice neutrons and 161 assistant vice neutrons. This gives it an atomic mass of 247. These 247 particles are held together in a nucleus by a force that involves the continuous exchange of meson-like particles called morons.

Since it has no electrons, Administratium is inert. However, it can be detected chemically as it impedes every reaction it comes into contact with. According to the discoverers, a minute amount of Administratium added to one reaction caused it to take over four days to complete. Without the Administratium the reaction ordinarily occurred in less than one second.

Administratium has a normal half life of approximately three years, at which time it does not actually decay but instead undergoes a reorganization in which assistant neutrons, vice neutrons and assistant vice neutrons exchange places. Studies seem to show the atomic number actually increasing after each reorganization.

Research indicates that Administratium occurs naturally in the atmosphere. It tends to concentrate in certain locations such as government agencies, large corporations and universities. It can usually be found in the newest, best-appointed and best-maintained buildings.

Scientists warn that Administratium is known to be toxic, and recommend plenty of fluids and bed rest after even low levels of exposure.

! 0   Æsop's Corporate Fables

FABLE 1

A crow was sitting on a tree, doing nothing all day. A small rabbit saw the crow, and asked him, "Can I also sit like you and do nothing all day long?" The crow answered: "Sure, why not."

So, the rabbit sat on the ground below the crow, and rested. All of a sudden, a fox appeared, jumped on the rabbit and ate it.

The moral of the story is:
To be sitting and doing nothing, you must be sitting very, very high ...

FABLE 2
A turkey was chatting with a bull.

"I would love to be able to get to the top of that tree," sighed the turkey, "but I haven't got the energy."

"Well, why don't you nibble on some of my droppings?" replied the bull. "They're packed with nutrients." The turkey pecked at a lump of dung and found that it actually gave him enough strength to reach the first branch of the tree.

The next day, after eating some more dung, he reached the second branch. Finally after a fortnight, there he was proudly perched at the top of the tree. He was promptly spotted by a farmer, who shot him out of the tree.

The moral of this story is:
Bullshit might get you to the top, but it won't keep you there.

FABLE 3
When the body was first made, all the parts wanted to be Boss.

The brain said, "I should be Boss because I control the whole body's responses and functions."

The feet said, "We should be Boss as we carry the brain about and get him to where he wants to go."

The hands said, "We should be the Boss because we do all the work and earn all the money."

And so it went on and on with the heart, the lungs and the eyes until finally the asshole spoke up. All the parts laughed at the idea of the asshole being the Boss. So the asshole went on strike, blocked itself up and refused to work.

Within a short time the eyes became crossed, the hands clenched, the feet twitched, the heart and lungs began to panic and the brain fevered.

Eventually they all decided that the asshole should be the Boss, so the motion (so to speak) was passed. All the other parts did all the work while the Boss just sat and passed out the shit!

The moral of this story is:
You don't need brains to be a Boss: any asshole will do.

Christmas Party

After the annual office Christmas party blow-out, John woke up with a pounding headache, cotton-mouthed, and utterly unable to recall the events of the preceding evening. After a trip to the bathroom he was able to make his way downstairs, where his wife put some coffee in front of him.

"Louise," he moaned, "tell me what went on last night. Was it as bad as I think?"

"Even worse," she assured him, voice dripping with scorn. "You made a complete ass of yourself, succeeded in antagonizing the entire board of directors, and insulted the president of the company to his face."

"He's an asshole – piss on him."

"You did," Louise informed him. "And he fired you."

"Well fuck him," said John.

'I did. You're back at work on Monday."

！ 🔟 Did I Get the Job?

In a survey, employers were asked about the most bizarre events that occurred during a job interview. Here are some of their answers:

1. A job applicant challenged the interviewer to an arm wrestle.

2. Interviewee wore a Walkman, explaining that she could listen to the interviewer and the music at the same time.

3. Candidate fell and broke arm during interview.

4. Candidate announced she hadn't had lunch and proceeded to eat a hamburger and French-fries in the interviewer's office.

5. Candidate explained that her long-term goal was to replace the interviewer.

6. Candidate said he never finished high school because he was kidnapped and kept in a closet in Mexico.

7. Balding candidate excused himself and returned to the office a few minutes later wearing a hairpiece.

8. Applicant said if he was hired he would demonstrate his loyalty by having the corporate logo tattooed on his forearm.

9. Applicant interrupted interview to phone her therapist for advice on how to answer specific interview questions.

10. Candidate brought large dog to interview.

11. Applicant refused to sit down and insisted on being interviewed standing up.

12. Candidate dozed off during interview.

The employers were also asked to list the "most unusual" things that job candidates have said.

1. "What is it that you people do at this company?"

2. "What is the company motto?"

3. "Why aren't you in a more interesting business?"

4. "What are the zodiac signs of all the board members?"

5. "Why do you want references?"

6. "Do I have to dress for the next interview?"

7. "I know this is off the subject, but will you marry me?"

8. "Will the company move my rock collection from California to Maryland?"

9. "Will the company pay to relocate my horse?"

10. "Does your health insurance cover pets?"

11. "Would it be a problem if I'm angry most of the time?"

12. "Does your company have a policy regarding concealed weapons?"

13. "Do you think the company would be willing to lower my pay?"

14. "Why am I here?"

15. "I am fascinated by fire."

16. "I would have been more successful if nobody had snitched on me."

17. "My legs are really hairy."

! 📎 East Coast, West Coast

Here's a handy guide for those of you who have to deal with vendors, customers, or other divisions on the other coast.

EAST COAST	WEST COAST
absolutely not	maybe
yes	maybe
action item by Feb 12 for Joe	Joe's working on the problem
bozo	subcontractor
brawl	design review
dictator	facilitator
do it and do it now	can you sign up for this program?
do it right or you're fired	I'm confident you'll get it done
fuck off	trust me
follow the spec	is there a spec?
get out of my office	let's get consensus on this one
he's a jerk	he's not signed on to our plan
he's a subordinate	he's a team player
I'll cover your butt	consider me your resource
ignore him, he's new	I'm bringing him up to speed
local bar	offsite facility
meet me in the parking lot	let's take that discussion offline
oh crap	thanks for bringing that to my attention
overdesigned	robust
punch his lights out	constructive confrontation
shut up!!	thank you for your input
shut up a minute	let me share this with you
that's totally incompetent	let me build on that point
unemployed	consulting
over budget	on schedule

under budget	we haven't started yet
we finished early	(no translation available)
we're done	how do you feel about that?
what's your problem?	I certainly understand your feelings
where's the spec?	what's a spec?
where's the schedule?	what's the game plan?
your plan sucks	let me share my feelings on this one

! 📎 Employee Appraisal Glossary

LOYAL	Can't get a job anywhere else
GREAT PRESENTATION SKILLS	Able to bullshit
GOOD COMMUNICATION SKILLS	Spends lots of time on phone
AVERAGE EMPLOYEE	Not too bright
EXCEPTIONALLY WELL QUALIFIED	Made no major blunders yet
ACTIVE SOCIALLY	Drinks a lot
FAMILY IS ACTIVE SOCIALLY	Spouse drinks, too
CHARACTER ABOVE REPROACH	Still one step ahead of the law
QUICK THINKING	Offers plausible excuses
CAREFUL THINKER	Won't make a decision
PLANS FOR ADVANCEMENT	Buys drinks for all the boys
AGGRESSIVE	Obnoxious
USES LOGIC ON DIFFICULT JOBS	Gets someone else to do it
INDEPENDENT WORKER	Nobody knows what he/she does
EXPRESSES THEMSELVES WELL	Speaks English
METICULOUS ATTENTION TO DETAIL	A nit picker
HAS LEADERSHIP QUALITIES	Is tall/has a loud voice
EXCEPTIONALLY GOOD JUDGEMENT	Lucky
OF GREAT VALUE TO THE ORGANIZATION	Gets to work on time
KEEN SENSE OF HUMOUR	Knows a lot of dirty jokes

CAREER MINDED   Back-stabber
RELAXED ATTITUDE   Sleeps at desk

Human Resource Management

At a goodbye lunch for an old and dear co-worker who was leaving the company due to 'rightsizing', our manager spoke up and said, "This is fun. We should have lunch like this more often."

Not another word was spoken. We just looked at each other like deer staring into the headlights of an approaching truck.

Knowledge is Power ...

Engineers and scientists will never make as much money as business executives. Now a rigorous mathematical proof that explains why this is true:

Postulate 1: Knowledge is Power.
Postulate 2: Time is Money.

As every engineer knows,

$$\frac{\text{Work}}{\text{Time}} = \text{Power}$$

Since Knowledge = Power, and Time = Money, we have

$$\frac{\text{Work}}{\text{Money}} = \text{Knowledge}$$

Solving for Money, we get:

$$\frac{\text{Work}}{\text{Knowledge}} = \text{Money}$$

Thus, as Knowledge approaches zero, Money approaches infinity regardless of the Work done.

Conclusion: The less you Know, the more Money you make.

Letter of Recommendation

Bob Smith, my assistant programmer, can always be found
hard at work in his cubicle. Bob works independently, without
wasting company time talking to colleagues. Bob never
thinks twice about assisting fellow employees, and he always
finishes given assignments on time. Often Bob takes extended
measures to complete his work, sometimes skipping coffee
breaks. Bob is a dedicated individual who has absolutely no
vanity in spite of his high accomplishments and profound
knowledge in his field. I firmly believe that Bob can be
classed as a high-caliber employee, the type which cannot be
dispensed with. Consequently, I duly recommend that Bob be
promoted to executive management, and a proposal will be
sent away as soon as possible.

Project Manager

A Memo was soon sent, following the letter:

That stupid idiot was reading over my shoulder when I wrote the report
sent to you earlier today. Kindly read every second line (i.e. 1, 3, 5, 7, 9 etc.)
for my true assessment of him.

Regards,
Project Manager

! Looking Back on the '90s

You know you worked in the '90s if ...

You've sat at the same desk for four years and worked for three different organizations.

Your CV is on a diskette in your pocket.

You get really excited about a 2% pay raise.

You learn about your layoff on the news.

Your biggest loss from a system crash is that you lose your best jokes.

Your supervisor doesn't have the ability to do your job.

Salaries of the members on the Executive Board are higher than all the Third World countries' annual budgets combined.

It's dark when you drive to and from work.

Communication is something your section is having problems with.

You see a good-looking person and know it is a visitor.

Free food left over from meetings is your main sustenance.

Being sick is defined as can't walk or you're in the hospital.

You're already late on the work task you just got.

You work 200 hours for the £100 bonus check and jubilantly say "Oh wow, thanks."

Your line manager's favourite lines are "when you get a few minutes", "in your spare time", "when you're free" and "I have an opportunity for you."

Holiday is something you roll over to next year or a cheque you get every January.

Your relatives and family describe your job as "works with computers".

You read this entire list and understood it.

Jobsearch Bullshit

"COMPETITIVE SALARY":
We remain competitive by paying less than our competitors.

"JOIN OUR FAST-PACED COMPANY":
We have no time to train you.

"CASUAL WORK ATMOSPHERE":
We don't pay enough to expect that you'll dress up.

"MUST BE DEADLINE ORIENTED":
You'll be six months behind schedule on your first day.

"SOME OVERTIME REQUIRED":
Some time each night and some time each weekend.

"DUTIES WILL VARY":
Anyone in the office can boss you around.

"MUST HAVE AN EYE FOR DETAIL":
We have no quality control.

"CAREER-MINDED":
Female applicants must be childless (and remain that way).

"APPLY IN PERSON":
If you're old, fat or ugly you'll be told the position has been filled.

"NO PHONE CALLS PLEASE":
We've filled the job; our call for resumes is just a legal formality.

"SEEKING CANDIDATES WITH A WIDE VARIETY OF EXPERIENCE:"
You'll need it to replace three people who just left.

"PROBLEM-SOLVING SKILLS A MUST":
You're walking into a company in perpetual chaos.

"REQUIRES TEAM LEADERSHIP SKILLS":
You'll have the responsibilities of a manager, without the pay or respect.

"GOOD COMMUNICATION SKILLS":
Management communicates, you listen, figure out what they want and do it.

"I'M EXTREMELY ADEPT AT ALL MANNER OF OFFICE ORGANIZATION":
I've used Microsoft Office.

"I'M HONEST, HARD-WORKING AND DEPENDABLE":
I pilfer office supplies.

"MY PERTINENT WORK EXPERIENCE INCLUDES":
I hope you don't ask me about all the McJobs I've had.

"I TAKE PRIDE IN MY WORK":
I blame others for my mistakes.

"I'M PERSONABLE":
I give lots of unsolicited personal advice.

"I'M EXTREMELY PROFESSIONAL":
I carry a Day-Timer.

"I AM ADAPTABLE":
I've changed jobs a lot.

"I AM ON THE GO":
I'm never at my desk.

"I'M HIGHLY MOTIVATED TO SUCCEED":
The minute I find a better job, I'm outta here.

PC Office Discourse

It has been brought to management's attention that some individuals throughout the company have been using foul language during the course of normal conversation with their co-workers. Due to complaints received from some employees who may be easily offended, this type of language will no longer be tolerated.

We do, however, realize the critical importance of being able to accurately express your feelings when communicating with co-workers. Therefore, a list of preferred new phrases has been provided so that proper exchange of ideas and information can continue in an effective manner without risk of offending our more sensitive employees:

PREFERRED PHRASE	OLD PHRASE
Perhaps I can work late	When the fuck do you expect me to do this?
I'm certain that is not feasible	No fucking way
Really?	You've got to be shitting me!
Perhaps you should check with ...	Tell someone who gives a shit
Of course I'm concerned	Ask me if I give a shit
I wasn't involved in that project	It's not my fucking problem
That's interesting behavior	What the fuck?!?!
I'm not sure I can implement this	Fuck it, it won't work

I'll try to schedule that sooner?	Why the hell didn't you tell me
Are you sure this is a problem?	Who the fuck cares?
He's not familiar with the problem	He's got his head up his ass
Excuse me sir?	Eat shit and die, mother-fucker
So you weren't happy with it?	Kiss my ass
I'm a bit overloaded at this moment	Fuck it, I'm on salary
I don't think you understand	Shove it up your ass
I love a challenge	This job sucks
You want me to take care of that?	Who the hell died and made you boss?
I see	Blow me
Yes, we really should discuss it	Another fucking meeting!!!!
I don't think this will be a problem	I really don't give a shit
He's somewhat insensitive	He's a fucking prick
I think you could use more training	You don't know what the fuck you're doing

Pert and Yielding Tightness

This is an actual quote from Abdul Aziz, Chief Minister of the Malaysian State of Kelantan, during a lecture to Government employees:

"There are far too many pretty women in the government offices at the moment, distracting male workers and lowering business efficiency with their pert and yielding tightness. We must be ever watchful for possible immoral activities and it is well-known that pretty women cause unhealthy activities that lead to insanity, blindness, sickness and bends. That is why from now on thorough ugliness must be considered a deciding factor at all job interviews. Since the prettier candidate has already been blessed by God it is only right that we should hire the uglier one. After all, if we do not choose the ugly candidates, who will?"

Six Phases of a Project

>> 1. Enthusiasm
>> 2. Disillusionment
>> 3. Panic
>> 4. Search for the Guilty
>> 5. Punishment of the Innocent
>> 6. Praise and reward for the non-participants

Stress Management Meditation

Picture yourself near a stream.

Birds are singing in the crisp, cool mountain air.

Nothing can bother you here.

No one knows this secret place.

You are in total seclusion from that place called the "real" world.

The smell of pine and blossom is on the gentle breeze.

The soothing sound of a gentle waterfall fills the air with a cascade of serenity.

The water is clear.

You can easily make out the face of the person whose head you're holding under the water.

There now – feeling better?

⚠ 📎 That Old Trick

One day while walking down the street a highly successful executive woman was tragically hit by a bus and killed. Her soul arrived up in heaven where she was met at the Pearly Gates by St. Peter himself.

"Welcome to Heaven," said St. Peter. "Before you get settled in though, it seems we have a problem. You see, strangely enough, we've never once had an executive make it this far and we're not really sure what to do with you."

"No problem, just let me in," said the woman.

"Well, I'd like to, but I have higher orders. What we're going to do is let you have a day in Hell and a day in Heaven and then you can choose whichever one you want to spend an eternity in."

"Actually, I think I've made up my mind ... I prefer to stay in Heaven," said the woman.

"Sorry, we have rules ..." And with that St. Peter put the executive in an elevator and it went down-down-down to Hell. The doors opened and she found herself stepping out onto the putting green of a beautiful golf course. In the distance was a country club. Standing in front of her were all her friends, fellow executives that she had worked with and they were all dressed in evening gowns and cheering for her. They ran up and kissed her on both cheeks and they talked about old times. They played an excellent round of golf and at night went to the country club where she enjoyed an excellent steak and lobster dinner. She met the Devil who was actually a really nice guy (kinda cute) and she had a great time telling jokes and dancing. She was having such a good time that before she knew it, it was time to leave.

Everybody shook her hand and waved good-bye as she got on the elevator. The elevator went up-up-up and opened back up at the Pearly Gates where St. Peter was waiting for her.

"Now it's time to spend a day in Heaven," he said. So she spent the next 24 hours lounging around on clouds and playing the harp and singing. She had a great time and before she knew it her 24 hours were up and St. Peter came and got her.

"So, you've spent a day in Hell and you've spent a day in Heaven. Now you must choose your eternity," he said.

The woman paused for a second and then replied, "Well, I never thought I'd say this – I mean, Heaven has been really great and all, but I think I had a better time in Hell."

So St. Peter escorted her to the elevator and again she went down-down-down back to Hell. When the doors of the elevator opened she found herself standing in a desolate wasteland covered in garbage and filth. She saw her friends were dressed in rags and were picking up the garbage and putting it in sacks. The Devil came up to her and put his arm around her.

"I don't understand," stammered the woman, "yesterday I was here and there was a golf course and a country club and we ate lobster and we danced and had a great time. Now all there is is a wasteland of garbage, and all my friends look miserable."

The Devil looked at her and smiled. "Yesterday," he said, "we were recruiting you; but today you're staff."

The Plan

In the beginning was the Plan.
And then came the Assumptions.
And the Assumptions were without form.
And the Plan was without substance.

And darkness was upon the face of the Workers.
And they spoke among themselves, saying, "It is a crock of shit and it
  stinketh."

And the Workers went unto the Supervisors, and said, "It's a pail of dung and we can't live with the smell."

And the Supervisors went unto the Managers, saying "It's a container of excrement, and it is very strong such that none may abide it."

And the Managers went unto the Directors saying, "It's a vessel of fertilizer, and none can stand against its strength."

And the Directors went unto the Vice-Presidents, saying, "It promotes growth, and it is very powerful."

And the Vice-Presidents went unto the President, saying, "This new plan will actively promote the growth and vigour of the company with very powerful effects."

And the President looked upon the Plan and he saw that it was good.

And the Plan became Policy.

10 Things to Say if Caught Sleeping at Work

10. They told me at the blood bank this might happen.
9. This is just a 15-minute power-nap like they raved about in that time management course you sent me to.
8. Whew! Guess I left the top off the Tip-ex. You probably got here just in time!
7. I wasn't sleeping! I was meditating on the mission statement and envisioning a new paradigm.
6. I was testing my keyboard for drool resistance.
5. I was doing a highly specific Yoga exercise to relieve work-related stress. Are you discriminatory towards people who practice Yoga?

4. Why did you interrupt me? I had almost figured out a solution to our biggest problem.
3. The coffee machine is broken.
2. Someone must've put decaf in the wrong pot.
1. ...in Jesus' name. Amen.

Tips for Bosses

1. Never give me work in the morning. Always wait until 4:00 p.m. and then bring it to me. The challenge of a deadline is refreshing.

2. If it's really a "rush job", run in and interrupt me every ten minutes to inquire how it's going. That helps. Or even better, hover behind me, advising me at every keystroke.

3. Always leave without telling anyone where you're going. It gives me a chance to be creative when someone asks where you are.

4. Wait until my yearly review and THEN tell me what my goals SHOULD have been. Give me a mediocre performance rating with a cost of living increase. I'm not here for the money anyway.

5. If you give me more than one job to do, don't tell me which is the priority. I like being a psychic.

6. Do your best to keep me late. I adore this office and really have nowhere to go or anything to do. I have no life beyond work.

7. If a job I do pleases you, keep it a secret. If that gets out, it could mean a promotion.

8. If you don't like my work, tell everyone. I like my name to be popular in conversations. I was born to be whipped.

9. If you have special instructions for a job, don't write them down. In fact, save them until the job is almost done. No use confusing me with useful information.

10. Never introduce me to the people you're with. I have no right to know anything. In the corporate food chain, I am plankton. When you refer to them later, my shrewd deductions will identify them.

11. Tell me all your little problems. No one else has any and it's nice to know someone is less fortunate. I especially like the story about having to pay so much tax on the bonus cheque you received for being such a good manager.

```
.... and more cow tales ....

>                (__)
>                (oo)
>          __[_]__\/
>      / |        ||
>    *  ||----||                    --  .
>    ^^        ^^
>    Portable Cow                Japanese model
>    (very handy)                 portable Cow
```

Do you keep falling asleep in meetings?

Here's something to change all of that.

WANK Word Bingo

How to play: Simply tick off 5 WANK Words
in one meeting and shout out BINGO!

It's that easy!

TESTIMONIAL FROM OTHER PLAYERS:

"I had only been in the meeting for five minutes
when I yelled BINGO."

"My attention span at meetings has improved dramatically."

"It's a wheeze, meetings will never be the same for me
after my first outright win."

"The atmosphere was tense at the last process workshop
as 32 of us listened intently for the elusive 5th."

"The facilitator was gobsmacked as we all screamed BINGO
for the 3rd time in 2 hours."

"I feel that the game has enhanced the overall quality
of meetings per se on a quid pro quo basis."

"People are now even listening to mumblers,
thanks to wank words."

"Bonza! You could have cut the atmosphere with a cricket
stump as we waited for the 5th delivery."

SYNERGY	REVISIT
TAKE THAT OFFLINE	GAME PLAN
STRATEGIC FIT	BANDWITH
AT THE END OF THE DAY	HARDBALL
GAP ANALYSIS	OUT OF THE LOOP
BEST PRACTICE	GO THE EXTRA MILE
THE BOTTOM LINE	BENCHMARK
CORE BUSINESS	THE BIG PICTURE
LESSONS LEARNT	VALUE-ADDED
TOUCH BASE	MOVERS AND SHAKERS

BALL PARK	RESULTS-DRIVEN
PROACTIVE, NOT REACTIVE	TOTAL QUALITY
WIN-WIN SITUATION	SLIPPERY SLIDE
THINK OUTSIDE THE BOX	TICKS IN BOXES
FAST TRACK	MINDSET
RESULT-DRIVEN	KNOCK-ON EFFECT
EMPOWER EMPLOYEES	PUT THIS ONE TO BED
NO BLAME	CLIENT-FOCUSED
STRETCH THE ENVELOPE	QUALITY-DRIVEN
KNOWLEDGE BASE	MOVE THE GOAL POSTS

One-liners

"Change is inevitable, except from a vending machine."

"I love cats ... they taste just like chicken."

"Out of my mind. Back in five minutes."

"Cover me. I'm changing lanes."

"As long as there are tests, there will be prayer in public schools."

"Happiness is a belt-fed weapon."

"Laugh alone and the world thinks you're an idiot."

"Sometimes I wake up grumpy. Other times I let her sleep."

"I want to die in my sleep like my grandfather ... not screaming and yelling like the passengers in his car."

"Montana – at least our cows are sane."

"The gene pool could use a little chlorine."

"I didn't fight my way to the top of the food chain to be a vegetarian."

"Don't blame me, I'm the thing from Uranus."

"Your kid may be an honor student, but you're still an IDIOT."

"It's as BAD as you think, and they ARE out to get you."

"When you do a good deed, get a receipt, in case heaven is like the Inland Revenue."

"Can you hang up the car phone long enough for me to call you stupid?"

"How d'you get your driver's license, a relative?"

"Wink – I'll do the rest."

"I took an IQ test and the results were negative."

"When there's a will, I want to be in it."

"Okay, who stopped the payment on my reality check?"

"If we aren't supposed to eat animals, why are they made of meat?"

"Time is the best teacher; unfortunately, it kills all its students."

"It's lonely at the top, but you eat better."

"Reality? That's where the pizza delivery guy comes from."

"Forget about World Peace ... Visualize using your turn signal."

"Give me ambiguity or give me something else."

"We are born naked, bloody and hungry, then it gets worse."

"Make it idiot-proof and someone will make a better idiot."

"He who laughs last thinks slowest."

"Always remember you're unique, just like everyone else."

"Lottery: A tax on people who are bad at math."

"Friends help you move. Real friends help you move bodies."

"Puritanism: The haunting fear that someone, somewhere may be having fun."

"Consciousness: That annoying time between naps."

"i souport publik edekasion"

"The sex was so good that even the neighbors had a cigarette."

"We are Microsoft. Resistance is futile. You will be assimilated."

"Be nice to your kids. They'll choose your nursing home."

"3 kinds of people: Those who can count and those who can't."

"Ever stop to think, and forget to start again?"

"Diplomacy is the art of saying 'Nice doggie' ...'til you can find a rock."

"2 + 2 = 5 for extremely large values of 2."

"I like you, but I wouldn't want to see you working with sub-atomic particles."

"I killed a 6-pack just to watch it die."

"Sex on television can't hurt you unless you fall off."

! Graffiti

Found in restrooms around the US:

The best way to a man's heart is to saw his breastplate open.
Women's restroom, Murphy's, Champaign, Illinois

Don't trust anything that bleeds for 5 days and doesn't die.
Men's restroom, Murphy's, Champaign, Illinois

If you voted for Clinton in the last election, you can't take a dump here.
Your asshole is in Washington.
Men's room Outback Steakhouse, Tacoma, Washington

Beauty is only a light switch away.
Perkins Library, Duke University, Durham, North Carolina

I've decided that to raise my grades I must lower my standards.
Houghton Library, Harvard University, Cambridge, Massachusetts

If life is a waste of time, and time is a waste of life, then let's all get wasted together and have the time of our lives.
Armand's Pizza, Washington, D.C.

If Bush were captain of the Titanic, he'd say we were stopping for ice.
Smoky Joe's, Philadelphia, Pennsylvania

Remember, it's not, "How high are you?" it's "Hi, how are you?"
Rest stop off Route 81, West Virginia

God made pot. Man made beer. Who do you trust?
The Irish Times, Washington, D.C.

No matter how good she looks, some other guy is sick and tired of putting up with her shit.
Men's Room, Linda's Bar and Grill, Chapel Hill, North Carolina

To do is to be – Descartes
To be is to do – Voltaire
Do be do be do – Frank Sinatra
Men's restroom, Greasewood Flats, Scottsdale, Arizona

At the feast of ego, everyone leaves hungry.
Bentley's House of Coffee and Tea, Tucson, Arizona

It's hard to make a comeback when you haven't been anywhere.
Written in the dust on the back of a bus, Wickenburg, Arizona

God is dead – Nietzsche
Nietzsche is dead – God
The Tombs Restaurant, Washington, D.C.

If voting could really change things, it would be illegal.
Revolution Books, New York, New York

A Woman's Rule of Thumb: If it has tires or testicles, you're going to have trouble with it.
Women's restroom, Dick's Last Resort, Dallas, Texas

JESUS SAVES! But wouldn't it be better if He had invested?
Men's restroom, American University, Washington, D.C.

Express Lane: Five beers or less.
Sign over one of the urinals, Ed Debevic's, Phoenix, Arizona

You're too good for him.
Sign over mirror in Women's restroom, Ed Debevic's, Beverly Hills, California

No wonder you always go home alone.
Sign over mirror in Men's restroom, Ed Debevic's, Beverly Hills, California

What are you looking up on the wall for? The joke is in your hands.
Men's restroom, Lynagh's, Lexington, Kentucky

! 🗩 Life's Little Annoyances

- The tiny red string on the Band-Aid wrapper never works for you.

- There are always one or two ice cubes that won't pop out of the tray.

- You have to try on a pair of sunglasses with that stupid little plastic tag in the middle of them.

- The person behind you in the supermarket runs his cart into the back of your ankle.

- The elevator stops on every floor and nobody gets on.

- There's always a car riding your tail when you're slowing down to find an address.

- You open a can of soup and the lid falls in.

- There's a dog in the neighborhood that barks at everything.

- You can never put anything back in a box the way it came.

- Three hours and three meetings after lunch you look in the mirror and discover a piece of parsley stuck to your front tooth.

- You drink from a soda can in which someone has extinguished a cigarette.

- You slice your tongue licking an envelope.

- Your tire gauge lets out half the air while you're trying to get a reading.

- A station comes in brilliantly when you're standing near the radio but buzzes, drifts and spits every time you move away.

- You wash a garment with a tissue in the pocket and your entire laundry comes out covered with lint.

- The car behind you blasts its horn because you let a pedestrian finish crossing.

- A piece of foil candy wrapper makes electrical contact with your filling.

- You set the alarm on your digital clock for 7 p.m instead of 7 a.m.

- You rub on hand cream and can't turn the bathroom doorknob to get out.

- Your glasses slide off your ears when you perspire.

- You can't look up the correct spelling of a word in the dictionary because you don't know how to spell it.

- You have to inform five different sales people in the same store that you're just browsing.

! Things That Get Me Annoyed

People who point at their wrist while asking for the time.
I know where my watch is buddy, where on earth is yours?
Do I point at my crotch when I ask where the bathroom is?

When people say, "Oh, you just want to have your cake and eat it too."
What good is a damn cake if you can't eat it?
What, should I eat someone else's cake instead?

When people say, "It's always in the last place you look."
Of course it is. Why would you keep looking after you've found it?
Do people do this?
Who and where are they?

When people say, while watching a movie, "Did you see that?"
No, moron, I paid $8.00 to come to the theatre and stare at the ceiling up there.
What did you come here for?

People who ask, "Can I ask you a question?"
Didn't really give me a choice there, did ya buddy?

When something is "new and improved", which is it?
If it's new, then there has never been anything before it.
If it's an improvement, then there must have been something before it.

When a cop pulls you over and then asks if you know how fast you were going.
You should know, you pulled me over.

❗ 🔟 Words of Wisdom

Don't kick a man when he's down unless you're certain he won't get up.

Indecision is the key to flexibility.

You can't tell which way the train went by looking at the track.

Be kind, everyone you meet is fighting a tough battle too.

This is as bad as it can get ... but don't bet on it.

There is no substitute for genuine lack of preparation.

By the time you can make ends meet, they move the ends.

Nostalgia isn't what it used to be.

Sometimes too much drink is not enough.

The facts, although interesting, are generally irrelevant.

The world gets a little better every day, and worse in the evening.

Someone who thinks logically is a nice contrast to the real world.

The other line always moves faster ... until you get in it.

Anything worth fighting for is worth fighting dirty for.

Everything should be made as simple as possible, but no simpler.

Friends may come and go but enemies accumulate.

It's hard to be nostalgic when you can't remember anything good.

I have seen the truth and it makes no sense.

If you think that there is good in everybody, you haven't met everybody.

If you can smile when things go wrong, you have someone in mind to blame.

One seventh of your life is spent on Monday.

The more you run over a dead cat, the flatter it gets.

Happiness is good health and a bad memory.

Do unto others.

Artificial Intelligence is no match for Natural Stupidity.

Plagiarism saves time.

Teamwork ... means never having to take all the blame yourself.

Never underestimate the power of very stupid people in large groups.

We waste time, so you don't have to.

Go the extra mile. It makes your boss look like an incompetent slacker.

The Romans did not create a great empire by having meetings; they did it by killing all those who opposed them.

If you can stay calm while all around you is chaos ... then you probably haven't completely understood the seriousness of the situation.

Sometimes I think the surest sign that intelligent life exists elsewhere in the universe is that none of it has tried to contact us.

As you journey through life take a minute every now and then to give a thought for the other fellow. He could be plotting something.

If you find something you like, buy a lifetime supply, because they will stop making it.

Always remember you're unique, just like everyone else.

Politics

! 📎 Crooked Company

Can you imagine working for the following company?
It has a little over 500 employees with the following statistics:

>>   29 have been accused of spousal abuse
>>   7 have been arrested for fraud
>>   19 have been accused of writing bad checks
>>   117 have bankrupted at least 2 businesses
>>   3 have been arrested for assault
>>   71 cannot get a credit card because of bad credit
>>   14 have been arrested on drug-related charges
>>   8 have been arrested for shoplifting
>>   21 are current defendants in lawsuits

In 1998 alone, 84 were stopped for drunk driving

Can you guess which organization this is?

Give up?

It is the 535 members of the Congress of the United States of America.

! 📎 Guide to Ideologies

FEUDALISM
You have two cows. Your lord takes some of the milk.

PURE SOCIALISM
You have two cows. The government takes them and puts them in a barn

with everyone else's cows. You have to take care of all the cows. The government gives you as much milk as you need.

BUREAUCRATIC SOCIALISM
You have two cows. The government takes them and puts them in a barn with everyone else's cows. They are cared for by ex-chicken farmers. You have to take care of the chickens the government took from the chicken farmers. The government gives you as much milk and as many eggs as the regulations say you should need.

FASCISM
You have two cows. The government takes both, hires you to take care of them and sells you the milk.

PURE COMMUNISM
You have two cows. Your neighbors help you take care of them, and you all share the milk.

RUSSIAN COMMUNISM
You have two cows. You have to take care of them, but the government takes all the milk.

DICTATORSHIP
You have two cows. The government takes both and shoots you.

SINGAPOREAN DEMOCRACY
You have two cows. The government fines you for keeping two unlicensed farm animals in an apartment.

MILITARISM
You have two cows. The government takes both and drafts you.

PURE DEMOCRACY
You have two cows. Your neighbors decide who gets the milk.

REPRESENTATIVE DEMOCRACY

You have two cows. Your neighbors pick someone to tell you who gets the milk.

AMERICAN DEMOCRACY

The government promises to give you two cows if you vote for it. After the election, the president is impeached for speculating in cow futures. The press dubs the affair "Cowgate".

BRITISH DEMOCRACY

You have two cows. You feed them sheeps' brains and they go mad. The government doesn't do anything.

BUREAUCRACY

You have two cows. At first the government regulates what you can feed them and when you can milk them. Then it pays you not to milk them. After that it takes both, shoots one, milks the other and pours the milk down the drain. Then it requires you to fill out forms accounting for the missing cows.

ANARCHY

You have two cows. Either you sell the milk at a fair price or your neighbors try to kill you and take the cows.

CAPITALISM

You have two cows. You sell one and buy a bull.

HONG KONG CAPITALISM

You have two cows. You sell three of them to your publicly listed company, using letters of credit opened by your brother-in-law at the bank, then execute a debt/equity swap with associated general offer so that you get all four cows back, with a tax deduction for keeping five cows. The milk rights of six cows are transferred via a Panamanian intermediary to a Cayman Islands company secretly owned by the majority shareholder, who sells the rights to all seven cows' milk back to the listed company. The annual report says that the company owns eight cows, with an option on one more. Meanwhile, you kill the two cows because the feng shui is bad.

ENVIRONMENTALISM
You have two cows. The government bans you from milking or killing them.

FEMINISM
You have two cows. They get married and adopt a veal calf.

TOTALITARIANISM
You have two cows. The government takes them and denies they ever existed. Milk is banned.

POLITICAL CORRECTNESS
You are associated with (the concept of "ownership" is a symbol of the phallo-centric, war-mongering, intolerant past) two differently aged (but no less valuable to society) bovines of non-specified gender.

COUNTER CULTURE
Wow, dude, there's like ... these two cows, man. You got to have some of this milk.

SURREALISM
You have two giraffes. The government requires you to take harmonica lessons.

Product Warnings

On a blanket from Taiwan:
NOT TO BE USED AS PROTECTION FROM A TORNADO.

On a helmet-mounted mirror used by US cyclists:
REMEMBER, OBJECTS IN THE MIRROR ARE ACTUALLY BEHIND YOU.

On a Taiwanese shampoo:
USE REPEATEDLY FOR SEVERE DAMAGE.

On the bottle-top of a (UK) flavoured milk drink:
AFTER OPENING, KEEP UPRIGHT.

On a New Zealand insect spray:
THIS PRODUCT NOT TESTED ON ANIMALS.

In a US guide to setting up a new computer:
TO AVOID CONDENSATION FORMING, ALLOW THE BOXES TO WARM
UP TO ROOM TEMPERATURE BEFORE OPENING.
(Sensible, but the instruction was INSIDE the box.)

On a Japanese product used to relieve painful haemorrhoids:
LIE DOWN ON BED AND INSERT POSCOOL SLOWLY UP TO THE
PROJECTED PORTION LIKE A SWORD-GUARD INTO ANAL DUCT.
WHILE INSERTING POSCOOL FOR APPROXIMATELY 5 MINUTES,
KEEP QUIET.

In some countries, on the bottom of Coke bottles:
OPEN OTHER END.

On a Sears hairdryer:
DO NOT USE WHILE SLEEPING.

On a bag of Fritos:
YOU COULD BE A WINNER! NO PURCHASE NECESSARY. DETAILS INSIDE.
(The shoplifter special!)

On a bar of Dial soap:
DIRECTIONS: USE LIKE REGULAR SOAP.
(And that would be how?)

On Tesco's Tiramisu dessert (printed on bottom of the box):
DO NOT TURN UPSIDE DOWN.

On Marks & Spencer Bread Pudding:
PRODUCT WILL BE HOT AFTER HEATING.

On a Korean kitchen knife:
WARNING KEEP OUT OF CHILDREN.

On a string of Chinese-made Christmas lights:
FOR INDOOR OR OUTDOOR USE ONLY.

On a Japanese food processor:
NOT TO BE USED FOR THE OTHER USE.

On Sainsbury's peanuts:
WARNING – CONTAINS NUTS.

On an American Airlines packet of nuts:
INSTRUCTIONS – OPEN PACKET, EAT NUTS.

On a Swedish chainsaw:
DO NOT ATTEMPT TO STOP CHAIN WITH YOUR HANDS OR GENITALS.

On a child's superman costume:
WEARING OF THIS GARMENT DOES NOT ENABLE YOU TO FLY.

On some Swann frozen dinners:
SERVING SUGGESTION: DEFROST.

On packaging for a Rowenta iron:
DO NOT IRON CLOTHES ON BODY.

On Boot's Children's Cough Medicine:
DO NOT DRIVE A CAR OR OPERATE MACHINERY AFTER TAKING THIS MEDICATION.

On Nytol Sleep Aid:
WARNING: MAY CAUSE DROWSINESS.

On a packet of Sunmaid raisins:
WHY NOT TRY TOSSING OVER YOUR FAVOURITE BREAKFAST CEREAL?

On a hotel-provided shower cap in a box:
FITS ONE HEAD.

Professionals

A defense attorney was cross-examining a police officer during a felony trial. The cross-examination went like this:

Q: Officer, did you see my client fleeing the scene?
A: No sir, but I subsequently observed a person matching the description of the offender running several blocks away.

Q: Officer, who provided this description?
A: The officer who responded to the scene

Q: A fellow officer provided the description of this so-called offender. Do you trust your fellow officers?
A: Yes sir, with my life.

Q: WITH YOUR LIFE? Let me ask you this then, officer: do you have a locker room in the police station, a room where you change your clothes in preparation for your daily duties?
A: Yes sir, we do.

Q: And do you have a locker in that room?
A: Yes sir, I do.

Q: And do you have a lock on your locker?
A: Yes sir.

Q: Now why is it, officer, IF YOU TRUST YOUR FELLOW OFFICERS WITH YOUR LIFE, that you find it necessary to lock your locker in a room you share with those officers?

A: You see sir, we share the building with a court complex, and sometimes defense attorneys have been known to walk through that room.

Accountants

What's the definition of an accountant?
Someone who solves a problem you didn't know you had in a way you
don't understand.

What's the definition of a good tax accountant?
Someone who has a loophole named after him.

When does a person decide to become an accountant?
When he realizes he doesn't have the charisma to succeed as an undertaker.

What does an accountant use for birth control?
His personality.

What's an extroverted accountant?
One who looks at your shoes while he's talking to you instead of his own.

What's an auditor?
Someone who arrives after the battle and bayonets all the wounded.

Why did the auditor cross the road?
Because he looked in the file and that's what they did last year.

What's an accountant's idea of trashing his hotel room?
Refusing to fill out the guest comment card.

How do you drive an accountant completely insane?
Tie him to a chair, stand in front of him and fold up a road map the
wrong way.

What's the most wicked thing a group of young accountants can do?
Go into town and gang-audit someone.

What do accountants suffer from that ordinary people don't?
Depreciation.

An accountant is someone who knows the cost of everything and the value of nothing.

There are three kinds of accountants in the world. Those who can count and those who can't.

An accountant is having a hard time sleeping and goes to see his doctor.
  "Doctor, I just can't get to sleep at night."
  "Have you tried counting sheep?"
  "That's the problem – I make a mistake and then spend three hours trying to find it."

A businessman was interviewing applicants for the position of divisional manager. He devised a simple test to select the most suitable person for the job. He asked each applicant the question, "What is two and two?"
  The first interviewee was a journalist. His answer was "twenty-two".
  The second applicant was an engineer. He pulled out a calculator and showed the answer to be between 3.999 and 4.001.
  The next person was a lawyer. He stated that in the case of Jenkins v. Commr of Stamp Duties (Qld), two and two was proven to be four.
  The last applicant was an accountant. The businessman asked him, "How much is two and two?"
  The accountant got up from his chair, went over to the door, closed it then came back and sat down. He leaned across the desk and said in a low voice, "How much do you want it to be?" He got the job.

! 📎 Delusions of Grandeur

Dr Smith died. When he got to the pearly gates, there was a very large crowd of people waiting to get into heaven.

Dr Smith went up to St. Peter and said, "I'm Dr Smith, and I want to get in there." St. Peter told Dr Smith "Yes . . . yes . . . you need to go to the back of the line."

Dr Smith became indignant and said, "You don't understand . . . my name is DOCTOR Smith!"

St. Peter again told him that he needed to go to the back of the line. Angrily, Dr Smith complied.

Then Dr Jones died. He went through the same scenario of going around the crowd and telling St. Peter that he wanted to enter the gates. As was Dr Smith, Dr Jones was told he needed to go to the back of the line and wait his turn.

"But you don't understand! I am DOCTOR Jones!" He was told again to go to the back of the line.

As Dr Smith and Dr Jones stood in line commiserating, they saw another man walk around the crowd and approach St. Peter. This man was wearing a white lab coat and had a stethoscope around his neck. He said something to St. Peter, then entered the gates of heaven. Now Dr Smith and Dr Jones were irate!

"How come he did not have to wait in line?" Dr Smith bellowed. A guy further up the line replied,

"Oh, that's just God. He thinks he's a doctor!"

Engineers, Physicists and Mathematicians

As an experiment, an engineer, a physicist and a mathematician are placed in separate rooms and left with a can of food, but no can-opener. A day later, the rooms are opened, one by one.

In the first room, the engineer is snoring, with a battered, opened and emptied can. When asked, he explains that when he got hungry, he beat the can to its failure point.

In the second room, the physicist is seen mouthing equations, with a can popped open beside him. When asked, he explains that when he got hungry, he examined the stress points of the can, applied pressure, and "pop!"

In the third room, the mathematician is found sweating and mumbling to himself, "Assume the can is open, assume the can is open ..."

Engineers think that equations approximate the real world.
Scientists think that the real world approximates equations.
Mathematicians are unable to make the connection ...

A mathematician, a biologist and a physicist are sitting in a street café watching people going in and coming out of the house on the other side of the street.

First they see two people going into the house. Time passes. After a while they notice three people coming out of the house.

The physicist: "The measurement wasn't accurate."
The biologist: "They have reproduced."

The mathematician: "If now exactly one person enters the house then it will be empty again."

An engineer, a physicist and a mathematician are shown a pasture with a herd of sheep, and told to put them inside the smallest possible amount of fence.

The engineer is first. He herds the sheep into a circle and then puts the fence around them, declaring, "A circle will use the least fence for a given area, so this is the best solution."

The physicist is next. She creates a circular fence of infinite radius around the sheep, and then draws the fence tight around the herd, declaring, "This will give the smallest circular fence around the herd."

The mathematician is last. After giving the problem a little thought, he puts a small fence around himself and then declares, "I define myself to be on the outside!"

A physicist, a mathematician and an engineer go for a job interview. They're put in isolated rooms for an hour with two ball-bearings and told to come up with something interesting.

At the end of the hour, the interviewers go and see the physicist. He says: "Well, I've worked out a series of experiments which calculate the thermal, mechanical and electrical properties of the ball-bearings, such as their electrical resistance and the mutual coefficient of elasticity."

"Well done", they reply, and go and see the mathematician. He says: "Well, after doing some straightforward mensuration, I tried to work out what would happen if the ball-bearings existed in a generalized n-dimensional vector space – this led to some pretty interesting non-linear algebra."

"Well done," they reply, and go to see the engineer. He says: "I lost one, and broke the other."

⚠ 📎 Five Surgeons

Five surgeons were taking a coffee break and were discussing their work.

The first said, "I think accountants are the easiest to operate on. You open them up and everything inside is numbered."

The second said, "I think librarians are the easiest to operate on. You open them up and everything inside is in alphabetical order."

The third said, "I like to operate on electricians. You open them up and everything inside is colour-coded."

The fourth one said, "I like to operate on lawyers. They're heartless, spineless, gutless and their heads and their asses are interchangeable."

The fifth surgeon said, "I like engineers. They always understand when you have a few parts left over at the end."

⚠ 📎 Fred West the Builder

The police have just arrested mass murderer Fred West. They take him down the station to the cells, beat him up and start to interrogate him.

"Right then, you evil shitbag," they say to him. "How many people have you killed?"

"Seventeen," says Fred.

So the coppers spend weeks digging up his house, and find 25 bodies. They go back to Fred, beat him up a bit more, and say, "You bastard, you told us you killed seventeen."

Fred says, "Aw, c'mon guys. I'm a builder. It was only an estimate."

! 📎 Lucky Thirteenth

A lawyer got married to a woman who had previously been married twelve times. On their wedding night, they settled into the bridal suite at their hotel and the bride said to her new groom, "Please, promise to be gentle. I am still a virgin."

This puzzled the groom, since after twelve marriages, he thought that at least one of her husbands would have been able to perform. He asked his new bride to explain the phenomenon.

She responded:

"My first husband was a Sales Representative who spent the entire marriage telling me, in grandiose terms, how great it was going to be.

"My second husband was from Software Services: he was never quite sure how it was supposed to function, but he promised he would send me documentation.

"My third husband was from Field Services and repeatedly said that everything was diagnostically OK, but couldn't get the system up.

"My fourth husband was from Educational Services, and you know the old saying – 'Those who can, do; those who can't, teach.'

"My fifth husband was from the Telemarketing Department. He knew he had the order, but he wasn't quite sure when he was going to be able to deliver.

"My sixth husband was an Engineer. He told me that he understood the basic process but needed three years to research, implement and design a new state-of-the-art method.

"My seventh husband was from Finance and Administration. He knew how, but he just wasn't sure whether it was his job or not.

"My eighth husband was from Standards and Regulations, and he told me that he met the minimum standards but regulations weren't clear on how to do it.

"My ninth husband was a Marketing Manager. Even though he had the product, he just wasn't sure how to position it.

"My tenth husband was a psychiatrist. All he ever wanted to do was talk about it.

"My eleventh husband was a gynaecologist, and all he ever wanted to do was look at it.

"My twelfth husband was a stamp collector, and all he ever wanted to do was ... God I miss him!

"So now I've married you, and I'm really excited."

"Why is that?" asked the lawyer.

"Well, it should be obvious! You're a lawyer! I just know I'm going to get screwed this time!"

! 📎 Relative Earnings

A neurosurgeon comes home and finds he has no water, so he calls a plumber.

The plumber walks in and has the water back on in five minutes. The plumber turns around and hands the doctor a bill for $275.00.

The outraged doctor stammers, "I'm a neurosurgeon, not some damn dumb plumber, and I don't even make that much for five minutes work!"

The plumber smiles and says, "Yeah, I know. I didn't make that much when I was a neurosurgeon either."

Roadkill

Q: What's the difference between a dead dog in the road and a dead lawyer in the road?
A: There are skid marks in front of the dog.

St Peter's Problem

On their way to a justice of the peace to get married, a couple had a fatal car accident. The couple found themselves sitting outside Heaven's Gate waiting on St. Peter to do an intake. While waiting, they wondered if they could possibly get married in Heaven. St. Peter finally showed up and they asked him. St. Peter said, "I don't know, this is the first time anyone has asked. Let me go find out." And he left.

The couple sat and waited for an answer ... for a couple of months ... and they began to wonder if they really should get married in Heaven, what with the eternal aspect of it all.

"What if it doesn't work?" they wondered, "Are we stuck together forever?" St. Peter returned after yet another month, looking somewhat bedraggled.

"Yes," he informed the couple. "You can get married in Heaven."

"Great," said the couple, "but what if things don't work out? Could we also get a divorce in Heaven?" St. Peter, red-faced, slammed his clipboard onto the ground.

"What's wrong?" asked the frightened couple.

"COME ON!" St. Peter shouted, "It took me three months to find a priest up here! Do you have any idea how long it will take me to find a lawyer?"

! 📎 The Helpful Accountant

An accountant was walking down the street when he came across a dishevelled chap in a shop doorway.

"Give us your loose change, Guv," he said.

"Why should I do that?" enquired the accountant.

"Because I'm skint and haven't got a penny to my name and nothing to eat," said the beggar.

"And how does this compare with the same quarter last year?"

! 📎 The Honest Lawyer

An investment counselor went out on her own. She was shrewd and diligent, so business kept coming in, and pretty soon she realized she needed an in-house counsel, so she began interviewing young lawyers.

"As I'm sure you can understand," she started off with one of the first applicants, "in a business like this, our personal integrity must be beyond question." She leaned forward. "Mr Peterson, are you an 'honest' lawyer?"

"Honest?" replied the job prospect. "Let me tell you something about honest. Why, I'm so honest that my father lent me fifteen thousand dollars for my education and I paid back every penny the minute I tried my very first case."

"Impressive! And what sort of case was that?"

"He sued me for the money."

! The Ultimatum

A group of terrorists burst into the conference room at the Ramada Hotel where the Estate Agents Society was holding its Annual Convention. More than 500 estate agents were taken as hostages.

The terrorist leader announced that, unless their demands were met, they would release one estate agent every hour.

! Three Questions

A man calls a lawyer and asks: "How much would you charge me to answer three questions?"

Lawyer: "Four hundred dollars."
Man: "That's a lot of money isn't it?"
Lawyer: "I guess so. What's your third question?"

Puns, Double Meanings and Wordplay

! 3M TA3

TRY TO FIGURE IT OUT WITHOUT LOOKING AT THE ANSWER.

It took the Division of Motor Vehicles six months to figure out and revoke this personalized license plate:

3M TA3

Can you tell why?

It spells out EAT ME in someone's rear view mirror.

! Anal Examination

A man goes to the doctor with a piece of lettuce sticking out of his bum. He says to the doctor that he is a little concerned.

Upon examination the doctor turns to his patient and says, "It's worse than I originally thought ... That's just the tip of the iceberg."

! Ark II

God called Noah one day and said, "Noah, I need you to build another ark."

"What, like the last one?" says Noah.

"Er, no ... I need this one to have six storeys."

"So do you want me to lead all the animals two by two into the ark?"

"No," says God. "I want you to take just fish on board."

"What kind of fish?"

"Just take carp onto the ark."

"Why just carp?"

"Because I have always wanted a multi-storey carp ark."

At the Vet's

A man runs into the vet's office carrying his dog, screaming for help. The vet rushes him back to an examination room and has him put his dog down on the examination table. The vet examines the still, limp body and after a few moments tells the man that his dog, regrettably, is dead. The man, clearly agitated and not willing to accept this, demands a second opinion.

The vet goes into the back room and comes out with a cat and puts the cat down next to the dog's body. The cat sniffs the body, walks from head to tail poking and sniffing the dog's body and finally looks at the vet and meows. The vet looks at the man and says, "I'm sorry, but Tiddles thinks that your dog is dead too." The man is still unwilling to accept that his dog is dead.

The vet brings in a black Labrador. The dog sniffs the body, walks from head to tail and finally looks at the vet and barks. The vet looks at the man and says, "I'm sorry, but Prince thinks your dog is dead too."

The man, finally resigned to the diagnosis, thanks the vet and asks how much he owes. The vet answers, "$650."

"$650 to tell me my dog is dead?" exclaimed the man ...

"Well," the vet replies, "I would only have charged you $50 for my initial diagnosis. The additional $600 was for the CAT scan and lab tests."

! 📎 Beethoven's Body

A tourist in Vienna is going through a graveyard and all of a sudden he hears some music. No one is around, so he starts searching for the source. He finally locates the origin and finds it is coming from a grave with a headstone that reads: 'Ludwig van Beethoven, 1770–1827'. Then he realizes that the music is the Ninth Symphony and it is being played backwards!

Puzzled, he leaves the graveyard and persuades a friend to return with him. By the time they arrive back at the grave, the music has changed. This time it is the Seventh Symphony, but like the previous piece, it is being played backwards.

Curious, the men agree to consult a music scholar. When they return with the expert, the Fifth Symphony is playing, again backwards. The expert notices that the symphonies are being played in the reverse order in which they were composed, the Ninth, then the Seventh, then the Fifth.

By the next day the word has spread and a throng has gathered around the grave. They are all listening to the Second Symphony being played backwards. Just then the graveyard's caretaker ambles up to the group. Someone in the group asks him if he has an explanation for the music.

"Don't you get it?" the caretaker says incredulously. "He's decomposing."

! 📎 Clyde Died

Clyde died in a fire and was burnt badly. The morgue needed someone to identify the body. So his two best friends, Clem and Zeke, were sent. Clem went in and the mortician pulled back the sheet. Clem said, "Yup, he's burnt pretty bad. Roll him over." So the mortician rolled him over and

Clem looked and said, "Nope, ain't Clyde."

The mortician thought that was rather strange. Then he brought Zeke to identify the body and Zeke took a look at him and said, "Yup, he's burnt real bad, roll him over." The mortician rolled him over and Zeke looked down and said, "No, it ain't Clyde."

The mortician asked, "How can you tell?" Zeke said, "Well, Clyde had two assholes."

"What? He had two assholes?" said the mortician.

"Yup, everyone in town knew he had two assholes. Every time we went to town, folks would say, 'Here comes Clyde with them two assholes.'"

! ◎ Comrade Rudolf

A Russian couple were walking down the street in Moscow one night, when the man felt a drop hit his nose.

"I think it's raining," he said to his wife.

"No, that felt more like snow to me," she replied.

"No, I'm sure it was just rain," he said.

Well, as these things go, they were about to have a major argument about whether it was raining or snowing. Just then, they saw a minor Communist Party official walking towards them.

"Let's not fight about it," the man said. "Let's ask Comrade Rudolph whether it's officially raining or snowing."

As the official approached, the man said, "Tell us, Comrade Rudolph, is it officially raining or snowing?"

"It's raining, of course!" he replied, and walked on. But the woman insisted: "I know that felt like snow!"

The man quietly replied: "Rudolph the Red knows rain, dear!"

! 📎 Fancy Dress

A man has a party to which the guests have to come as a human emotion. The day of the party comes and his first guest arrives wearing a green T-shirt with an N and a V on it.

HOST: What have you come as?
GUEST 1:   I'm green with envy
HOST: Oh, very good. Come in and get a drink

Then there is a second knock at the door, and a gorgeous girl arrives in the tiniest pink dress with tassels on.

HOST: What have you come as?
GUEST 2:   I'm tickled pink
HOST: Oh, very good. Come in and get a drink!

Later on there is another knock at the door and there stand two Rastafarians, completely bollock naked: one has his knob in a bowl of custard and the other has a pear on his knob.

HOST: What the fuck have you come as?
RASTAFARIAN: I'm fuckin' dis custard and he's fuckin' dis pear.

Meanwhile, behind the two Rastafarians, a bloke turns up just wearing his boxer shorts.

"I'm premature ejaculation; I've come in my pants."

! 📎 Focus

Two nuns were on a remote beach. They decided to go behind a sand dune and sunbathe in the nude.

They were lying there for a while when a photographer came by and pointed a camera at them. The first nun asked him, "Aren't you going to focus?"

The second nun said, "Quiet sister! Let him take his picture first."

Gandhi

Mahatma Gandhi, as you know, walked barefoot most of the time, which produced an impressive set of callouses on his feet. He also ate very little, which made him rather frail and with his odd diet, he suffered from bad breath.

This made him what?

A super-calloused fragile mystic plagued with halitosis.

If Lawyers are Disbarred...

If lawyers are disbarred and clergymen defrocked, doesn't it follow that electricians can be delighted, musicians denoted, cowboys deranged, models deposed and dry cleaners depressed?

Laundry workers could decrease, eventually becoming depressed and depleted! Even more, bedmakers will be debunked, baseball players will be debased, landscapers will be deflowered, bulldozer operators will be degraded, organ donors will be delivered, software engineers will be detested, the BVD company will be debriefed and even musical composers will eventually decompose.

On a more positive note, though, perhaps we can hope politicians will be devoted.

! 📎 Man in Bar

A man walks into a bar – he sits down and orders a drink. The barman gives him his drink, accompanied by a bowl of peanuts. To his surprise, a voice comes from the peanut bowl.

"You look great tonight!" it says. "You really look fantastic ... and that aftershave is just wonderful!" The man is obviously a little confused, but tries to ignore it.

Realizing he has no cigarettes he wanders over to the cigarette machine. After inserting his money, another voice comes from the machine.

"You BASTARD ... Oh my god you STINK ... Do you know, you're almost as ugly as your mother?"

By now, the man is extremely perplexed. He turns to the barman for an explanation.

"Ah yes, sir," the barman responds. "The peanuts are complimentary, but the cigarette machine is out of order."

! 📎 Mistranslations

Hotel room notice, Chiang-Mai, Thailand:
PLEASE DO NOT BRING SOLICITORS INTO YOUR ROOM

Hotel brochure, Italy:
THIS HOTEL IS RENOWNED FOR ITS PEACE AND SOLITUDE. IN FACT CROWDS FROM ALL OVER THE WORLD FLOCK HERE TO ENJOY ITS SOLITUDE.

Hotel lobby, Bucharest:
THE LIFT IS BEING FIXED FOR THE NEXT DAY. DURING THAT TIME WE REGRET THAT YOU WILL BE UNBEARABLE

In a Leipzig elevator:
DO NOT ENTER THE LIFT BACKWARDS, AND ONLY WHEN LIT UP.

Hotel elevator, Belgrade:
TO MOVE THE CABIN, PUSH BUTTON FOR WISHING FLOOR. IF THE CABIN SHOULD ENTER MORE PERSONS, EACH ONE SHOULD PRESS A NUMBER OF WISHING FLOOR. DRIVING IS THEN GOING ALPHABET-ICALLY BY NATIONAL ORDER.

Hotel elevator, Paris:
PLEASE LEAVE YOUR VALUES AT THE FRONT DESK.

Hotel, Athens:
VISITORS ARE EXPECTED TO COMPLAIN AT THE OFFICE BETWEEN THE HOURS OF 9 AND 11 AM DAILY.

Hotel, Yugoslavia:
THE FLATTENING OF UNDERWEAR WITH PLEASURE IS THE JOB OF THE CHAMBERMAID.

Hotel, Japan:
YOU ARE INVITED TO TAKE ADVANTAGE OF THE CHAMBERMAID.

In the lobby of a Moscow hotel across from a Russian Orthodox monastery:
YOU ARE WELCOME TO VISIT THE CEMETERY WHERE FAMOUS RUSSIAN AND SOVIET COMPOSERS, ARTISTS AND WRITERS ARE BURIED DAILY EXCEPT THURSDAY.

Hotel catering to skiers, Austria:
NOT TO PERAMBULATE THE CORRIDORS IN THE HOURS OF REPOSE IN THE BOOTS OF ASCENSION.

Taken from a menu, Poland:
SALAD A FIRM'S OWN MAKE; LIMPID RED BEET SOUP WITH CHEESY
DUMPLINGS IN THE FORM OF A FINGER; ROASTED DUCK LET LOOSE;
BEEF RASHERS BEATEN UP IN THE COUNTRY PEOPLE'S FASHION.

Supermarket, Hong Kong:
FOR YOUR CONVENIENCE, WE RECOMMEND COURTEOUS, EFFICIENT
SELF-SERVICE.

Dry cleaner's, Bangkok:
DROP YOUR TROUSERS HERE FOR THE BEST RESULTS.

Outside a dress shop, Paris:
DRESSES FOR STREET WALKING.

Outside a dress shop, Hong Kong:
LADIES HAVE FITS UPSTAIRS.

Tailor shop, Rhodes:
ORDER YOUR SUMMERS SUIT. BECAUSE IS BIG RUSH, WE WILL
EXECUTE CUSTOMERS IN STRICT ROTATION.

From the *Soviet Weekly*:
THERE WILL BE A MOSCOW EXHIBITION OF ARTS BY 15,000 SOVIET
REPUBLIC PAINTERS AND SCULPTORS. THESE WERE EXECUTED
OVER THE PAST TWO YEARS.

In an East African newspaper:
A NEW SWIMMING POOL IS RAPIDLY TAKING SHAPE SINCE THE
CONTRACTORS HAVE THROWN IN THE BULK OF THEIR WORKERS.

Hotel, Vienna:
IN CASE OF FIRE, DO YOUR UTMOST TO ALARM THE HOTEL PORTER.

A sign posted in Germany's Black Forest:
IT IS STRICTLY FORBIDDEN ON OUR BLACK FOREST CAMPING SITE THAT PEOPLE OF DIFFERENT SEX, FOR INSTANCE, MEN AND WOMEN, LIVE TOGETHER IN ONE TENT UNLESS THEY ARE MARRIED WITH EACH OTHER FOR THIS PURPOSE.

Hotel, Zurich:
BECAUSE OF THE IMPROPRIETY OF ENTERTAINING GUESTS OF THE OPPOSITE SEX IN THE BEDROOM, IT IS SUGGESTED THAT THE LOBBY BE USED FOR THIS PURPOSE.

An advertisement by a Hong Kong dentist:
TEETH EXTRACTED BY THE LATEST METHODISTS.

From a Russian book on chess:
A LOT OF WATER HAS BEEN PASSED UNDER THE BRIDGE SINCE THIS VARIATION HAS BEEN PLAYED.

A laundry in Rome:
LADIES, LEAVE YOUR CLOTHES HERE AND SPEND THE AFTERNOON HAVING A GOOD TIME.

Tourist agency, Czechoslovakia:
TAKE ONE OF OUR HORSE-DRIVEN CITY TOURS. WE GUARANTEE NO MISCARRIAGES.

Advertisement for donkey rides, Thailand:
WOULD YOU LIKE TO RIDE ON YOUR OWN ASS?

In the window on a Swedish furrier:
FUR COATS MADE FOR LADIES FROM THEIR OWN SKIN.

The box of a clockwork toy made in Hong Kong:
GUARANTEED TO WORK THROUGHOUT ITS USEFUL LIFE.

Detour sign in Kyushi, Japan:
STOP. DRIVE SIDEWAYS.

In a Swiss mountain inn:
SPECIAL TODAY – NO ICE-CREAM.

Airline ticket office, Copenhagen:
WE TAKE YOUR BAGS AND SEND THEM IN ALL DIRECTIONS.

On the door of a Moscow hotel room:
IF THIS IS YOUR FIRST VISIT TO THE USSR, YOU ARE WELCOME TO IT.

Cocktail lounge, Norway:
LADIES ARE REQUESTED NOT TO HAVE CHILDREN IN THE BAR.

At a Budapest zoo:
PLEASE DO NOT FEED THE ANIMALS. IF YOU HAVE ANY SUITABLE FOOD, GIVE IT TO THE GUARD ON DUTY.

Doctors office, Rome:
SPECIALIST IN WOMEN AND OTHER DISEASES.

Hotel, Acapulco:
THE MANAGER HAS PERSONALLY PASSED ALL THE WATER SERVED HERE.

In a Tokyo shop:
OUR NYLONS COST MORE THAN COMMON, BUT YOU'LL FIND THEY ARE THE BEST IN THE LONG RUN.

Information booklet about using a hotel air conditioner, Japan:
COOLES AND HEATES: IF YOU WANT JUST CONDITION OF WARM AIR IN YOUR ROOM, PLEASE CONTROL YOURSELF.

Car rental brochure, Tokyo:
WHEN PASSENGER OF FOOT HEAVE IN SIGHT, TOOTLE THE HORN.
TRUMPET HIM MELODIOUSLY AT FIRST, BUT IF HE STILL OBSTACLES
YOUR PASSAGE THEN TOOTLE HIM WITH VIGOR.

Sign from a Majorcan shop entrance:
ENGLISH WELL TALKING HERE SPEECHING AMERICAN

! 📎 Nelson Mandela

Nelson Mandela is sitting at home enjoying his retirement, watching the telly when he hears a knock at the door. When he opens it, he is confronted by a little Japanese man, clutching a clipboard and yelling, "Ahhhhh! You sign! You sign!" Behind him is an enormous truck full of car exhausts. Nelson is standing there in complete amazement when the Japanese man starts to yell louder, "You sign! You sign!"

Nelson says to him, "Look mate, you've obviously got the wrong bloke. Get lost!" and shuts the door in the Japanese man's face.

The next day he hears a knock at the door again. When he opens it, the little Japanese man is back, with a huge truck full of brake pads. He thrusts his clipboard under Nelson's nose, yelling, "Ahh, you sign! You sign!"

Mr Mandela is getting a bit hacked off by now, so he shoves the little Japanese man back, shouting: "Look, get lost! You've got the wrong bloke! I don't want them!" and then slams the door in the Japanese man's face again.

The following day Nelson is resting, and late in the afternoon, hears a knock on the door again. Upon opening the door, the little Japanese man thrusts the same clipboard under his nose, shouting, "Ahhhhhhh, You sign! You sign!" Behind him are TWO large trucks full of wing mirrors. Nelson loses his temper completely, picks the little man up by his shirt front and yells at him: "Look mate, I don't want these! Do you understand? You must have the wrong man! Who do you really want to give these to?"

The little Japanese man looks at him a bit puzzled, consults his clipboard, and says: "You not Nissan Maindealer?"

New Meanings for Old Words

The *Washington Post* recently had a contest for readers in which they were asked to supply alternative meanings for various words. The following were some of the winning entries:

Abdicate *v.* to give up all hope of ever having a flat stomach.

Carcinoma *n.* a valley in California, notable for its heavy smog.

Esplanade *v.* to attempt an explanation while drunk.

Willy-nilly *adj.* impotent

Flabbergasted *adj.* appalled over how much weight you have gained.

Negligent *adj.* describes a condition in which you absentmindedly answer the door in your nightie.

Lymph *v.* to walk with a lisp.

Gargoyle *n.* an olive-flavored mouthwash.

Bustard *n.* a very rude Metrobus driver.

Coffee *n.* a person who is coughed upon.

Flatulence *n.* the emergency vehicle that picks you up after you are run over by a steamroller.

Balderdash *n.* a rapidly receding hairline.

Testicle *n.* a humorous question in an exam.

Semantics *n.* pranks conducted by young men studying for the priesthood, including such things as glueing the pages of the priest's prayer book together just before vespers.

Rectitude *n.* the formal, dignified demeanor assumed by a proctologist immediately before he examines you.

Marionettes *n.* residents of Washington who have been jerked around by the mayor.

Oyster *n.* a person who sprinkles his conversation with Yiddish expressions.

! 📎 New Words

BLAMESTORMING: Sitting around in a group, discussing why a deadline was missed or a project failed, and who was responsible.

UMFRIEND: A sexual relation of dubious standing or a concealed intimate relationship, as in "This is Dylan, my … um … friend."

SEAGULL MANAGER: A manager who flies in, makes a lot of noise, criticizes everything and then leaves.

CHAINSAW CONSULTANT: An outside expert brought in to reduce the employee headcount, leaving the top brass with clean hands.

CUBE FARM: An office filled with cubicles.

IDEA HAMSTERS: People who always seem to have their idea generators running.

MOUSE POTATO: The on-line, wired generation's answer to the couch potato.

PRAIRIE DOGGING: When someone yells or drops something loudly in a cube farm, and people's heads pop up over the walls to see what's going on.

SITCOMs (Single Income, Two Children, Oppressive Mortgage): What Yuppies turn into when they have children and one of them stops working to stay home with the kids.

SQUIRT THE BIRD: To transmit a signal to a satellite.

STARTER MARRIAGE: A short-lived first marriage that ends in divorce with no kids, no property and no regrets.

STRESS PUPPY: A person who seems to thrive on being stressed out and whiny.

SWIPED OUT: An ATM or credit card that has been rendered useless because the magnetic strip is worn away from extensive use.

TOURISTS: People who take training classes just to get a vacation from their jobs. "We had three serious students in the class; the rest were just tourists."

TREEWARE: Hacker slang for documentation or other printed material.

XEROX SUBSIDY: Euphemism for swiping free photocopies from one's workplace.

ALPHA GEEK: The most knowledgeable, technically proficient person in an office or work group.

ASSMOSIS: The process by which some people seem to absorb success and advancement by kissing up to the boss rather than working hard.

FLIGHT RISK: Used to describe employees who are suspected of planning to leave a company or department soon.

IRRITAINMENT: Entertainment and media spectacles that are annoying but you find yourself unable to stop watching them. The O.J. trials were a prime example. Bill Clinton's shameful video Grand Jury testimony is another.

PERCUSSIVE MAINTENANCE: The fine art of whacking the heck out of an electronic device to get it to work again.

UNINSTALLED: Euphemism for being fired. Heard on the voice-mail of a vice president at a downsizing computer firm: "You have reached the number of an Uninstalled Vice President. Please dial our main number and ask the operator for assistance." *(Syn: decruitment.)

SALMON DAY: The experience of spending an entire day swimming upstream only to get screwed and die in the end.

CLM (Career Limiting Move): Used among microserfs to describe ill-advised activity. Trashing your boss while he or she is within earshot is a serious CLM.

ADMINISPHERE: The rarefied organizational layers beginning just above the rank and file. Decisions that fall from the adminisphere are often profoundly inappropriate or irrelevant to the problems they were designed to solve.

404: Someone who's clueless. From the World Wide Web error message "404 Not Found" meaning that the requested document could not be located. "Don't bother asking him ... he's 404, man."

OHNO-SECOND: That minuscule fraction of time in which you realize that you've just made a BIG mistake, e.g. as a rude email joke leaves your Outbox, bound for an inappropriate recipient.

! 🗐 Oasis Soup

Liam Gallagher is sitting in a restaurant and sees "Oasis soup" on the menu and says to the waiter, "I'll have the Oasis soup."

The waiter brings back the soup and Liam says, "Here! That looks like tomato soup to me. Why's that Oasis soup?"

The waiter says, "Well, you've got a roll with it."

Positive-Negative

A linguistics professor was lecturing to his class one day.

"In English," he said, "a double negative forms a positive. In some languages, though, such as Russian, a double negative is still a negative. However, there is no language wherein a double positive can form a negative."

A voice from the back of the room piped up, "Yeah, right."

'Second Funniest Joke in the World'

"Doctor, I can't pronounce my F's, T's and H's."
"Well you can't say fairer than that then."

Sick Bag

A paper bag goes to the doctor and complains of feeling really ill. The doctor does a lot of tests and tells the paper bag to come back next week for the results. The following week the paper bag is extremely distressed to be told by his doctor that he is HIV positive.

"But how can this be?" he cries, "I'm only a paper bag!"

"Well, have you had unprotected sex in the last year?" asks the doctor.

"No, how can I?" he shouts. "I'm only a paper bag!"

"How about sharing needles, giving blood, anything like that?"

"I've said to you before," the paper bag sobs, "how can I? I'm only a paper bag."

"Ahhhh," says the doctor shaking his head sadly. "As I suspected ... your mother must have been a carrier."

! 🔟 Start Groaning Now

My wife's gone to the West Indies.
Jamaica?
No, she went of her own accord.

(that's the original one, now prepare for a deluge of variations ...)

My wife's gone to the Indian coast.
Goa?
Phwoar! I'll say!

My wife's gone to St Petersburg.
Is she Russian?
No, she's taking her time.

My wife's gone to Northern Italy.
Genoa?
I should think so, we've been married for 20 years.

My wife's had an accident on a volcano.
Krakatoa?
No. She broke her leg.

My wife's gone mad in Venezuela.
Caracas?
Yes, absolutely loopy.

My wife's gone to the Welsh border.
Wye?
Search me.

My wife's gone to the botanical gardens.
Kew?
Yes, it was rather busy.

My wife's gone to Malawi.
Lilongwe?
Yes, about 5000 miles.

My wife's got an upset tummy in Laos.
Inkhazi?
Yes, constantly.

My wife's gone to see relatives in France.
Nice?
(... need I say more ...)

My wife's gone on a singing tour of South Korea
Seoul?
No, R&B

My wife caught a cold in the Gulf.
Qatar?
Yes, she was coughing up greenies for weeks.

My wife had an accident in Slovenia.
Bled?
Like a stuck pig.

My wife's parents are from Croatia.
Split?
No, they're still happily married.

My wife went to a very bad concert in South East Asia.
Singapore?
Terrible. And the rest of the band was even worse.

My wife went on a sailing course in Poole.
In Dorset?
Yes, she'd recommend it to anyone.

The Bells, The Bells

After the death of Quasimodo the bishop decides to have an audition for a new bellringer. Five candidates turn up and the last to go wants to climb the tower.

"We usually pull the ropes down here," says the bishop.

"I do it my special way," the man replies.

They climb up to the belfry and the man starts ringing by bashing the bells with his face. This strange technique produces a wonderful mellow tone and the bishop is just about to give him the job when the man slips and falls to his death. Horrified, the bishop runs down to where a crowd has gathered around the body.

"Who was he?" they say.

"Don't know," says the bishop, "but his face rings a bell."

(and there's more ...)

The dead man's brother turns up and demands that he be given the job to compensate for his poor brother's death. The bishop agrees to an audition but during the ringing, the biggest bell comes off its rocker and crashes down on top of the ringer, killing him instantly. The crowd rush into the church and once again ask who has been killed.

"Don't know," says the bishop, "but he's a dead ringer for his brother."

The Jagger Collateral

A frog goes into a bank and approaches the teller. He can see from her nameplate that her name is Patricia Whack. So he says, "Hello Patricia Whack, I'd like to get a loan to buy a boat and go on a long vacation."

Patti looks at this frog in disbelief and asks how much he wants to borrow. The frog says $30,000, and the teller asks his name, and the frog says it's Kermit Jagger, he's the adopted pet of Mick Jagger and that it's OK, he knows the bank manager. Patti explains that $30,000 is a substantial amount of money and that he will need to secure some collateral against the loan. She asks if he has anything he can use as collateral. The frog says, "Sure. I have this," and produces a tiny pink porcelain elephant, about an inch tall, bright pink and perfectly formed.

Very confused, Patti explains that she'll have to consult with the manager and leaves the room. She finds the manager and says, "There is a frog called Kermit Jagger out there who claims to know Mick Jagger and wants to borrow $30,000. And he wants to use this as collateral." She holds up the tiny pink elephant and asks, "What the heck is this?" The bank manager looks her in the eye and says:

"It's a knick knack, Patti Whack, give the frog a loan. His old man's a Rolling Stone."

The Missing Viking

A famous Viking explorer returned home from a voyage and found his name missing from the town register. His wife insisted on complaining to the local civic official who apologized profusely saying, "I must have taken Leif off my census."

The Road and the Bus Lane

A bit of black tarmac walks into a bar and orders a pint. He's just starting his pint when a bit of red tarmac walks in.

"Oi! Mate!" says the black tarmac. "I'm a piece of black tarmac, so that makes me a road. What are you?"

"I'm a bus lane," says the piece of red tarmac.

"Well it's nice to meet you," says road. "Come and join me for a pint." After a few beers the road says, "Ere, do you fancy going to that new club in town?" and the bus lane says, "No mate, I'm a lightweight, I always end up getting my head kicked in." So road says, "Don't worry about it, I'm a bit of a hard case, I'll look after you." So bus lane says "Fair enough, as long as you'll look after me." So off they go.

After a few more beers in the club, three bits of green tarmac walk in. As soon as he sees them, road hides under a table, the bits of green tarmac take one look at bus lane and start kicking him, punching him and generally having a laugh. After a while they get bored and walk out. Bus lane pulls his battered body over to the table and wipes his blood up and turns to road and says, "I thought you were going to look after me?"

"I was!" says road, "But those bits of green tarmac are fucking cycle paths!"

! 📎 They Never Forget

An elephant is drinking out of a river when he spots a turtle asleep on a log. The elephant ambles over and kicks the unsuspecting turtle clear across the river.

"Why did you do that?" asks a passing giraffe.

"Because I recognized it as the same turtle that took a nip out of my trunk 47 years ago."

"Wow, what a memory!" says the giraffe.

"Yes," says the elephant. "Turtle Recall."

! 📋 Tonto Cooling Silver

After a long, gruelling ride through the desert, The Lone Ranger and Tonto (faithful Indian companion) come to a small town. The Lone Ranger says to Tonto: "Silver here is really hot and tired. I want you to run around him flapping your arms to cool him off whilst I enter yon saloon for a drink."

After several minutes of relaxing in the saloon, drinking his milk, a man comes in through the swinging doors and asks who owns the white horse tied up out front. The Lone Ranger responds: "That would be me."

Then the guy says: "Well, you left your injun runnin'!"

! 📋 Two Whales

Two whales are crashing majestically through the North Sea when they spy a whaling ship.

"Oh dear," says one, "let's make a run for it."

"NO!" says the other, "I'm tired of running from these ships, I say we take a stand!"

"OK," replies the first whale, "but what are we going to do?"

"I know, we'll swim underneath and capsize their boat by blasting it out of the water with the jets from our blow holes!"

"I'm with you – let's go."

So, the ship is overturned and the survivors are flailing about in the water.

It isn't enough for the second whale, though, and he shouts to the first, "C'mon, let's chew up and spit out the survivors!"

"Oh no," says the other whale. "I don't mind the blow job but I'm not eating seamen."

Religion

! 🔟 Communion Lite

The Roman Catholic Church is bringing out a new, low-fat communion wafer. It's going to be called "I Can't Believe It's Not Jesus."

! 🔟 Guide to Religions

Taoism   Shit happens.

Buddhism   If shit happens, it's not a real shit.

Islam   If shit happens, it's the will of Allah.

Protestantism   Shit happens because you don't work hard enough.

Judaism   Why does shit always happen to me?

Hinduism   This shit happened before.

Catholicism   Shit happens because you're bad.

Hare Krishna   Shit happens, rama rama.

TV Evangelism   Send more shit!

Atheism   No shit.

Jehovah's Witnesses Knock, knock. Shit happens.

Hedonism   There's nothing like good shit.

Christian Science   Shit happens in your mind.

Agnosticism	Maybe shit happens, maybe it doesn't.
Existentialism	What is shit anyway?
Stoicism	This shit doesn't bother me.
Rastafarian	Let's smoke this shit!
Zen	What is the sound of shit happening?

Just a Second

Mortal:	What is a million years like to you?
God:	Like one second.
Mortal:	What is a million dollars like to you?
God:	Like one penny.
Mortal:	Can I have a penny?
God:	Just a second …

Lottery

A Jewish guy called Jacob finds himself in dire straits. His business has gone bust and he's in serious financial trouble. He's so desperate that he decides to ask God for help. He goes into the synagogue and begins to pray.

"God, please help me, I've lost my business and if I don't get some money, I'm going to lose my house as well, please let me win the lotto."

Lotto night comes and somebody else wins it. Jacob goes back to the synagogue.

"God, please let me win the lotto, I've lost my business, my house and I'm going to lose my car as well."

Lotto night comes and Jacob still has no luck. Back to the synagogue.

"My God, why have you forsaken me? I've lost my business, my house, my car and my wife and children are starving. I don't often ask you for help and I have always been a good servant to you. Why won't you just let me win the lotto this one time so I can get my life back in order?"

Suddenly there is a blinding flash of light as the heavens open and Jacob is confronted by the voice of GOD himself:

"JACOB, MEET ME HALFWAY ON THIS ONE. BUY A TICKET."

Moses

Nine-year-old Joey was asked by his mother what he had learned in Sunday School.

"Well, Mom, our teacher told us how God sent Moses behind enemy lines on a rescue mission to lead the Israelites out of Egypt. When he got to the Red Sea, he had his engineers build a pontoon bridge, and all the people walked across safely. Then he used his walkie-talkie to radio headquarters and call in an air strike. They sent in bombers to blow up the bridge and all the Israelites were saved."

"Now, Joey, is that REALLY what your teacher taught you?" his mother asked.

"Well, no, Mom, but if I told it the way the teacher did, you'd never believe it."

Priestly Guidance

Sean and Murphy are two teenagers out on the razzle one night. Well, Sean's better looking than his mate and, consequently, he scores with a local chick and goes back to her place – abandoning Murphy with a wink.

Next morning, Sunday as it happens, Sean turns up at Murphy's place with bags under his eyes, a dry throat, spotty chin and all the rest of it …

he looks like death warmed up, and appears to have all the symptoms of going into a diabetic coma, even though he's not a diabetic . . . and Murphy asks how it went.

"Great," says Sean. "But I'm knackered and I think I really ought to go to confession you know, after what I did with this girl last night."

Murphy tells him to get a move on 'cause the church has already started morning service and so the pair of them get down there, whereupon Murphy says he'll wait at the door on account he hasn't got any sins to confess.

Sean reaches the confessional and the voice of the priest whispers to him through the screen, "Speak up and reveal your sins to God young man," and so Sean goes on to describe his night of debauchery in detail . . . adding that it all happened with a local girl . . . and the priest says, "Young man, your sins can be forgiven, but you must tell me the name of the poor girl, she may be in greater danger than you."

Sean doesn't think he can bring himself to give her name and says, "Father, I've come to confess my own sins, the girl can do the same, it wouldn't be proper of me to speak her name now would it?"

The priest asks him, in an annoyed tone, "Was it Mary O'Flannagan then, young man?" and Sean cries "No Father . . . it's the girl's own business . . . I'll not say . . .", which perplexes the priest more still, leading him to demand, "Well then, was it Lucy O'Hara, you young idiot?" and Sean replies, "No Father . . . it's the girl's own business . . . I'll not say . . ." and the priest gets even more annoyed and asks in a sterner voice still, "Was it Susan O'Flaherty then, you rapscallion?" and Sean screams back, "No Father . . . it's the girl's own business . . . I'll not say . . . I demand you pardon me for my own sins and let me leave."

The priest issues Sean with 50 Hail Mary's and orders him to clean the church after the service; he is thus absolved of his sins.

On rejoining Murphy at the door Murphy smiles and asks, "How did it go then Sean, what did you get?" to which Sean says "Oh, a few Hail Mary's and a bit of cleaning to do after the service . . . and three fucking red hot tips for next Saturday."

! 🔖 The Going Rate

A priest is hearing confessions one afternoon when he has to go to the bathroom. He calls the janitor over to take his place. The janitor resists, saying he isn't a Catholic or a priest and will not know what to say. The priest assures him that everything will be fine if he just follows the chart in the confessional.

"If someone comes in and says they have stolen, you tell them to say two Hail Mary's and don't do it again," explains the priest. "Just follow the chart." And with that, the priest leaves.

The janitor sits down, and in walks a man to confess.

"Forgive me father for I have sinned. I have had anal sex with another man."

The janitor is shocked! He keeps going over the chart, trying to find a reference to anal sex and can't find any. He starts to get worried and opens the confession door, and asks a nearby choirboy, "What does the father give for anal sex?"

"Well," says the choirboy, "usually it's a T-shirt and a candy bar."

! 🔖 The Power of Prayer

An old Jewish man is walking on the beach with his only grandson, when a giant wave crashes on shore, sweeping the boy out to sea.

The man looks up to the heavens and says: "Oh Lord, this is my only grandson. How can you take him away from me like this? My son will not understand. My daughter-in-law will die from grief."

Another wave comes by, and deposits the boy at the old man's feet.

The grandfather looks to the heavens again and says, "He had a hat!"

Sex, Lays
and Duct Tape

A sweet young thing thought she might have some fun with a stiff-looking military man at a cocktail party, so she walked over and asked him when was the last time he had had sex.

"1956," was his immediate reply.

"No wonder you look so uptight!" she exclaimed. "Honey, you need to get out more."

"I'm not sure I understand you," he answered, glancing at his watch.

"It's only 2014 now."

! 🔗 A Week in Hell

A guy dies and finds himself in hell. As he wallows in despair, he meets with the devil.

Devil: Why so glum, chum?
Guy: Why do you think? I'm in hell.

Devil: Hell's not so bad. We actually have a lot of fun down here. You a drinkin' man?
Guy: Sure, I love to drink.

Devil: Well, you're going to love Mondays then. On Mondays, all we do is drink: whisky, tequila, wine coolers, Goose Island beer, anything, every-

thing! We drink 'til we throw up, and then we drink some more.
Guy: Gee, that sounds great.

Devil: You a smoker?
Guy: You better believe it.

Devil: All right! You're gonna love Tuesdays. We get the finest cigars from around the world and smoke our lungs out. If you get cancer, it's okay: you're already dead!
Guy: Golly!

Devil: I bet you like to gamble.
Guy: Yes, as a matter of fact, I do.

Devil: Good, because Wednesday is gambling day. Craps, blackjack, horse races, you name it. We even opened up a roulette table.
Guy: Gosh, I never played roulette before.

Devil: Well, now you can. You like to do drugs?
Guy: Yes, I love to do drugs. You don't mean ...

Devil: That's right! Thursday is drug day. Help yourself to a great, big bowl of coke, smoke a joint the size of a submarine. You can do all the drugs you want, and if you overdose, it's okay: you're already dead!
Guy: Neat! I never realized hell was such a swinging place.

Devil: You gay?
Guy: No!

Devil: Oooooh! You're gonna hate Fridays!

! 📎 Almost Perfect

A young single guy on a cruise ship is having the time of his life. On the second day of the cruise, the ship sinks, but our guy manages to grab on to a piece of driftwood and, using every last ounce of strength, swims a few miles through the shark-infested sea to a remote island.

Lying on the shore nearly passed out from exhaustion, he turns his head and sees a woman lying near him, unconscious, barely breathing. She's also managed to be washed up on shore from the sinking ship. He makes his way over to her, and with some mouth-to-mouth assistance he manages to get her breathing again. She looks up at him, wide-eyed and grateful and says, "You saved my life, I'm so grateful, you're my hero." He suddenly realizes the woman is Cindy Crawford!

Days and weeks go by. Cindy and our guy are living on the island. They've set up a hut, there's plenty of fruit on the trees, they're in heaven. Cindy's fallen madly in love with our man, and they're making passionate love morning, noon and night.

One day she notices he's looking kind of sad.

"What's the matter, sweetheart?" she asks. "We have a wonderful life together, I'm in love with you. Is there something wrong? Is there anything I can do?"

He says, "Actually, there is. Would you mind putting on my shirt?"

"Sure," she says, "if it will help." He takes off his shirt and she puts it on.

"Now would you put on my pants?" he asks.

"Sure, honey, if it's really going to make you feel better," she says.

"Okay, would you put on my hat now, and draw a little moustache on your face?" he asks.

"Whatever you want, sweetie," she says, and does.

Then he says, "Now, would you start walking around the edge of the island?" She starts walking around the perimeter of the island. He sets off in the other direction. They meet up half way around the island a few minutes later. He rushes up to her, grabs her by the shoulders and says,

"Mate! You'll never believe who I'm shagging!"

An Interesting Fact About Semen

This one actually happened at Harvard University in a biology class.

The Prof was discussing the high glucose levels found in semen. A young female (freshman) raised her hand and asked, "If I understand, you're saying there is as much glucose in semen as in sugar?" "That's correct," responded the Prof, going on to add statistical info. Raising her hand again, the girl asked, "Then why doesn't it taste sweet?"

After a stunned silence, the whole class burst out laughing, the poor girl's face turned bright red and as she realized exactly what she had inadvertently implied, she picked up her books without a word and walked out of class ... and never returned.

However, as she was going out the door, the Prof's reply was classic. Totally straight-faced, he answered her question. "It doesn't taste sweet because the taste-buds for sweetness are on the tip of your tongue and not the back of your throat."

! ◻ Chicken

A sailor who has been at sea for several months comes into port and heads for a brothel. He tells the man at the desk he'd like some sex, but he doesn't have much money. The man tells him a girl will cost him $40 and a sex show $20.

The sailor is desperate as he only has $5, having lost most of his money in card games aboard ship.

"You've got to help me out! I've been at sea for months and I really need some sex. You've got to do something for me. Please!"

The man thinks for a moment, takes the money and directs the sailor to one of the upstairs rooms. Once inside the room the sailor looks around but the only thing he sees is a chicken. Desperate for some action, he resigns himself to fucking the chicken and quickly leaves.

Two weeks later, he returns, this time having won a few bucks on ship. "What do you have for $20?" he asks.

The man directs him upstairs once again to a different room. Opening the door, the room is packed with men shoulder to shoulder all watching lesbians through a one-way mirror on the wall. The sailor's eyes light up as he watches and he remarks to a man standing next to him, "This is great."

The man replies, "If you think this is great, you should have been here two weeks ago. There was a guy fucking a chicken!"

! 📎 Dirty Verse

>>   There was a young lady from Leith
>>   Who would circumcise men with her teeth
>>   It wasn't for fame,
>>   Or love of the game
>>   But to get at the cheese underneath.
>>
>>   There was a young actress from Crewe,
>>   Who remarked, as the vicar withdrew,
>>   "The Bishop was quicker
>>   And thicker and slicker,
>>   And two inches longer than you."
>>
>>   There was a young vampire called Mabel,
>>   Whose periods were always quite stable,
>>   At every full moon,
>>   She took out a spoon,
>>   And drank herself under the table.

>> There was a young plumber from Lee,
>> Who was plumbing his girl with great glee,
>> She said stop your plumbing,
>> I think someone's coming,
>> Said the plumber, still plumbing, "It's me!"
>>
>> A kinky young girl from Coleshill,
>> Tried a dynamite stick for a thrill,
>> They found her vagina,
>> In North Carolina,
>> And bits of her tits in Brazil.
>>
>> There was a young man from Pitlochrie,
>> Making love to his girl in the rock'ry,
>> She said, "Look you've cum,
>> All over my bum,
>> This isn't a shag it's a mock'ry."
>>
>> There was a young lassie from Morton,
>> Who had one long tit and one short 'un,
>> On top of all that,
>> A great hairy twat,
>> And a fart like a six-fifty Norton.

Dopey

The Seven Dwarfs are vacationing in Rome when they get to meet the Pope. Dopey somewhat reluctantly approaches the Pope and asks, "Pope, are there any Dwarf Nuns in the Vatican?" The Pope responds, "No Dopey, we do not have any Dwarf Nuns in the Vatican." Dopey sees the other six Dwarfs smile at each other.

Dopey, now a little more nervous, asks, "Pope, are there any Dwarf Nuns in Rome?" The Pope responds again, "No Dopey, I don't believe there are any Dwarf Nuns in Rome." The other six Dwarfs all begin to snicker.

Dopey asks again, sweat showing on his brow, "Pope, aren't there any Dwarf Nuns anywhere in Italy?" The Pope responds, "Dopey, there is not one Dwarf Nun in all of Italy." All six Dwarfs are laughing openly and slapping each other on the back.

Dopey tries one last time, "Please Pope, isn't there just one Dwarf Nun anywhere in the world?" The Pope responds "NO, not anywhere in the world."

All six Dwarfs are rolling on the ground, yelling, "Dopey Fucked a Penguin, Dopey Fucked a Penguin ..."

! Epidemic

A worried father telephoned his family doctor and said that he was afraid that his teenaged son had come down with VD. "He says he hasn't had sex with anyone but the maid, so it has to be her."

"Don't worry so much," advised the doctor. "These things happen."

"I know, doctor," said the father, "but I have to admit that I've been sleeping with the maid also. I seem to have the same symptoms."

"That's unfortunate."

"Not only that, I think I've passed it to my wife."

"Oh God," said the doctor. "That means we all have it."

! Faulty Watch

007 walks into a bar and takes a seat next to a very attractive woman. He gives her a quick glance, then casually looks at his watch for a moment.

The woman notices this and asks, "Is your date running late?"

"No," he replies. "Q's just given me this state-of-the-art watch, and I was just testing it."

The intrigued woman says, "A state-of-the-art watch? What's so special about it?"

"It uses alpha waves to talk to me telepathically," he explains.

"What's it telling you now?"

"Well, it says you're not wearing any knickers ..."

The woman giggles and replies, "Well it must be broken because I am wearing knickers!"

007 tuts, taps his watch and says, "Damn thing must be an hour fast."

Forgiveness

Sister Mary Catherine and Sister Mary Elizabeth are walking through the park when they are jumped by two thugs. Their habits are ripped from them and the men begin to sexually assault them.

Sister Mary Catherine casts her eyes heavenward and cries, "Forgive him Lord, for he knows not what he is doing!"

Mary Elizabeth turns and says, "Mine does ..."

Grab a Hold of This

A chicken and a horse are playing together in a barn yard. Suddenly the horse falls into a pit. He yells to the chicken, "Go get the farmer, save me, save me!" The chicken goes looking for the farmer but can't find him. So she gets the farmer's BMW and drives it over to the mud pit, lassoes the horse, ties it to the car and pulls him out.

The horse says, "Thank you, thank you. I owe you my life ..." Then a couple of days later they are playing there again and this time the chicken falls into the mud pit and the chicken says, "Help me. Help me! Go get the farmer!" So the horse says, "No, No, No, I think I can get to you." The horse stretches across the mud pit and tells the chicken, "Grab onto my dick." The chicken grabs on, the horse stretches back and the horse saves the chicken's life.

So what's the moral of the story?

If you have a dick the size of a horse, then you don't need a BMW to pick up chicks.

Headache Cure

A guy is suffering from severe headaches for years with no relief. After trying all the usual cures he's referred to a headache specialist by his family doctor.

The doctor asks him what his symptoms are and he replies, "I get these blinding headaches; kind of like a knife across my scalp and ..." He is interrupted by the doctor, "And a heavy throbbing right behind the left ear."

"Yes! Exactly! How did you know?"

"Well I am the world's greatest headache specialist, but I myself suffered from that same type of headache for many years. It is caused by a tension in the scalp muscles. This is how I cured it: Every day I would give my wife oral sex. When she came she would squeeze her legs together with all her strength and the pressure would relieve the tension in my head. Try that every day for two weeks and come back and let me know how it goes."

Two weeks go by and the man is back, "Well, how do you feel?" the doctor asks. "Doc, I'm a new man! I feel great! I haven't had a headache since I started this treatment! I can't thank you enough. And, by the way – nice house!"

Health Plan

Queen Elizabeth was visiting one of Canada's top hospitals, and during her tour of the floors she passed a room where a male patient was masturbating.

"Oh my God," said the Queen, "that's disgraceful. What is the meaning of this?"

The doctor leading the tour explained, "I am sorry your majesty, this man has a very serious condition in which his testicles rapidly fill with semen. If he doesn't do that at least five times a day, he'll become swollen."

"Oh, I am so sorry," said the Queen. "I was unaware that such a medical problem existed."

On the same floor, they soon passed a room where a young nurse was giving a patient oral sex.

"Oh my God," said the Queen. "What's happening in there?"

The doctor replied, "Same problem, better health plan."

How Did You Get Here?

Two men waiting at the Pearly Gates strike up a conversation.

"How d'you die?" the first man asks the second.

"I froze to death," says the second.

"That's awful," says the first man. "How does it feel to freeze to death?"

"It's very uncomfortable at first," says the second man. "You get the shakes, and you get pains in all your fingers and toes. But eventually, it's a very calm way to go. You get numb and you kind of drift off, as if you're sleeping. How about you, how did you die?"

"I had a heart attack," says the first man. "You see, my wife was cheating on me, so one day I showed up at home unexpectedly. I ran up to the bedroom, and found her alone, knitting. I ran down to the basement, but no one was hiding there. I ran up to the second floor, but no one was hiding there, either. I ran as fast as I could to the attic, and just as I got there, I had a massive heart attack and died." The second man shakes his head.

"That's so ironic," he says.

"What do you mean?" asks the first man.

"If you had only stopped to look in the freezer, we'd both still be alive."

¦ 🗑 I Say, I Say ...

Q: What's the difference between oral sex and anal sex?
A: Oral sex makes your day, anal sex makes your hole weak.

Q: How is pubic hair like parsley?
A: You push it to the side before you start eating.

Q: What's the difference between a bitch and a whore?
A: A whore sleeps with everybody at the party, and a bitch sleeps with everybody at the party except you.

Q: What's the difference between love, true love and showing off?
A: Spitting, swallowing and gargling

Q: What are three words you dread the most while making love?
A: "Honey, I'm home."

Q: What's the difference between a Catholic wife and a Jewish wife?
A: A Catholic wife has real orgasms and fake jewellery.

Q: Do you know why women fake orgasm?
A: Because men fake foreplay.

Q: What's the difference between a G-spot and a golf ball?
A: A guy will actually search for a golf ball.

Q: Why does a bride smile when she walks up the aisle?
A: She knows she's given her last blow job.

Q: What did the elephant say to the naked man?
A: It's cute, but can you pick up peanuts with it?

Q: What has seventy-five balls and screws old ladies?
A: Bingo!

Q: What's the definition of a Yankee?
A: Same thing as a "quickie", only you do it yourself.

Q: Why did God invent alcohol?
A: So fat, smelly people can get laid too.

Q: How do you get three little old ladies to say the "F" word?
A: Have a fourth one yell "Bingo!"

Q: What do you get if you cross a pit bull with a hooker?
A: Your last blow job.

Jimmy the Rooster

A farmer has about 200 hens but no rooster, and he wants chicks. So he goes down the road to the next farmer and asks if he has a rooster to sell. The other farmer says, "Yeah, I've this great rooster named Jimmy. He'll service every chicken you've got, no problem."

Well, Jimmy the rooster cost a lot of money, but the farmer decides he'd be worth it. So, he buys Jimmy. The farmer takes Jimmy home and sets him down in the barnyard, first giving the rooster a pep talk:

"Jimmy, I want you to pace yourself now. You've got a lot of chickens to service here, and you cost me a lot of money. Consequently, I'll need you to do a good job. So, take your time and have some fun," the farmer says with a chuckle.

Jimmy seems to understand, so the farmer points toward the hen house, and Jimmy takes off like a shot. WHAM! Jimmy nails every hen in the hen house three or four times, and the farmer is really shocked.

After that the farmer hears a commotion in the duck pen. Sure enough, Jimmy is in there. Later, the farmer sees Jimmy after the flock of geese down by the lake. Once again, WHAM! He gets all the geese. By sunset he sees Jimmy out in the fields chasing quail and pheasants. The farmer is distraught – worried that his expensive rooster won't even last 24 hours.

Sure enough, the farmer goes to bed and wakes up the next day to find Jimmy dead as a doornail – stone cold in the middle of the yard with buzzards circling overhead.

The farmer, saddened by the loss of such a colorful and expensive animal, shakes his head and says, "Oh, Jimmy, I told you to pace yourself. I tried to get you to slow down, now look what you've done to yourself."

Jimmy opens one eye, nods toward the buzzards circling in the sky, and says, "Shhh, they're getting closer ..."

Keeping It Up

A guy walks into a pharmacy and says to the pharmacist,

"Listen, I have three girls coming over tonight. I've never had three girls at once, so I need something to keep me horny ... keep me potent."

The pharmacist reaches under the counter, unlocks the bottom drawer and takes out a small cardboard box marked with a label "Viagra Extra Strength" and says, "Here, if you eat this, you'll go nuts for twelve hours." The guy says, "Gimme three boxes."

The next day the guy walks into the same pharmacy, limps up to the counter and pulls down his pants. The pharmacist looks in horror as he notices the man's penis is black and blue, and skin is hanging off in some places. In a pained voice, the man moans out, "Gimme a bottle of Deep Heat." The pharmacist replies in horror, "You can't put Deep Heat on that!" The man replies, "No, it's for my arms. The girls didn't show up."

❗ 📎 Ladder to Success

A man was walking along the street when he saw a ladder going into the clouds. As any of us would do, he climbed the ladder. He reached a cloud, upon which was sat a rather plump and very ugly woman.

"Shag me or climb the ladder to success," she said.

No contest, thought the man, so he climbed the ladder to the next cloud. On this cloud was a slightly thinner woman, who was slightly easier on the eye.

"Shag me or climb the ladder to success," she said.

"Well," thought the man, "might as well carry on."

On the next cloud was an even slimmer female who, this time, was quite attractive.

"Shag me or climb the ladder to success," she uttered. He realized it was getting better as he went on, so on he went.

On the next cloud was an absolute beauty. Slim, attractive, the lot.

"Shag me or climb the ladder to success," she flirted. Unable to imagine what could be waiting, and being a gambling man, he decided to climb again.

When he reached the next cloud, there was a old fat bloke sat there.

"Who are you?" the man asked.

"Hello," said the fat bloke. "My name's Cess!"

! 回 Luring the Moose

Two hunters went moose hunting every winter without success. Finally, they came up with a foolproof plan. They got a very authentic female moose costume and learned the mating call of a female moose. The plan was to hide in the costume, lure the bull, then come out of the costume and shoot the bull. They set themselves up on the edge of a clearing, donned their costume and began to give the moose love call.

Before long, their call was answered as a bull came crashing out of the forest and into the clearing. When the bull was close enough, the guy in front said, "Okay, let's get out and get him."

After a moment that seemed like an eternity, the guy in the back shouted, "The zipper is stuck! What are we going to do!?"

The guy in the front says, "Well, I'm going to start nibbling grass, but you'd better brace yourself."

! 回 Making Babies

Dad came home one day in an exceptionally horny mood and took his wife upstairs for sex. Just when they were really getting into it, their young son entered the room and started to cry.

"What's wrong, son?" the father asked. "Why are you crying?"

"You're hurting my mommy," the little boy replied.

"No, no," the father reassured him. "I'm not hurting her. We are making babies." This seemed to calm the boy, and when he left the room the couple got back to their business.

The next day the father came home early from work and found his son on the steps, crying.

"What's the matter NOW?" asked Dad.

"It's those babies you were making with mommy yesterday," the boy answered.

"The mailman is upstairs eating them."

Making It Better

Two women were playing golf one sunny afternoon. The first of the twosome teed off and watched in horror as the ball headed directly toward a foursome of men playing the next hole. Sure enough, the ball hit one of the guys, and he immediately clasped his hands together at his crotch, fell to the ground and proceeded to roll around in agony.

The woman rushed over and immediately began to apologize. She then explained that she was a physical therapist and offered to help ease his pain.

"Ummph, ooh, nnooo, I'll be all right ... I'll be fine in a few minutes," he replied as he remained in the fetal position, still clasping his hands together at his crotch. But she persisted, and he finally allowed her to help him. She gently took his hands away and laid them to the side, loosened his pants and put her hands inside, beginning to massage him.

"Does that feel better?" she asked.

"Not really," he wheezed. "It's so sore." So she massaged some more.

"Better yet?" she asked. The man screwed his eyes up.

"Throbbing," he gasped. So she kept on massaging until the man practically passed out, a glazed smile on his face.

"How's that now?" she asked.

"Ohhh, yeah ... It feels really great," he replied. "But my thumb still hurts like hell!"

! ◎ Medical Ethics

A woman is in her doctor's office, and suddenly shouts out, "Doctor, kiss me." The doctor looks at her and says that it would be against his code of ethics to kiss her.

About 20 minutes later the woman again shouts out, "Doctor, please, kiss me just once." Again he refuses, apologetically, but says that as a doctor he simply cannot kiss her.

Another 15 minutes pass, and the woman pleads with the doctor "Doctor, Doctor, please kiss me just once!"

"Look," he says, "I am sorry. I just CANNOT kiss you.

"In fact, I probably shouldn't even be fucking you!"

! ◎ Mother Gets the Message

A mother had three daughters and after their weddings she asked each one of them to write home and tell her about their married life. The first wrote back on the second day. The letter arrived with a single message, "Maxwell House Coffee". The Mother was confused but finally noticed a Maxwell coffee ad, and it said, "Satisfaction to the last drop". Mother was happy.

Then the second daughter got married and after a week she sent home her reply. The message read: "Rothmans". Mother looked for the Rothmans ad, and it said, "LIFE SIZE, KING SIZE". Again, Mother was happy.

Then it was the third one's wedding. Mother was anxious. It took four weeks for a message to come through. When it did the message was simply "BRITISH AIRWAYS". Mother was concerned. She frantically went through all the newspapers at home looking for a BA ad. She found one and fainted.

The ad read: "TWO TIMES A DAY, SEVEN DAYS A WEEK, BOTH WAYS".

! Moths

The lovers passionately embraced while lying on her bed. Their bodies fused together as they gyrated and panted. Then suddenly the woman cocked her ear.

"Quick, my husband is coming through the front door. Hide in the bathroom," she cried.

Her lover ran into the bathroom as she hid his clothes under the bed. Just as she turned back, her husband came through the bedroom door.

"What are you doing lying naked on the bed?" he asked.

"Darling, I heard you coming up the drive way and got ready to receive you," she replied with a wink and a smile.

"Great," he said, "I'll just run into the bathroom and I'll be with you in two shakes."

She panicked. Before she could stop him, he was in the bathroom. He found a man clapping his hands together in mid-air. Dumbfounded, he asked, "Who the devil are you?"

"I'm from the exterminator company. Your wife called me in to get rid of these pesky moths," the lover replied. The husband yelled, "But you've got no clothes on!"

The lover looked down at his body, jumped backwards in surprise and said, "The little bastards."

! Oops

A girl asks her boyfriend to come over Friday night and have dinner with her parents. Since this is such a big event, the girl announced to her boyfriend that, after dinner, she would like to go out and make love for the first time.

The boy is ecstatic, but he has never had sex before, so he takes a trip to the pharmacist to get some condoms. The pharmacist helps the boy for about an hour. He tells the boy everything there is to know about condoms and sex. At the cash register, the pharmacist asks the boy how many condoms he'd like to buy: a 3-pack, 10-pack or a family pack.

"I'm really going to put it to this girl," the boy tells the pharmacist. "I intend to plug every orifice in her body at least twice." The pharmacist, with a laugh, suggests the family pack, saying the boy will be rather busy, it being his first time and all.

That night, the boy shows up at the girl's parents' house and meets his girlfriend at the door. "Oh, I'm so excited for you to meet my parents, come on in!" The boy goes inside and is taken to the dinner table where the girl's parents are seated. The boy quickly offers to say grace and bows his head. A minute passes, and the boy is still deep in prayer with his head down. Ten minutes pass, and still no movement from the boy.

Finally, after twenty minutes with his head down, the girlfriend finally leans over and whispers to the boyfriend, "I had no idea you were this religious."

The boy turns, and whispers back, "I had no idea your father was a pharmacist."

Paying For It

A girl walks into a hardware store as she needs a new hinge for a door at home. As she brings it to the counter, the clerk asks, "Wanna screw for that hinge?"

To which she replies, "No, but I'll suck you off for that toaster on the top shelf."

! Putting Your Mouth
Where the Money is

A man and a woman were waiting at the hospital donation center.

Man: "What are you doing here today?"

Woman: "Oh, I'm here to donate some blood. They're going to give me $5 for it."

Man: "Hmm, that's interesting. I'm here to donate sperm, myself. But they pay me $25."

The woman looked thoughtful for a moment and they chatted some more before going their separate ways. Several months later, the same man and woman meet again in the donation center.

Man: "Oh, hi there! Here to donate blood again?"

Woman: [shaking her head with mouth closed] "Unh unh."

! Ralph's 20-inch Penis

When Ralph first noticed that his penis was growing larger and staying erect longer, he was delighted, as was his wife. But after several weeks his penis had grown to nearly twenty inches! Ralph became quite concerned, so he and his wife went to see a prominent urologist.

After an initial examination, the physician explained to the couple that though rare, Ralph's condition could be cured through corrective surgery.

"How long will Ralph be on crutches?" the wife asked anxiously.

"Crutches? Why would he need crutches?" responded the surprised doctor.

"Well," said the wife coldly, "you're planning to lengthen Ralph's legs, aren't you?"

! ✐ Sex Therapy

Two women had been having a friendly lunch when the subject turned to sex. "You know, John and I have been having some sexual problems," Linda told her friend.

"That's amazing!" Mary replied. "So have Tom and I."

"We're thinking of going to a sex therapist," said Linda.

"Oh, we could never do that! We'd be too embarrassed!" responded Mary. "But after you go, will you please tell me how it went?"

Several weeks passed and the two friends met for lunch again.

"So, how did the sex therapy work out, Linda?" Mary asked.

"Things couldn't be better!" Linda exclaimed. "We began with a physical exam, and afterward the doctor said he was certain he could help us. He told us to stop at the grocery store on the way home and buy a bunch of grapes and a dozen doughnuts. He told us to sit on the floor nude, and toss the grapes and doughnuts at each other. Every grape that went into my vagina, John had to get it out with his tongue. Every doughnut that I ringed his penis with, I had to eat. Our sex life is wonderful, in fact it's better than it's ever been!"

With that endorsement, Mary talked her husband into an appointment with the same sex therapist. After the physical exams were completed the doctor called Mary and Tom into his office.

"I'm afraid there is nothing I can do for you," he said.

"But doctor," Mary complained, "you did such good for Linda and John, surely you must have a suggestion for us! Please, please, can't you give us some help? Any help at all?"

"Well, OK," the doctor answered. "On your way home, I want you to stop at the grocery store and buy a sack of apples and a box of Cheerios ..."

! Sign Job

Two deaf people get married. During the first week of marriage, they find that they are unable to communicate in the bedroom when they turn off the lights (because they can't see each other using sign language, natch).

After several nights of fumbling around and misunderstandings, the wife proposes a solution.

"Honey," she signs, "why don't we agree on some simple signals? For instance, at night, if you want to have sex with me, reach over and squeeze my left breast one time. If you don't want to have sex, reach over and squeeze my right breast one time."

The husband thinks this is a great idea and signs back to his wife, "Great idea! Now if you want to have sex with ME, reach over and pull on my penis one time."

"And if you don't want to have sex, reach over and pull on my penis fifty times."

! Superman Needs a Shag

Superman was flying around thinking, "I need a shag." He was horny as a horndog. The Man of Steel was gagging for it. He passed over Gotham City when he saw Batman, so he flew down for some advice.

"Hey, Batty, who's a good shag?" Batman replied, "Well Supe, everyone knows that Wonderwoman is the best sex in comicland, why don't you try her?"

"I'd love to, but Wonderwoman and I are friends, so I don't really want to take advantage of her ..."

"Damn shame," said Batman, and waved goodbye to Superman as he flew off.

A few minutes later he was flying low over a city when he saw Spiderman swinging from rooftop to rooftop. He flew down.

"Hey Spidey, I'm cruisin' for a piece of ass, who's the best shag in comicland?"

"Hey, Big S, everyone knows that Wonderwoman is far and away the best shag in comicland, why don't you try her?"

"Well, we are sort of friends," said Superman, "but I didn't realize she had gotten around so much," and he flew off in frustration.

Minutes later he was flying over a field when he saw Wonderwoman lying naked, in the middle of the field, with her legs apart and up in the air. Superman was tempted. "Goddamn it!" he thought to himself, "I'm faster than a speeding bullet, I can be in and out of there before she even knows I'm here." So with a blur and a sonic boom he was down, in and gone.

Wonderwoman stared up into the sky with a glazed expression. "What the fuck was that?" she exclaimed.

"I don't know," said the Invisible Man as he rolled off, "but my arse is killing me."

The Gorilla and the Gay

Two gay guys are walking through a zoo. They come across the gorillas and after a while they notice that the male gorilla has a massive hard-on. Naturally the guys are fascinated so they watch some more.

One of the guys just can't bear it any longer and he reaches into the cage to touch it. The gorilla grabs him, drags him into the cage and fucks his brains out for six hours solid. When he's done the gorilla throws him back over the cage. An ambulance is called and he's taken away to the hospital.

Next day his friend visits him and asks, "Are you hurt?"

"AM I HURT?" he shouts. "He hasn't called, he hasn't written ..."

! 📎 The Man from Melbourne

An Australian guy goes into a bar in the Greek Islands. Jill, the barmaid, takes his order and notices his Australian accent.

Over the course of the night they talk quite a bit. At the end of the night he asks her if she wants to have sex with him. Although she is attracted to him she says no. He then offers to pay her $200 for the deed. Jill is travelling the world and because she is short of funds she agrees.

The next night the guy turns up again and after showing her plenty of attention throughout the night he asks if she will sleep with him again for $200. She figures in for a penny in for a pound – and it was fantastic the night before – so she agrees.

This goes on for five nights. On the sixth night the guy comes into the bar. But this night he orders a beer and just goes and sits in the corner.

The girl is disappointed and thinks that maybe she should pay him more attention. She goes over and sits next to him. She asks him where he is from and he tells her Melbourne.

"So am I," she says. "What suburb in Melbourne?"

"Glen Iris," he says.

"That's amazing," she says. "So am I – what street?"

"Cameo Street," he says.

"This is unbelievable," she says. "What number?" He says, "Number 20," and she is astonished.

"You are not going to believe this," she says. "I'm from number 22 – my parents still live there!"

"I know," he says. "Your father gave me $1,000 and asked me to give it to you."

! The Papal Stiffy

The Pope wakes up one morning with a huge erection. Thinking that it isn't very Catholic, he tries to get rid of it. Unfortunately, walking around the room, thinking about West Ham and even getting some fresh air on the balcony all fail to soften him up. With only one option left, he sits down on the balcony and relieves himself. Later, the Pope is walking around Rome, when a man with a camera approaches him.

"Hello, Mr ... Pope," the man says. "Six o'clock this morning, on the balcony, I think you know what I'm talking about."

"I'm sorry, I don't know what you mean," the Pope replies.

"Oh, I think you do," the man retorts, "and 50 thousand will buy you the camera." Panicky and confused, the Pope pays up and takes the camera.

Back in the Vatican, one of the Pope's aides asks about the camera.

"A chap in town sold it to me for 50 thousand," the Pope explains.

"50 thousand?" says the aide.

"Blimey, he must've seen you coming."

! The Pickle Slicer

Bill worked in a pickle factory. He had been employed there for a number of years when he came home one day to confess to his wife that he had a terrible compulsion. He had an urge to stick his penis into the pickle slicer. His wife suggested that he should see a sex therapist to talk about it, but Bill indicated that he'd be too embarrassed. He vowed to overcome the compulsion on his own.

One day a few weeks later, Bill came home absolutely ashen. His wife could see at once that something was seriously wrong.

"What's wrong, Bill?" she asked.

"Do you remember that I told you how I had this tremendous urge to put my penis into the pickle slicer?"

"Oh, Bill, you didn't."

"Yes, I did."

"My God, Bill, what happened?"

"I got fired."

"No, Bill. I mean, what happened with the pickle slicer?"

"Oh ... she got fired too."

! 🔘 The Purest Woman

There was a man who wanted a pure wife. So he started to attend church to find a woman. He met a gal who seemed nice, so he took her home. When they got there, he whips out his manhood and asks, "What's this?" She replies, "A cock." He thinks to himself that she is not pure enough.

A couple of weeks later he meets another gal and soon takes her home. Again, he pulls out his manhood and asks the question. She replies, "A cock." He is pissed because she had seemed more pure than the first but ... oh well.

A couple of weeks later he meets a gal who seems real pure. She won't go home with him for a long time but eventually he gets her to his house. He whips it out and asks, "What is this?" She giggles and says, "A pee-pee." He thinks to himself that he has finally found his woman.

They get married, but after several months every time she sees his member she giggles and says, "That's your pee-pee." He finally breaks down and says, "Look, this is not a pee-pee, it is a cock."

She laughs and says, "No it's not. A cock is ten inches long and black."

! 🔟 Three Wishes

As an elderly lady sat on her front porch reflecting on her long life, a Fairy Godmother suddenly appeared and offered to fulfill three wishes for her.
"Well," said the woman, "I guess I'd like to be rich."

Poof! The Fairy Godmother turned her rocking chair into solid gold.

"And I wouldn't mind being a young and beautiful princess."

Poof! The Fairy Godmother turned the old woman into an exquisite young princess, with a priceless crown of jewels.

"Your third wish?" asked the Fairy Godmother.
The elderly woman's dog raised his head and uttered a single, weak hoarse woof.
"Could you possibly turn my wonderful dog into a handsome prince?"

Poof! There, in front of the old woman, who has now turned into a beautiful princess, stood the most handsome young man anyone had ever seen. More handsome than anyone could possibly imagine.

She stared at him in awe, completely smitten. As he came toward her, her knees weakened. He bent down, brushing his lips across her ear as he whispered,

"I'll bet you are sorry you had me neutered."

! 🔟 War is Hell

The elderly Italian man went to his parish priest and asked if the priest would hear his confession.
"Of course, my son," said the priest.

"Well, Father, at the beginning of World War Two, a beautiful woman knocked on my door and asked me to hide her from the Germans. I hid her in my attic, and they never found her."

"That's a wonderful thing, my son, and nothing that you need to confess," said the priest.

"It's worse, Father. I was weak and told her that she had to pay for rent of the attic with her sexual favors," continued the old man.

"Well, it was a very difficult time, and you took a large risk. You would have suffered terribly at their hands if the Germans had found you hiding her. I know that God, in his wisdom and mercy, will balance the good and the evil and judge you kindly," said the priest.

"Thanks, Father," said the old man. "That's a load off of my mind. Can I ask another question?"

"Of course, my son," said the priest.

The old man asked, "Do I have to tell her that the war is over?"

What a Man Needs

A travelling salesman checked into a futuristic motel. Realizing he needed a haircut before his next day's meeting, he called down to the desk clerk and asked if there was a barber on the premises.

"I'm afraid not, sir," the clerk told him, "but down the hall is a special machine that should serve your purposes."

Sceptical but intrigued, the salesman located the appropriate machine, inserted fifty cents and stuck his head in the opening, at which time the machine started to buzz and whirl. Fifteen seconds later the salesman pulled out his head and surveyed it in the mirror, which reflected the best haircut he ever received in his life.

Down the hall was another machine with a sign that read, "Manicures – 25 cents."

"Why not?" thought the salesman. He paid the money, inserted his hands into the slot and pulled them out perfectly manicured.

The next machine had a huge sign that read, "This Machine Provides What Men Need Most When Away from Their Wives – cost 50 cents."

The salesman was embarrassed and looked both ways. Seeing nobody around he put in fifty cents, then unzipped his pants and stuck his "thing" into the opening – with great anticipation, since he had been away from his wife for two weeks.

When the machine started buzzing, the guy let out a shriek of agony. Fifteen seconds later it shut off and, with trembling hands, the salesman was able to withdraw his throbbing penis ...

... which now had a button sewn on the tip.

! What Dad Was Doing

A small boy was woken in the middle of the night by strange noises coming from his parents' room, so he decided to investigate. As he entered his parents' bedroom, he was shocked to see his mum and dad shagging for all they were worth.

"Dad!" he shouted. "What are you doing?"

"It's OK, son," replied his father. "Your mother wants to have another baby, that's all." The small boy, excited at the prospect of a new baby brother, was pleased and went back to bed with a smile on his face.

Several weeks later, the little boy was walking past the bathroom and was shocked to discover his mother on her knees sucking furiously on his father's penis.

"Dad!" he shouted, "What are you doing now?"

"Son, there's been a slight change of plan," his dad replied.

"Now she wants a BMW."

The Magic of Married Life

! 📎 A Priest, a Nun and a Blanket

A priest and nun are on their way back home from a convention when their car breaks down. They are unable to get repairs completed and it appears that they will have to spend the night in a motel. The only motel in this town has only one room available so they have a minor problem.

PRIEST: Sister, I don't think the Lord would have a problem, under the circumstances, if we spent the night together in this one room. I'll sleep on the couch and you take the bed.
SISTER: I think that would be okay.

They prepare for bed and each one takes their agreed place in the room. Ten minutes later ...

SISTER: Father, I'm terribly cold.
PRIEST: Okay, I'll get up and get you a blanket from the closet.

Ten minutes later ...

SISTER: Father, I'm still terribly cold.
PRIEST: Okay Sister, I'll get up and get you another blanket.

Ten minutes later ...

SISTER: Father, I'm still terribly cold. I don't think the Lord would mind if we acted as man and wife just for this one night.
PRIEST: You're probably right ... Get up and get your own damn blanket.

❗ 📎 A Woman's Choice

A married couple were enjoying a dinner out when a statuesque brunette walked over to their table, exchanged warm greetings with the husband and walked off.

"Who was that?" the wife demanded.

"If you must know," the husband replied, "that was my mistress."

"Your mistress? That's it! I want a divorce!" The husband looked her straight in the eye and said, "Are you sure you want to give up our big house in the suburbs, your Mercedes, your furs, your jewellery and our vacation home in Mexico?"

For a long time they continued dining in silence. Finally, the woman nudged her husband and said, "Isn't that Howard over there? Who's he with?"

"That's HIS mistress," her husband replied.

"Oh," she said, taking a bite of dessert. "Ours is much cuter."

❗ 📎 Bedroom Statues

A woman was in bed with her lover when she heard her husband opening the front door.

"Hurry!" she said. "Stand in the corner!" She quickly rubbed baby oil all over him and then she dusted him with talcum powder.

"Don't move until I tell you to," she whispered. "Just pretend you're a statue."

"What's this, honey?" the husband asked as he entered the room.

"Oh, it's just a statue," she replied nonchalantly. "The Joneses bought one for their bedroom. I liked the idea so much, I got one for us, too."

No more was said about the statue. Not even later that night when they went to sleep. Around two in the morning the husband got out of bed, went into the kitchen and returned with a sandwich and a glass of milk.

"Here," he said to the statue, "eat this. I stood like an idiot at the Joneses' for three days and nobody offered me so much as a glass of water."

! 📎 Before They Met

A man met a beautiful woman and he decided he wanted to marry her right away. She said, "But we don't know anything about each other." He said, "That's all right, we'll learn about each other as we go along." So she consented, and they were married and went on a honeymoon to a very nice resort.

So one morning they were lying by the pool, when he got up off of his towel, climbed up to the 10-meter board and did a two and a half tuck gainer, this followed by three rotations in jack-knife position, where he straightened out and cut the water like a knife.

After a few more demonstrations, he came back and laid down on the towel. She said, "That was incredible!" He said, "I used to be an Olympic diving champion. You see, I told you we'd learn more about each other as we went along." So she got up, jumped in the pool and started doing laps.

After about thirty laps she climbed back out and laid down on her towel hardly out of breath. He said, "That was incredible! Were you an Olympic endurance swimmer?"

"No," she said. "I was a hooker in Venice and I worked both sides of the canal . . ."

! 📎 Deathbed Confession

Jake was on his deathbed, with his wife, Becky, maintaining a steady vigil by his side. As she held his fragile hand, her warm tears ran silently down her face, splashed onto his face and roused him from his slumber.

He looked up and his pale lips began to move slightly. "My darling Becky," he whispered.

"Hush, my love," she said. "Go back to sleep. Shhh, don't talk." But he was insistent.

"Becky," he said in his tired voice. "I have to talk. I have something I must confess to you."

"There's nothing to confess," replied the weeping Becky. "It's all right. Everything's all right, Go to sleep now."

"No, no. I must die in peace, Becky. I slept with your sister, your best friend and our next door neighbour." Becky mustered a pained smile and stroked his hand.

"Hush now, Jake. Don't torment yourself. I know all about it," she said.

"Why do you think I poisoned you?"

! 📎 Deathbed Reassurance

A man lies on his deathbed, surrounded by his weeping wife and their four children.

Three of the children are tall, good looking and athletic, but the fourth and youngest is an ugly runt.

"Darling wife," the husband whispers, "assure me that the youngest child really is mine. I want to know the truth before I die, I will forgive you if ..." The wife gently interrupts him.

"Yes, my dearest, absolutely, no question, I swear on my mother's grave that you are his father." The man then dies, happy. The wife mutters under her breath:

"Thank God he didn't ask about the other three."

Divorced Barbie

A man walks into a store to buy a Barbie doll for his daughter.
"How much is that Barbie in the window?" he asks the shop assistant.

>> In a condescending manner she responds, "Which Barbie? We have:
>> Barbie Goes to the Gym for $19.95,
>> Barbie Goes to the Ball for $19.95,
>> Barbie Goes Shopping for $19.95,
>> Barbie Goes to the Beach for $19.95,
>> Barbie Goes the Night Club for $19.95,
>> Barbie Goes to College for $19.95,
>> Barbie Goes to the Opera for $19.95,
>> and Divorced Barbie for $265.00."

The man asks, "Why is Divorced Barbie $265.00 when all the others are only $19.95?"

"That's obvious," the assistant states. "Divorced Barbie comes with Ken's house, Ken's car, Ken's boat, Ken's Rolex, Ken's furniture ..."

Doctor's Orders

A woman accompanied her husband to the doctor's office. After his check-up, the doctor called the wife into his office alone. He said: "If you don't do the following, your husband will surely die:

1. Each morning, fix him a healthy breakfast.
2. Be pleasant and make sure he is in a good mood.
3. For lunch, make him a nutritious meal.
4. For dinner, prepare him an especially nice meal.
5. Don't burden him with chores as he probably had a hard day.
6. Don't discuss your problems with him.
7. And most importantly, have sex with him several times a week and satisfy his every whim."

On the way home, the husband asked his wife what the doctor said to her.

"You're going to DIE," she replied.

🎙 📎 Doing Without

Three couples, an elderly couple, a middle-aged couple and a young, newly-wed couple, wanted to join a church. The pastor said, "We have special requirements for new parishioners. You must abstain from having sex for two weeks."

The couples agreed and came back at the end of two weeks. The pastor went to the elderly couple and asked, "Were you able to abstain from sex for two weeks?" The old man replied, "No problem at all, Pastor."

"Congratulations! Welcome to the church!" said the pastor.

The pastor went to the middle-aged couple and asked, "Well, were you able to abstain from sex for the two weeks?" The man replied, "The first week was not too bad. The second week I had to sleep on the couch for a few nights but, yes, we made it."

"Congratulations! Welcome to the church!" said the pastor.

The pastor then went to the newly-wed couple and asked, "Well, were you able to abstain from sex for the two weeks?"

"No Pastor, we were not able to go without sex for the two weeks," the young man replied sadly.

"What happened?" inquired the pastor.

"My wife was reaching for a can of paint on the top shelf and dropped it. When she bent over to pick it up, I was overcome with lust and took advantage of her right there."

"You understand, of course, this means you will not be welcome in our church," stated the pastor.

"We know," said the young man.

"We're not welcome at the local supermarket anymore either!"

! ◍ Economizing

During a heated spat over finances the husband said, "Well, if you'd learn to cook and were willing to clean this place, we could fire the maid."

The wife, fuming, shot back, "Oh yeah??? Well, if you'd learn how to make love, we could fire the chauffeur and the gardener."

! ◍ Golfing Etiquette

Two men were having an awfully slow round of golf because the two women in front of them managed to get into every sand trap, lake and rough on the course. They didn't bother to wave the men on through, which is proper golf etiquette.

After two hours of waiting and waiting, one man said, "I think I'll walk up there and ask those gals to let us play through."

He walked out the fairway, got halfway to the women, stopped, turned around and came back, explaining, "I can't do it. One of those women is my wife and the other is my mistress! Maybe you'd better go talk to them."

The second man walked toward the ladies, got halfway there and, just as his partner had done, stopped, turned around and walked back and said:

"Small world."

It Could Be You

A man runs home and bursts in yelling, "Pack your bags, sweetheart! I've just won the lottery, all six numbers." She says, "Oh wonderful! Should I pack for the beach or the big city?"

He replies, "I don't care ... just fuck off!"

Love, Lust and Marriage

LOVE	When your eyes meet across a crowded room.
LUST	When your tongues meet across a crowded room.
MARRIAGE	When you lose your child in a crowded room.
L.	When you share everything you own.
L.	When you steal everything they own.
M.	When the bank owns everything.
L.	When you phone each other just to say, "Hi".
L.	When you phone each other to pick a hotel room.
M.	When you phone each other to bitch.
L.	When you write poems about your partner.
L.	When all you write is your phone number.
M.	When all you write is cheques.
L.	When you show concern for your partner's feelings.
L.	When you couldn't give a hoot.

M.   When your only concern is what's on TV.

L.   When your farewell is "I love you, darling ..."
L.   When your farewell is "So, same time next week ..."
M.   When your farewell is a relief.

L.   When you are proud to be seen in public with your partner.
L.   When you only see each other naked.
M.   When you never see each other awake.

L.   When your heart flutters every time you see them.
L.   When your groin twitches every time you see them.
M.   When your wallet empties every time you see them.

L.   When nobody else matters.
L.   When nobody else knows.
M.   When everybody else matters and you don't care who knows.

L.   When all the songs on the radio describe how you feel.
L.   When the song on the radio determines how you do it.
M.   When you listen to talk radio.

L.   When breaking up is something you try not to think about.
L.   When staying together is something you try not to think about.
M.   When just getting through today is your only thought.

L.   When you're only interested in doing things with your partner.
L.   When you're only interested in doing things TO your partner.
M.   When you're only interested in your golf score.

L.   When intercourse is called "making love".
L.   When intercourse is called "screwing".
M.   What the hell are you talking about?

L.   When it doesn't matter if you don't climax . . .
L.   When the relationship is over if you don't climax . . .
M.   What's a climax?

On Her Knees

There were three guys talking in the pub. Two of them are talking about the amount of control they have over their wives, while the third remains quiet.

After a while one of the first two turns to the third and says, "Well, what about you, what sort of control do you have over your wife?"

The third fellow says, "I'll tell you. Just the other night my wife came to me on her hands and knees."

The first two guys were amazed.

"What happened then?" they asked.

"She said, 'Get out from under the bed and fight like a man.'"

One Question Too Many

A wife asks her husband, "Honey, if I died, would you remarry?"

"After a considerable period of grieving, I guess I would. We all need companionship."

"If I died and you remarried," the wife asks, "would she live in this house?"

"We've spent a lot of money getting this house just the way we want it. I'm not going to get rid of my house. I guess she would."

"If I died and you remarried, and she lived in this house," the wife asks, "would she sleep in our bed?"

"Well, the bed is brand new, and it cost us $2,000. It's going to last a long time, so I guess she would."

"If I died and you remarried, and she lived in this house and slept in our bed, would she use my golf clubs?"

"Oh, no," the husband replies.

"She's left-handed."

! Say It With Flowers

One Friday afternoon two women are talking about nothing in particular when one of them spots the other's husband and says, "Oh look, Gloria! He's bought you a lovely bunch of flowers."

Gloria turns to look and replies, "Oh bloody hell, that's me on my back with my legs open all weekend."

Her friend looks surprised and asks, "You don't have a vase, then?"

! Sticky Fingers

A couple were in bed one night. The wife had curled up ready for sleep and the husband put his bed lamp on to read a book.

As he was reading, he stopped and reached over to his wife and started fondling her pussy. He did this only for a very short while and then went back to reading his book. The wife got up and started stripping off in front of him.

The husband asked, "What are you doing taking all your jammies off?" The wife replied, "You were playing with my pussy. I thought it was for something a bit heavier."

The husband said, "No, not at all. I couldn't turn the pages of my book."

🎤 📎 Stumpy and Martha

Every year, Stumpy and his wife Martha went to the State Fair. And every year, Stumpy would say, "Martha, I'd like to ride in that there airplane." And every year, Martha would reply, "I know, Stumpy, but that airplane ride costs ten dollars, and ten dollars is ten dollars."

One year Stumpy and Martha went to the fair and Stumpy said,

"Martha, I'm 71 years old. If I don't ride that airplane this year I may never get another chance." Martha replied, "Stumpy, that there airplane ride costs ten dollars, and ten dollars is ten dollars."

The pilot overheard them and said, "Folks, I'll make you a deal. I'll take you both up for a ride. If you can stay quiet for the entire ride and not say one word, I won't charge you, but if you say one word it's ten dollars." Stumpy and Martha agreed, and up they went.

The pilot performed all kinds of twists and turns, rolls and dives, but not a word was heard. He even did a nose dive, pulling up 15 feet above the ground, but still not a word.

They landed and the pilot turned to Stumpy.

"By golly, I did everything I could think of to get you to yell out, but you didn't."

Stumpy replied, "Well, I was gonna say something when Martha fell out … but ten dollars is ten dollars!"

🎤 📎 Talcum Powder

A man's wife asks him to go to the store to buy some cigarettes. He walks down to the store only to find it closed, so he goes into a nearby bar to use the vending machine. At the bar he sees a beautiful woman and starts talking to her. They have a couple of beers and one thing leads to another and they end up in her apartment.

When they've had their fun, he realizes it's 3 a.m. and says, "Oh, shit! It's so late, my wife is going to kill me! Have you got any talcum powder?" She gives him some talcum powder, which he proceeds to rub on his hands. Then he goes home.

His wife is waiting for him in the doorway and she is pretty pissed.

"Where the hell have you been!?!"

"Well, honey, it's like this. I went to the store like you asked, but they were closed. So I went to the bar to use the vending machine. I saw this great-looking chick there and we had a few drinks and one thing led to another and I ended up in bed with her."

"Oh yeah? And what is that on your hands?" She sees his hands are covered with powder and screams,

"You &%@&%!* liar! You went bowling again!!!"

! 📎 Ten More Years

A funeral service is being held in a church for a woman who has just passed away.

At the end of the service, the pall-bearers are carrying the casket out when they accidentally bump into a wall, jarring the casket. They hear a faint moan. They open the casket and find that the woman is actually still alive. She lives for ten more years and then dies.

A ceremony is again held at the same church and at the end of the ceremony, the pall bearers are again carrying out the casket.

As they are walking, the husband cries out, "WATCH OUT FOR THAT WALL!"

! 📎 The Best Friend

A woman is in bed with her husband's best friend. They make love for hours, and afterwards, while they're just lying there, the phone rings. Since it is the woman's house, she picks up the receiver and chats away cheerfully. Her lover looks over at her and listens, only hearing her side of the conversation.

"Hello? Oh, hi. I'm so glad that you called. Really? That's wonderful. I am so happy for you. That sounds terrific. Great! Thanks. Okay. Bye-bye." She hangs up the telephone and her lover asks, "Who was that?"

"Oh," she replies, "that was my husband telling me all about the wonderful time he's having on his fishing trip with you."

! 📎 The Sleeping Wife

Two married pals are out drinking one night when one turns to the other and says, "You know, I don't know what else to do. Whenever I go home after we've been out drinking I turn the headlights off before I get to the driveway. I shut off the engine and coast into the garage. I take my shoes off before I go into the house, I sneak up the stairs, I get undressed in the bathroom, I ease into bed and my wife STILL wakes up and yells at me for staying out so late!"

His mate looks at him and says, "Well, you're obviously taking the wrong approach. I screech up into the driveway, slam the door, storm up the steps, throw my shoes into the cupboard, jump into bed, rub my cold hands on my wife's warm arse and say, "How about a blow job?" ... and she's always sound asleep."

! The Typical Husband

A husband and wife are staying in a hotel and after a romantic evening wining and dining they go off to bed. However, as soon as they settle down, the man (not quite ready for slumber) leans over and whispers softly, "Hey snuggle boopy doops, your little hubby wubby isn't ready for nighty-night yet." The wife takes the hint and says, "OK, but I have to use the bathroom first."

So off she goes. On her way back, however, she trips over a piece of carpet and lands flat on her face. Her husband jumps up and exclaims in a concerned tone, "Oh my precious little honey bunny, is your nosey-wosey all righty?"

No harm is done, so she jumps into bed and they have mad passionate sex for three hours. Afterwards, the wife goes off to the bathroom again, but on her way she trips over the same piece of carpet and again lands flat on her face on the floor.

Her husband looks over and grunts, "Clumsy bitch."

! Three Wishes

A woman was out golfing one day, and hit her ball into the woods. She went into the woods to look for it and found a frog in a trap.

The frog said to her, "If you release me from this trap, I will grant you three wishes."

The woman freed the frog and the frog said, "Thank you, but I forgot to mention that there was a condition to your wishes – that whatever you wish for, your husband will get 10 times more or better."

The woman said, "That'll be fine."

For her first wish she wanted to be the most beautiful woman in the world. The frog warned her, "You do realize that this wish will also make your husband the most handsome man in the world, an Adonis, and that women will flock to him." The woman replied, "That will be okay, because I will be the most beautiful woman and he will only have eyes for me." So, poof! She becomes the most beautiful woman in the world.

For her second wish, she wanted to be the richest woman in the world. The frog said, "That will make your husband the richest man in the world, and he will be 10 times richer than you." The woman said, "That will be okay, because what is mine is his, and what is his is mine ..." So, poof! She becomes the richest woman in the world.

The frog then enquired about her third wish, and she answered, "I'd like a mild heart attack."

Tornadoes and Marriage

Q: How are tornadoes and marriage alike?
A: They both begin with a lot of sucking and blowing, and in the end you lose your house.

Without Him

Two elderly ladies meet at the launderette after not seeing one another for a while. One asked how the other's husband was doing.

"Oh! Ted died last week. He went out to the garden to dig up a cabbage for dinner, had a heart attack and dropped down dead right there in the middle of the vegetable patch!"

"Oh dear! I'm very sorry," replied her friend. "What did you do?"

"Opened a can of peas instead."

To Protect and Serve

A young bloke has started work on a property, and the boss sends him up the back paddock to do some fencing work, but come evening he's half an hour late. The boss gets on the CB radio to check if he's all right.

"I've got a problem, Boss. I'm stuck here. I've hit a pig!"

"Ah well, these things happen sometimes," the boss says. "Just drag the carcass off the road so nobody else hits it in the dark."

"But he's not dead, boss. He's gotten tangled up on the bull bar, and I've tried to untangle him, but he's kicking and squealing, and he's real big, boss. I'm afraid he's gonna hurt me!"

"Never mind," says the boss. "There's a .303 under the tarp in the back. Get that out and shoot him. Then drag the carcass off the road and come on home."

"Okay, boss."

Another half an hour goes by, but there's still not a peep from the young fella. The boss gets back on the CB.

"What's the problem, son?"

"Well, I did what you said boss, but I'm still stuck."

"What's up? Did you drag the pig off the road like I said?"

"Yeah boss, but his motorcycle is still jammed under the truck."

! 🔟 The Feds

The phone rings at FBI headquarters.

"Hello?"

"Hello, is this FBI?"

"Yes. What do you want?"

"I'm calling to report my neighbor Tom. He is hiding marijuana in his firewood."

"This will be noted."

Next day, the FBI comes over to Tom's house. They search the shed where the firewood is kept, break every piece of wood, find no marijuana, swear at Tom and leave.

The phone rings at Tom's house.

"Hey, Tom! Did the FBI come?"

"Yeah!"

"Did they chop your firewood?"

"Yeah they did."

"Okay, now it's your turn to call. I need my garden plowed."

! 🔟 Unique Animal

Q: What's the only animal with an arsehole in the middle of its back?

A: A police horse.

! 🔟 Worst Things to Say to a Policeman

I can't reach my license unless you hold my beer.

Sorry, Officer, I didn't realize my radar detector wasn't plugged in.

Aren't you the guy from the Village People?

Hey, you must've been doin' about 125 mph to keep up with me! Good job!

I thought you had to be in relatively good physical condition to be a police officer.

I was going to be a cop, but I decided to finish high school instead.

Bad cop! No donut!

You're not gonna check the trunk, are you?

Gee, that gut sure doesn't inspire confidence.

Didn't I see you get your butt kicked on Cops?

Wow, you look just like the guy in the picture on my girlfriend's nightstand.

I pay your salary!

So, uh, you on the take, or what?

Gee, Officer! That's terrific. The last officer only gave me a warning, too!

Do you know why you pulled me over? Okay, just so one of us does.

I was trying to keep up with traffic. Yes, I know there is no other car around – that's how far ahead of me they are.

What do you mean, "Have I been drinking?" You're the trained specialist.

Well, when I reached down to pick up my bag of crack, my gun fell off my lap and got lodged between the brake pedal and the gas pedal, forcing me to speed out of control.

Hey, is that a 9 mm? That's nothing compared to this .44 magnum.

World of Blondes

What do you call an eternity?
Four blondes in four cars at a four way stop.

Why do blondes have TGIF written on their shoes?
Toes Go In First.

What do smart blondes and UFOs have in common?
You always hear about them but never see them.

What did the blonde say when she opened the box of Cheerios?
Oh look, Daddy ... Doughnut seeds.

Why did the blonde stare at the can of frozen orange juice?
Because it said concentrate.

Why do blondes always smile during lightning storms?
They think their picture is being taken.

How can you tell when a blonde sends you a fax?
It has a stamp on it.

Why can't blondes dial 911?
They can't find the 11 on the phone!

What do you do if a blonde throws a pin at you?
Run, she's got a grenade in her mouth!

How can you tell if a blonde has been using your computer?
There is Tipp-Ex all over the monitor.

Why shouldn't blondes have coffee breaks?
It takes too long to retrain them.

A blonde and a brunette were walking outside when the brunette said, "Oh look at the dead bird."
The blonde looked skyward and said, "Where, where?"

How do you drown a blonde?
Put a scratch & sniff sticker at the bottom of the pool.

Why does it take longer to build a blonde snowman as opposed to a regular one?
You have to hollow out the head.

How do you get a twinkle in a blonde's eye?
Shine a flashlight in her ear.

Hear about the blonde that got an AM radio?
It took her a month to realize she could play it at night.

What happened to the blonde ice hockey team?
They drowned in Spring training.

What did the blonde say when she saw the sign in front of the YMCA?
"Look! They spelled MACY'S wrong!"

How do you make a blonde laugh on Saturday?
Tell her a joke on Wednesday.

What's the difference between a blonde and an ironing board?
It's difficult to open the legs of an ironing board.

Why do blondes have more fun?
They are easier to keep amused.

What do you call a smart blonde?
A golden retriever.

! 🗋 Dumb Blonde, Smart Blonde

Two blondes were working on a house. The one who was nailing down siding would reach into her nail pouch, pull out a nail and either toss it over her shoulder or nail it in.

The other blonde, figuring this was worth looking into, asked, "Why are you throwing those nails away?"

The first blonde explained, "If I pull a nail out of my pouch and it's pointed TOWARD me I throw it away 'cause it's defective. If it's pointed toward the HOUSE, then I nail it in!"

The second blonde got completely pissed off and yelled, "You MORON!!!

"The nails pointed toward you aren't defective!

"They're for the OTHER side of the house!!"

```
.... more cow tales ....

>                          (__)
>              *           '(OO)'
>            \_/--------\/ '
>             ||        ||_. '
>          %_/ ~------\
>                         ~
>
>    _____
>    // // // //  |  \\  \\  \\ \\
>
>        Cow on a hot tin roof
```

! 0 Road Safety

The stoplight on the corner buzzes when it is safe to cross the street. I was crossing with a blonde co-worker of mine, when she asked if I knew what the buzzer was for. I explained that it signals to blind people when the light is red.

She responded, appalled, "What on earth are blind people doing driving?"

! 0 Stereotyping

A young ventriloquist is touring the clubs and stops to entertain at a bar in a small town.

He's going through his usual run of stupid blonde jokes, when a big blonde woman in the fourth row stands on her chair and says: "I've heard just about enough of your denigrating blonde jokes, asshole. What makes you think you can stereotype women that way? What do a person's physical attributes have to do with their worth as a human being? It's guys like you who keep women like me from being respected at work and in my community, of reaching my full potential as a person ... because you and your kind continue to perpetuate discrimination against not only blondes but women at large ... all in the name of humour."

Flustered, the ventriloquist begins to apologize, when the blonde pipes up,

"You stay out of this mister, I'm talking to that little bastard on your knee!"

Ten Blondes on Everest

Eleven women were clinging precariously to a wildly swinging rope suspended from a crumbling outcropping on Mount Everest.

Ten were blonde, one was a brunette.

As a group they decided that one of the party should let go. If that didn't happen the rope would break and everyone would perish. For an agonizing few moments no-one volunteered.

Finally the brunette gave a truly touching speech saying she would sacrifice herself to save the lives of the others.

The blondes applauded.

The Blonde and the Blanket

A brunette, a redhead and a blonde escape a burning building by climbing to the roof. The firemen are on the street below, holding a blanket for them to jump into.

The firemen yell to the brunette, "Jump! Jump! It's your only chance to survive!"

The brunette jumps and SWISH! The firemen yank the blanket away ... the brunette slams into the sidewalk like a tomato.

"C'mon! Jump! You gotta jump!" say the firemen to the redhead.

"Oh no! You're gonna pull the blanket away!" says the redhead.

"No! It's brunettes we can't stand! We're OK with redheads!"

"OK," says the redhead, and she jumps. SWISH! The firemen yank the blanket away, and the lady is flattened on the pavement like a pancake.

Finally, the blonde steps to the edge of the roof. Again, the firemen yell "Jump! You have to jump!"

"No way! You're just gonna pull the blanket away!" yelled the blonde.

"No! Really! You have to jump! We won't pull the blanket away!"

"Look," the blonde says, "nothing you say is gonna convince me that you're not gonna pull the blanket away!"

"So what I want you to do is put the blanket down, and back away from it . . ."

! 🔖 The Double Suicide

A blonde and a redhead were each enjoying a beer at a bar. They were discussing their day, when the 6 p.m. news came on the TV over the bar. The news program was about a man who was threatening to jump from a local bridge.

The blonde turned to the redhead and said, "I'll bet you $50 that he doesn't jump!" The redhead agreed to the bet and they both sat and watched. Within ten minutes the man jumped from the bridge.

"Damn!!!" said the blonde. "Well, a bet's a bet! Here's your $50!"

The redhead began to feel guilty and then explained, "I'm sorry, I can't take your money . . . you see . . . I saw this story on the news at 5:00 p.m."

The blonde then said, "No, no, it's okay. Take the money. I saw the news at 5 p.m. too, but I didn't think he would jump again!"

! 🔖 The Smart Blonde

A lawyer and a blonde are sitting next to each other on a long flight from London to New York. The lawyer leans over to her and asks if she would like to play a fun game. The blonde just wants to take a nap, so she politely declines and rolls over to the window to catch a few winks.

The lawyer persists and explains that the game is really easy and a lot of fun. He explains, "I ask you a question, and if you don't know the answer, you pay me £5, and vice-versa." Again, she politely declines and tries to get some sleep.

The lawyer, now somewhat agitated, says, "Okay, if you don't know the answer you pay me £5, and if I don't know the answer, I will pay you £50!" This catches the blonde's attention and, figuring that there will be no end to this torment unless she plays, she agrees to the game.

The lawyer asks the first question.

"What's the distance from the earth to the moon?" The blonde doesn't say a word, reaches into her purse, pulls out a five pound note and hands it to the lawyer.

Now, it's the blonde's turn. She asks the lawyer: "What goes up a hill with three legs, and comes down with four?" The lawyer looks puzzled. He takes out his laptop computer and searches all his references. He taps into the Airphone with his modem and searches the Net and the Library of Congress. Frustrated, he sends e-mails to all his co-workers and friends. All to no avail.

After over an hour, he wakes the blonde and hands her £50. The blonde politely takes the £50 and turns away to get back to sleep.

The lawyer wakes the blonde and asks, "Well, so what IS the answer!?"

Without a word, the blonde reaches into her purse, hands the lawyer £5 and goes back to sleep.

The Sophisticated Blonde

A wealthy playboy met a beautiful young blonde girl in an exclusive lounge. He took her up to his lavish apartment where he soon discovered she was not a tramp, but was well groomed and apparently very intelligent.

Hoping to impress her, he began showing her his collection of expensive paintings and first editions of famous authors, and offered her a glass of wine. He asked her if she preferred port or sherry and she said, "Oh, sherry by all means. To me it is the nectar of the gods. Just looking at it in a crystal-clear decanter fills me with a glorious sense of anticipation. When the stopper is removed and the gorgeous liquid is poured into my glass, I inhale the enchanting aroma and I'm lifted on the wings of ecstasy. It seems as though I'm about to drink a magic potion and my whole being begins to glow. The sounds of a thousand violins being softly played fills my ears and I am transported into another world.

"On the other hand, port makes me fart."

Why Did The Blonde...

A blonde is out for a walk. She comes to a river and sees another blonde on the opposite bank.

"Yoohoo!" she shouts. "How can I get to the other side?"

The second blonde looks up the river then down the river then shouts back,

"You are on the other side."

Xenophobes' Corner

Two men were sitting next to each other in a pub in Kilburn. After a while, one guy looks at the other and says, "I can't help but think, from listening to you, that you're from Ireland." The other guy responds proudly, "Yes, that I am!"

The first guy says, "So am I! And whereabouts from Ireland might you be?" The other guy answers, "I'm from Dublin, I am."

The first guy responds, "Sure and begorra, and so am I! And what street did you live on in Dublin?" The other guy says, "A lovely little area it was, I lived on McCleary Street in the old central part of town."

The first guy says, "Faith and it's a small world, so did I! And to what school would you have been going?" The other guy answers, "Well now, I went to St. Mary's of course."

The first guy gets really excited, and says, "And so did I. Tell me, what year did you graduate?" The other guy answers, "Well, now, I graduated in 1964."

The first guy exclaims, "The Good Lord must be smiling down upon us! I can hardly believe our good luck at winding up in the same bar tonight. Can you believe it, I graduated from St. Mary's in 1964 my own self."

About this time, another guy walks into the bar, sits down and orders a beer. The bartender walks over shaking his head and mutters,

"It's going to be a long night tonight, the Murphy twins are drunk again."

！◎ Adam & Eve

A Brit, a Frenchman and a Russian are viewing a painting of Adam and Eve frolicking in the Garden of Eden.

"Look at their reserve, their calm," muses the Brit. "They must be British."

"Nonsense," the Frenchman disagrees. "They're naked, and so beautiful. Clearly, they are French."

"No clothes, no shelter," the Russian points out, "they have only an apple to eat, and they're being told this is paradise. They are Russian."

！◎ Aussie Afterplay

An Italian, a Frenchman and an Australian are discussing their relative performance in bed.

The Italian says – "When I've a finsheda makina da love with my girlfriend I go down and gently tickle the back of her knees, she floatsa 6 inches abovea da bed in ecstasy."

The Frenchman replies – "Zat is nossing, when Ah 'ave finished making love wiz my girlfriend Ah kiss all ze way down her body and zen Ah lick zer soles of her feet wiz mah tongue and she floats 12 inches above ze bed in pure ecstasy."

The Aussie says – "That's nothing, when I've finished shaggin my Sheila, I get out of bed, walk over to the window and wipe my dick clean on the curtains. She hits the fucking roof!!!"

! 🔖 Dig, Dig, Fill, Fill

There were two Irishmen working for the city. One would dig a hole, he would dig, dig, dig; the other would come behind him and fill the hole, fill, fill, fill. These two men worked furiously. One digging a hole, the other filling it up again.

A man was watching from the sidewalk and couldn't believe how hard these men were working, but couldn't understand what they were doing. Finally he had to ask them. He said to the hole digger, "I appreciate how hard you work, but what are you doing? You dig a hole and your partner comes behind you and fills it up again!"

The hole digger replied, "Oh yeah, it must look funny, but the guy who plants the trees is sick today."

! 🔖 Earthly Balance

Once upon a time in the Kingdom of Heaven, God went missing for six days. Eventually, Michael the Archangel found him on the seventh day, resting.

He inquired of God, "Where have you been?" God sighed a deep sigh of satisfaction and proudly pointed downwards through the clouds. "Look Michael, look what I've made," said God. Archangel Michael looked puzzled and said, "What is it?"

"It's a planet," replied God, "and I've put LIFE on it. I'm going to call it Earth and it's going to be a great place of balance."

"Balance?" inquired Michael, still confused. God explained, pointing to different parts of Earth ...

"For example, North America will be a place of great opportunity and wealth while South America is going to be poor; the Middle East over there will be a hot spot and Russia will be a cold spot. Over there I've placed a continent of white people and over there is a continent of black people."

God continued, pointing to different countries "This one will be extremely hot and arid while this one will be very cold and covered in ice."

The Archangel, impressed by God's work, then pointed to a small land mass and said, "What's that one?"

"Ah," said God. "That's Britain, the most glorious place on Earth. There are beautiful lakes, rivers, streams and hills. The people from Britain are going to be modest, intelligent and humorous and they're going to be found travelling the world. They'll be extremely sociable, hard-working and high-achieving and they will be known throughout the world as diplomats and carriers of peace."

Michael gasped in wonder and admiration but then exclaimed, "What about balance, God? You said there will be balance!"

God replied wisely, "Wait until you see the wankers I'm putting next to them in France."

❗ 📎 G'day, You Bastard

Q: What's the definition of Australian aristocracy?
A: A man who can trace his lineage back to his father.

❗ 📎 High Speed Chicken

Scientists at NASA built a gun specifically to launch dead chickens at the windshields of airliners, military jets and the space shuttle, all traveling at maximum velocity. The idea is to simulate the frequent incidents of collisions with airborne fowl to test the strength of the windshields. British engineers heard about the gun and were eager to test it on the windshields of their new high speed trains. Arrangements were made, and a gun was sent to the British engineers.

When the gun was fired, the engineers stood shocked as the chicken hurtled out of the barrel, crashed into the shatterproof shield, smashed it to smithereens, blasted through the control console, snapped the engineer's backrest in two and embedded itself in the back wall of the cabin, like an arrow shot from a bow.

The horrified Brits sent NASA the disastrous results of the experiment, along with the designs of the windshield, and begged the US scientists for suggestions.

NASA responded with a one-line memo: "Thaw the chicken."

! Iraqi Education

Q: Why don't they teach driver's education and sex education on the same day in Iraq?
A: They don't want to wear out the camel.

! Irish Air Disaster

Ireland's worst air disaster occurred today when a small two-seater Cessna plane crashed into a cemetery early this afternoon in central Ireland.

Irish search and rescue workers have recovered 826 bodies so far and expect that number to climb as digging continues into the night.

! 0 Irish Wedding

A wedding took place just outside Cavan in Ireland. To keep tradition going, everyone got extremely drunk and the bride's and groom's families had a storming row and began wrecking the reception room and generally kicking the living daylights out of each other. The police were called in to break up the fight.

The following week, all members of both families appeared in court. The fight continued in the courtroom until the judge finally brought calm with the use of his hammer, shouting "Silence in Court." The courtroom went silent and Paddy (the best man) stood up and said: "Judge. I was the best man at the wedding and I think I should explain what happened." The judge agreed and asked Paddy to take the stand.

Paddy began his explanation by telling the court that it is traditional in a Cavan wedding that the best man gets the first dance with the bride. The judge said, "OK".

"Well," said Paddy, "after I had finished the first dance, the music kept going, so I continued dancing to the second song, and after that the music kept going and I was dancing to the third song ... when all of a sudden the groom leapt over the table, ran towards us and gave the bride an unmerciful kick right between her legs."

Shocked, the judge said, "God, that must have hurt!"

"Hurt!" Paddy replies. "You're not feckin kiddin'. He broke three of my fingers."

! 0 Kissing in the Dark

There were an Englishman, a Frenchman and Claudia Schiffer sitting together in a train carriage going through Provence. Suddenly the train went through a tunnel and, being one of the older-style trains with no carriage lighting, it went completely dark.

Then there was a kissing sound, followed by the sound of a really loud slap. When the train came out of the tunnel, Claudia Schiffer and the Englishman were sitting as if nothing had happened and the Frenchman had a nasty red slap mark on his face.

The Frenchman was thinking, "The Englishman must have kissed Claudia Schiffer and she missed him and slapped me instead."

Claudia Schiffer was thinking, "The Frenchman must have tried to kiss me and actually kissed the Englishman and got slapped for it."

The Englishman was thinking, "This is great. The next time the train goes through a tunnel, I'll make another kissing noise and slap that French wanker again!"

Like a Melon

In the middle of a gynaecology conference, an English and a French gynaecologist are discussing various cases they have recently treated.

The Frenchman says, "Only last week, zare was a woman oo came to see me, and 'er cleetoris – eet was like a melon!"

The Englishman says, "Don't be absurd, it couldn't have been that big, my good man, she wouldn't have been able to walk if it was."

"Aaah," sighs the Frenchman, "you Eenglish, zare you go again, always talkeeng about ze size ... I was talkeeng about ze flaveur!"

Mexican Olympiasts

Q: Why doesn't Mexico have an Olympic team?
A: Because all the Mexicans who can run, jump and swim are already in the U.S.

! On a Desert Island

On a beautiful deserted island in the middle of nowhere, the following people are stranded:

>> 2 Italian men and 1 Italian woman
>> 2 French men and 1 French woman
>> 2 German men and 1 German woman
>> 2 Greek men and 1 Greek woman
>> 2 English men and 1 English woman
>> 2 Polish men and 1 Polish woman
>> 2 Japanese men and 1 Japanese woman
>> 2 American men and 1 American woman
>> 2 Australian men and 1 Australian woman
>> 2 New Zealand men and 1 New Zealand woman
>> 2 Irish men and 1 Irish woman

One month later, the following things have occurred:

One Italian man killed the other Italian man for the Italian woman.

The two French men and the French woman are living happily together having loads of sex.

The two German men have a strict weekly schedule of when they alternate with the German woman.

The two Greek men are sleeping with each other and the Greek woman is cleaning and cooking for them.

The two English men are waiting for someone to introduce them to the English woman.

The Polish men took a long look at the endless ocean and one look at the Polish woman and started swimming.

The two Japanese men have faxed Tokyo and are waiting for instructions.

The two American men are contemplating the virtues of suicide, while the American woman keeps on bitching about her body being her own, the true nature of feminism, how she can do everything that they can do, about the necessity of fulfilment, the equal division of household chores, how her last boyfriend respected her opinion and treated her much nicer and how her relationship with her mother is improving. But at least the taxes here are low and it is not raining.

The two Australian men beat each other senseless fighting over the Australian woman, who is checking out all the other men, after calling them both "bloody wankers".

Both New Zealand men are searching the island for sheep.

The Irish began by dividing the island into North and South and by setting up a distillery. They do not remember if sex is in the picture because it gets sort of foggy after the first few litres of coconut whiskey, but they are satisfied that at least the English are not getting any.

! ◍ Tendjewberrymud

A telephone exchange between a hotel guest and room service at a hotel in Asia, which was recorded and published in the *Far East Economic Review*.

Room Service: Morny. Ruin sorbees.
Guest :   Sorry, I thought I dialled room-service.
RS: Rye. Ruin sorbees. Morny! Djewish to odor sunteen?
G: Uh ... yes ... I'd like some bacon and eggs.
RS: Ow July den?

G: What?

RS: Ow July den? ... pry, boy, pooch?

G : Oh, the eggs! How do I like them? Sorry, scrambled please.

RS: Ow July dee bayhçem. Crease?

G: Crisp will be fine.

RS: Hokay. An San tos?

G: What?

RS: San tos. July San tos?

G: I don't think so.

RS: No? Judo one toes??

G: I feel really bad about this, but I don't know what "judo one toes" means.

RS: Toes! toes! ... why djew Don Juan toes? Ow bow singlish mopping we bother?

G: English muffin! I've got it! You were saying 'Toast'. Fine. Yes, an English muffin will be fine.

RS: We bother?

G: No. Just put the bother on the side.

RS: Wad?

G: I mean butter. Just put it on the side.

RS: Copy?

G: Sorry?

RS: Copy? tea mill?

G: Yes. Coffee please, and that's all.

RS: One Minnie. Ass ruin torino fee, strangle ache, crease baychem, tossy singlish mopping we bother honey sigh and copy. Rye??

G: Whatever you say.

RS: Tendjewberrymud.

G : You're welcome.

! 🔟 The Thick Irish Wife

An Englishman, an Irishman and a Scotsman are sitting in a bar, drinking and discussing how stupid their wives are.

The Englishman says, "I tell you, my wife is so stupid. Last week she went to the supermarket and bought £100 worth of meat because it was on sale and we don't even have a fridge to keep it in."

The Scotsman agrees that she sounds pretty thick, but says his wife is thicker.

"Just last week, she went out and spent $17,000 on a new car," he laments. "And she doesn't even know how to drive!"

The Irishman nods wisely, and agrees that these two women sound like they both walked through the stupid forest and got hit by every branch. However, he still thinks his wife is dumber.

"Ah, it kills me every time I think of it," he chuckles. "My wife recently left to go on a trip to Greece. I watched her packing her bag, and she must have put about 100 condoms in there and she doesn't even have a penis!"

! 🔟 Two Paddys, Two Pigs

Paddy and Paddy, two Irishmen, went out one day and each bought a pig.

When they got home, Paddy turned to Paddy and said, "Paddy, me ol' mate, how we gonna tell who owns which feckin pig?" Paddy says, "Well Paddy, I'll cut one a ta ears off my feckin pig, and ten we can tell 'em apart."

"Ah tat'd be grand," says Paddy.

This worked fine until a couple of weeks later when Paddy stormed into the house.

"Paddy," he said, "your feckin pig has chewed the ear off a my feckin pig. Now we got two feckin pigs with only one ear each. How we goin ter tell who owns which feckin pig?"

"Well Paddy," said Paddy, "I'll cut ta other ear off my feckin pig. Ten we'll av two feckin pigs and only one of them will have an ear."

"Ah, tat'd be grand," says Paddy.

Again this worked fine until a couple of weeks later when Paddy again stormed into the house.

"Paddy," he said, "your feckin pig has chewed the other ear offa my feckin pig. Now we got two feckin pigs with no feckin ears. How we goin ter tell who owns which feckin pig?"

"Ah tis is serious, Paddy," said Paddy. "I'll tell ya what I'll do. I'll cut ta tail offa my feckin pig. Ten we'll have two feckin pigs with no feckin ears, and only one feckin tail."

"Ah tat'd be grand," says Paddy.

Another couple of weeks went by, and you guessed it, Paddy stormed into the house once more.

"PADDY," shouted Paddy, "YOUR FECKIN PIG HAS CHEWED THE FECKIN TAIL OFFA MY FECKIN PIG AND NOW WE GOT TWO FECKIN PIGS WITH NO FECKIN EARS AND NO FECKIN TAILS! HOW THE FECK ARE WE GOIN TER FECKIN TELL 'EM APART?"

"Ah feck it," says Paddy. "How about you have the black one, and I'll have the white one?"

❗ 📎 Very Sporting

On a train from London to Manchester, an American was telling off the Englishman sitting across from him in the compartment.

"You English are too stuffy. You set yourselves apart too much. Look at me ... in me, I have Italian blood, French blood, a little Indian blood and some Swedish blood. What do you say to that?"

The Englishman said, "Very sporting of your mother."

Why Americans Should Never Be Allowed to Travel

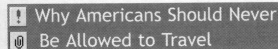

The following are actual stories provided by travel agents:

- I had someone ask for an aisle seat so that her hair wouldn't get messed up by being near the window.

- A client called in inquiring about a package to Hawaii. After going over all the cost info, she asked, "Would it be cheaper to fly to California and then take the train to Hawaii?"

- I got a call from a woman who wanted to go to Cape Town. I started to explain the length of the flight and the passport information when she interrupted me with: "I'm not trying to make you look stupid, but Cape Town is in Massachusetts." Without trying to make her look like the stupid one, I calmly explained, "Cape Cod is in Massachusetts, Cape Town is in Africa." Her response ... click.

- A man called, furious about a Florida package we did. I asked what was wrong with the vacation in Orlando. He said he was expecting an ocean-view room. I tried to explain that is not possible, since Orlando is in the middle of the state. He replied, "Don't lie to me. I looked on the map and Florida is a very thin state."

- I got a call from a man who asked, "Is it possible to see England from Canada?" I said, "No." He said, "But they look so close on the map."

- Another man called and asked if he could rent a car in Dallas. When I pulled up the reservation, I noticed he had a one-hour lay over in Dallas. When I asked him why he wanted to rent a car, he said, "I heard Dallas was a big airport, and I need a car to drive between the gates to save time."

- A nice lady just called. She needed to know how it was possible that her flight from Detroit left at 8:20am and got into Chicago at 8:33am. I tried to explain that Michigan was an hour ahead of Illinois, but she could not understand the concept of time zones. Finally I told her the plane went very fast, and she bought that!

- A woman called and asked, "Do airlines put your physical description on your bag so they know who's luggage belongs to who?" I said, "No, why do you ask?" She replied, "Well, when I checked in with the airline, they put a tag on my luggage that said FAT. Since I'm overweight, I wondered if there is any connection?" After putting her on hold for a minute while I "looked into it" (I was actually laughing), I came back and explained the city code for Fresno is FAT, and that the airline was just putting a destination tag on her luggage.

- I just got off the phone with a man who asked, "How do I know which plane to get on?" I asked him what exactly he meant, which he replied, "I was told my flight number is 823, but none of these darn planes have numbers on them."

- A woman called and said, "I need to fly to Pepsi-cola on one of those computer planes." I asked if she meant to fly to Pensacola on a commuter plane. She said, "Yeah, whatever."

- A businessman called and had a question about the documents he needed in order to fly to China. After a lengthy discussion about passports, I reminded him he needed a visa. "Oh no I don't, I've been to China many times and never had to have one of those." I double checked and sure enough, his stay required a visa. When I told him this he said, "Look, I've been to China four times and every time they have accepted my American Express."

- A woman called to make reservations, "I want to go from Chicago to Hippopotamus, New York." The agent was at a loss for words. Finally, the agent: "Are you sure that's the name of the town?" "Yes, what flights do you have?" replied the customer. After some searching, the agent came back with, "I'm sorry, ma'am, I've looked up every airport code in the country and can't find a Hippopotamus anywhere." The customer retorted, "Oh don't be silly. Everyone knows where it is. Check your map!" The agent scoured a map of the state of New York and finally offered, "You don't mean Buffalo, do you?" "That's it! I knew it was a big animal!"

Yeeeurch!

The story is told of two civil servants (a man and a woman) who met at a party in Highgate. Powerfully attracted to one another, they repaired at the earliest discreet opportunity to his flat, where they embarked on a night of torrid sex, moving swiftly from an 'entrée' of conventional intercourse to oral sex and a variety of excitingly athletic positions. Exhausted, but still feeling horny, they concluded their sexual feast with a 'digestif' of buggery. Waking up in the early morning, the male civil servant was troubled by a feeling of discomfort in his groin and a vague sense of unease. Concerned, and by now in some pain, he repaired to the bathroom to investigate the problem. In the dawn's early light he gingerly rolled back his foreskin, and was appalled to discover a piece of sweetcorn adhering to his glans.

! 📎 Pâté on a Bed of Seaweed

The following is a short true story, as seen recently by millions of viewers on a Spanish TV channel.

The parents of a teenage girl decided to put their daughter's name forward for a popular "surprise" game show. She idolized teeny-bopper pop star Ricky Martin, and it was arranged for TV cameras to be discreetly placed throughout the house. The house was then left empty with Ricky Martin himself hidden in the wardrobe in the girl's bedroom

– all set to give the daughter a wonderful surprise when she returned home from school. Meanwhile, the parents were in the show's studio, in front of a live studio audience.

Upon returning home from school, the daughter didn't go straight to her room and open the wardrobe as expected. Instead, she began to investigate the house, calling out the names of her family to ascertain who was at home.

Having established that she was on her own, the daughter made her way down to the kitchen where she opened the fridge and removed a large tin of pâté; at this stage the live TV audience is wondering what the hell is going on. She then went back upstairs to her bedroom where she quickly proceeded to remove all her clothes. She spread her legs – and then spread the pâté. At this stage Ricky Martin is still hidden inside the wardrobe, and half of Spain is seeing a nubile young girl, stark naked on the bed with pâté all over her crotch.

As if the parents were not shocked enough by this, the daughter then calls the family dog, who obediently trots up the stairs to settle down to his favourite meal of "pâté on a bed of seaweed".

The broadcast is abruptly cut. A set of acutely embarrassed parents are left in front of a deadly quiet studio audience, while a few million Spaniards sit in front of their TVs and piss themselves with laughter.

Consequently, sales of tinned pâté have rocketed.

Semen Detection

Three women, a brunette, a redhead and a blonde, all come home from work at the same time and get in the elevator.

The brunette notices a blob on the elevator wall and says: "Oooohhh, that looks like semen." She reaches out and touches the blob with her fingers and says, "It feels like semen."

The redhead reaches out and touches it with her fingers, smells it and says "It smells like semen."

Judi, the blonde, reaches out and touches it with her fingers and then puts her fingers in her mouth and says,

"It doesn't taste like anyone in this building …"

Sperm Bank

A guy in a balaclava bursts into a sperm bank with a shotgun.

"Open the fucking safe," he yells at the girl behind the counter.

"But we're not a real bank," she replies. "We don't have any money, this is a sperm bank."

"Don't argue, open the fucking safe or I'll blow your head off," says the guy with the gun. She obliges and once she's opened the safe door the guy says, "Take out one of the bottles and drink it."

"But it's full of sperm!" she replies nervously.

"Don't argue, just drink it," he says. She prises the cap off and gulps it down.

"Take out another one and drink it too," he demands. She takes out another and drinks it as well.

Suddenly the guy pulls off the balaclava and to the girl's amazement it's her husband.

"There," he says. "It's not that fucking difficult, is it?!"

Tales From the Emergency Room

Mother Hen

A 50-year-old woman was brought into a New York emergency room complaining of abdominal pains. During an examination, doctors found that the woman's labia were pinned together with old safety pins. Further inside, they found the dismembered body of a chicken. The woman explained that she inserted the chicken pieces, convinced that they would grow into a baby.

Late Delivery

A 63-year-old widow was admitted to hospital in Receive, Brazil, suffering abdominal pains. X-rays showed that she was carrying a 20-inch long skeleton of a fetus which she conceived a decade earlier. It had become lodged outside the womb and was never expelled from her body.

Female Sofa

A 500lb woman from Illinois was examined in hospital. During the examination, an asthma inhaler fell from under her armpit, a dime was found under one of her breasts and a remote control was found lodged between the folds of her vulva.

Tight Fit

A couple hobbled into a Washington emergency room covered in bloody restaurant towels. The man had his around his waist, and the woman had hers around her head. They eventually explained to doctors that they had gone out that evening for a romantic dinner. Overcome with passion, the woman crept under the table to administer oral sex to the man. While in the act, she had an epileptic fit, which caused her teeth to clamp down on the man's member and wrench it from side to side. In agony and desperation, the man grabbed a fork and stabbed her in the head until she let go.

Sex Education

A Californian doctor examining a young woman with abdominal pains asked her if she was sexually active. She said that she wasn't. A later examination showed that she was pregnant. Asked why she said that she was not sexually active, the woman replied, "I'm not, I just lie there." When asked if she knew who the father was, with a puzzled look she replied, "No. Who?"

Blind Drunk

A drunk staggered into a Pennsylvania ER complaining of severe pain while trying to remove his contact lenses. He said that they would come out half way, but they always popped back in. A nurse tried to help using a suction pump, but without success. Finally, a doctor examined him and discovered that the man did not have his contact lenses in at all. He had been trying to rip out the membrane of his cornea.

Growing Season

An old woman in a North Carolina ER complained of green vines growing from her vagina. Investigation revealed a large potato trapped in her womb. The woman then suddenly remembered that she had inserted it two weeks previously, because she thought that her uterus was falling out.

Prickly Pair

In Michigan, a man came into the ER with lacerations to his penis. He complained that his wife had "a rat in her pussy" and it bit him during sex. After an examination of his wife, if was revealed that she had a surgical needle left inside her after a recent hysterectomy.

Last Stand

A Cambridge man hobbled into casualty complaining of a permanent erection. He admitted to doctors that while on holiday in Cuba, he frequented many brothels, and in one he was given some erectile cream to keep him hard. He was told to use it sparingly. However, since he was having so much fun, he kept using more and more. By the time he came to casualty, all the blood vessels in his penis were swollen and his testicles had ballooned in size. Doctors could do nothing except prescribe painkillers, and told him that it would return to normal in a few days. They also told him to enjoy his erection while it lasted, because it was going to be his last.

Juicy Lucy

In Kentucky, a woman complained of a purple discharge from her vagina. She thought it might have something to do with the diaphragm that her doctor had recently given her. "I followed all the instructions to the letter," she told her doctor, "and used it with the jelly." When asked which kind of jelly she had used, she replied, "Grape."

Call The Bum Squad!

A World War II veteran came into a London clinic with a haemorrhoid problem. One painful pile would often hang down from the man's anus and he was in the habit of pushing it back up with an artillery shell. On this occasion, the shell got stuck. Doctors were going to remove it but the man told them the shell was still live. So the hospital called in the army bomb disposal squad, who built a lead box around the man's anus to defuse the shell before it could be removed.

🗑 Klingons Around Uranus

A 20-year-old man came to casualty with a stony mass in his rectum. He said that he and his boyfriend were fooling around with concrete mix, when his boyfriend had the idea of pouring the mix into his anus using a funnel. The concrete then hardened, causing constipation and pain. Under general anaesthesia, a perfect concrete cast of the man's rectum was removed, along with a stray ping-pong ball.

❗ 🎙 The Newly-Married Angler

A man is on a fishing holiday, just him and his rod and a bit of peace and quiet. He's been sitting in the same spot every day for a week, and every day he's seen another man on the other side of the lake, quietly fishing. After a week he wanders round to the man to engage in a bit of angling-related banter.

"On a fishing holiday are you?" our man enquires.

"Nah, I'm on my honeymoon," says the second man.

"Honeymoon?" says the first geezer. "Shouldn't you be with your wife making love to her like a frenzied weasel?"

"Can't do that mate," says the newlywed. "She's got crabs, herpes and ripping vaginal lesions."

"That's unfortunate," replies the fisherman, "but can't you go brown and give it to her up the old tradesman's entrance?"

"No chance," says the hapless bridegroom, "she's got anal chancroids, bleeding haemorrhoids and a bad case of bacterial dysentry."

"Sounds nasty," comments our man, "but surely she can give you a blow job?"

"I'd rather not," says the newlywed. "She's got foot and mouth and her teeth are green and rotting."

"She sounds horrific," comments the fisherman. "Why the fuck did you marry her?"

"For the maggots."

! 📎 Three Vampires

Three vampires walk into a pub. One after the other they go to the bar and order their drinks.

First vampire: "Can I have a pint of blood and a packet of crisps?"
Barman replies, "Sorry mate, we don't serve blood."
First vampire: "Just give me the crisps then."
The first vampire then goes and sits at a table to wait for his two friends.

Second vampire: "Can I have a pint of blood and a packet of peanuts?"
Once again the barman replies, "Sorry mate, we don't serve blood."
Second vampire: "Just give me the peanuts then."
The second vampire then goes and sits down with his friend and waits for the third vampire.

Third vampire: "Can I have a pint of warm water?"
Barman: "Sure, no problem."
The third vampire then sits down with his two friends and his pint of warm water.

The other two vampires, looking very confused, ask,

"Why are you drinking warm water? We're vampires – we only drink blood."

As soon as this has been said, the third vampire pulls a used tampon from his pocket and says,

"Never heard of teabags then?"

❗️📎 Tuna Mayonnaise

A strange but true story (allegedly) emphasizing the importance of food hygiene.

A woman had been absent from college for a number of weeks. When she returned one of her close friends was curious as to why she had been sick for so long. The following story emerged.

The woman and her boyfriend enjoyed involving food in their fore-play – Mars bars, cream, syrup, gravy, peanut butter, you name it.

One day the boyfriend, before going to work, made his sandwiches for the day, tuna mayonnaise, leaving the leftover tuna mayo lying out on the kitchen top. He went to work, came home, had dinner and relaxed for a night in with his girlfriend. Time passed and the pair of them got in the mood and started "doing the do". The boyfriend leapt up, after yodeling in the canyon for a while, and remembered the tuna mayo. He got the tuna mayo off the kitchen table, began to slap it all over his girlfriend's body (applying volu-minous amounts to her vaginal area) and started to lick it off.

Two days later after their night of tuna mayo lust had passed, the couple started to feel very ill. The boyfriend first, he seemed to be unable to stop vomiting, and the girlfriend later who kept on getting severe stomach cramps. The boyfriend put this down to eating the tuna mayo that had been lying out uncovered all day, and sure enough his jippy belly soon eased off after day or so.

His girlfriend, however, continued to feel ill, her pain worsening and her abdominal area becoming increasingly sore and tender. This went on for a few more days until the girlfriend couldn't even get out of her bed for the pain in her crotch and abdominal area. So her boyfriend took her to the doctor, who recommended she saw a gynaecologist. Thinking she might have cervical cancer, the gynaecologist checked her out and to his horror discovered far inside the woman's vagina a swarm of maggots that had been eating into her upper vaginal cavity.

Apparently what happened was the tuna mayo, after being left uncovered in the sun, attracted a number of flies, who naturally laid their eggs, which the boyfriend ate and the girlfriend "incubated"!

Valentine Card

Q: How can you tell if a valentine card is from a leper?
A: The tongue's still in the envelope.

```
.... and more cow tales ....

>          (__)                    (__)                     __)
>          (oo)                    (oo)                     o)
>    /-------\/            /-------\/
>   /  |   o  ||           *  ||----||
> *    ||----||               ||    ||
>       ^^    ^^              ^^    ^^
> Cow that gives       Cow that gives      Cow that gives
> (w)hole milk.        low-fat milk.          2% milk.
```

Zone of Unclassifiability

! ⓤ Advantageous Terms

Before going to Europe on business, a man drove his Rolls-Royce to a downtown NY City bank and went in to ask for an immediate loan of $5,000. The loan officer, taken aback, requested collateral.

"Well, then, here are the keys to my Rolls-Royce," the man said. The loan officer promptly had the car driven into the bank's underground parking for safe keeping, and gave him $5,000.

Two weeks later, the man walked through the bank's doors, and asked to settle up his loan and get his car back.

"That will be $5,000 in principal, and $15.40 in interest," the loan officer said. The man wrote out a check and started to walk away.

"Wait sir," the loan officer said. "While you were gone, I found out you are a millionaire. Why in the world would you need to borrow $5,000?"

The man smiled. "Where else could I park my Rolls-Royce in Manhattan for two weeks and pay only $15.40?"

! ⓤ Give Us a Push

A man is in bed with his wife when there's a rat-a-tat-tat on the door. He rolls over and looks at his clock, and it's half three in the morning. Fuck that for a game of soldiers, he thinks, and rolls over. Then, a louder knock follows.

"Aren't you going to answer that?" says his wife, so he drags himself out of bed, and goes downstairs. He opens the door and this bloke is stood outside.

"Eh mate," says the stranger, "can you give us a push?"

"No, fuck off, it's half three. I was in bed," says the man and shuts the door. He goes back up to bed and tells his wife what happened and she says "Dave, you are an arsehole. Remember that night we broke down in the pouring rain on the way to pick the kids up from the babysitter and you had to knock on that man's door to get us started again? What would have happened if he'd told us to fuck off?" So he gets out of bed again, gets dressed and goes downstairs.

He opens the door, and not being able to see the stranger anywhere he shouts: "Eh mate, do you still want a push?" and he hears a voice cry out, "Yeah please, mate." So, still being unable to see the stranger he shouts, "Where are you?"

The stranger replies: "I'm over here on the swings."

```
....and more cow tales ....
>              (__)
>            __(oo)
>          /   \/  (__)
>         /    \\   (oo)
>        /|  /-^^---\/                    /---------\ /
>       / | /|      ||              / |        ||o
>      *   || ||----||            *  ||@\---||
>          ^^ ^^     ^^              ^^       ^^
>        Cows that give            Cow that
>        homogenized milk.         gives cream.
```

! Indian Names

The little Indian boy asked his father Chief Running Bull "Father, how do we Indians get our names?"

"Well," said his father, "take when your sister was born. I walked out of the teepee and saw the white clouds flying and I thought 'I'll call her White Cloud Flying.' Then when your brother was born I walked out of the teepee and I saw a buffalo stamping and I thought 'I'll call him Buffalo Stamping.' So you see, that's how we Indians get our names.

"Why do you ask, Two Dogs Fucking?"

! Murphy's Nails

Murphy owned a factory that made nails. He decided to give things a boost, so he called in an advertising agency to make an ad for TV. Three weeks later the agency rang saying his new ad would get its first showing on the following Wednesday night during "NYPD Blue".

Murphy invited all his friends and relations round to his house to see the ad. The ad came on and the camera zoomed in on a grassy field and there was lovely background music. The camera then moved over the grass and up the side of a hill. At the top of the hill it came to the bottom of a cross. It slowly moved up the cross ... to reveal Jesus on the cross. It moved out to his hands to show the nails driven through. A voice then said, "Always use Murphy's nails." Murphy and his friends were appalled.

Next day all newspapers and media chat shows were discussing the tasteless and irreverent ad for Murphy's nails. Murphy became the most hated man in the country and business slumped. Murphy rang the advertising agency in despair and asked them to change the ad.

Three weeks later they rang saying there would be a new ad the following night. Murphy got all his friends in again. The ad came on as before: the camera focused on the grass, same background music.

"Shit, I'm fucked," says Murphy.

The camera went up the hill and came to a cross, but this time there was no-one on it. The camera looked off into the distance ... and there was Jesus legging it across the fields.

A voice rang out, "They should have used Murphy's nails!"

Screwed

An explorer in the deepest, darkest part of the Amazon suddenly finds himself surrounded by a bloodthirsty native tribe. Upon surveying the situation, he whispers to himself, "I'm screwed."

Suddenly there is a clap of thunder, a flash of lightning and a ray of light descends from the sky, accompanied by a booming voice.

"No, you are not screwed. Pick up that stone at your feet and bash in the head of the chief standing in front of you." The explorer can't believe his ears, but he obeys, picking up the stone and bashing the life out of the chief. He is breathing heavily while standing above the lifeless body; surrounding him are the 100 warriors, astonished by what they have seen.

"OK," says the voice, booming out again. "NOW you're screwed."

Telemarketing Tips

1. If they want to loan you money, tell them you just filed for bankruptcy and you could sure use some money.

2. If they start out with, "How are you today?" say, "Why do you want to know?" Alternatively, you can tell them, "I'm so glad you asked,

because no one these days seems to care, and I have all these problems; my arthritis is acting up, my eyelashes are sore, my dog just died ..." When they try to get to the sell, just keep talking about your problems.

3. If they say they're John Doe from XYZ Company, ask them to spell their name. Then ask them to spell the company name. Then ask them where it is located. Continue asking them personal questions or questions about their company for as long as necessary.

4. This works great if you are male: Telemarketer: "Hi, my name is Judy and I'm with XYZ Company ..." You: Wait for a second and with a real husky voice ask, "What are you wearing?"

5. Cry out in surprise, "Judy! Is that you? Oh my God! Judy, how have you been?" Hopefully, this will give Judy a few brief moments of terror as she tries to figure out where the hell she could know you from.

6. Say "No", over and over. Be sure to vary the sound of each one, and keep a rhythmic tempo, even as they are trying to speak. This is most fun if you can do it until they hang up.

7. If MCI calls trying to get you to sign up for the Family and Friends plan, reply, in as SINISTER a voice as you can, "I don't have any friends ... would you be my friend?"

8. If the company cleans rugs, respond: "Can you get out blood? Can you get out GOAT blood? How about HUMAN blood?"

9. After the telemarketer gives their spiel, ask him/her to marry you. When they get all flustered, tell them that you could not just give your credit card number to a complete stranger.

10. Tell the telemarketer that you work for the same company, they often can't sell to employees.

11. Answer the phone. As soon as you realize it is a telemarketer, set the receiver down, shout or scream "Oh my God!!!" and then hang up.

12. Tell the telemarketer you are busy at the moment and ask them if they will give you their home phone number so you can call them back. When the telemarketer explains that they cannot give out their home number, you say, "I guess you don't want anyone bothering you at home, right?" The telemarketer will agree and you say, "Now you know how I feel!" Hang up.

13. Ask them to repeat everything they say, several times.

14. Tell them it is dinner time, but ask if they would please hold. Put them on your speaker phone while you continue to eat at your leisure. Smack your food loudly and continue with your dinner conversation.

15. Tell the telemarketer you are on "home incarceration" and ask if they could bring you some beer.

16. Ask them to fax the information to you, and make up a number.

17. Tell the telemarketer, "Okay, I will listen to you. But I should probably tell you, I'm not wearing any clothes."

18. Insist that the caller is really your buddy Leon, playing a joke. "Come on Leon, cut it out! Seriously, Leon, how's your momma?"

19. Tell them you are hard of hearing and that they need to speak up ... louder ... louder ... louder ...

20. Tell them to talk VERY SLOWLY, because you want to write EVERY WORD DOWN.

The Morning Song
(For Non-Morning People)

>> I woke early one morning,
>> The earth lay cool and still
>> When suddenly a tiny bird
>> Perched on my window sill,
>>
>> He sang a song so lovely
>> So carefree and so gay,
>> That slowly all my troubles
>> Began to slip away.
>>
>> He sang of far-off places
>> Of laughter and of fun,
>> It seemed his very trilling,
>> Brought up the morning sun.
>>
>> I stirred beneath the covers
>> Crept slowly out of bed,
>> And gently lowered the window
>> And crushed his fucking head.
>>
>>
>>
>>
>>
>>
>>

❗📎 The Ultimate Urban Myth Chain Letter

Please sign this UN petition.

I know this guy whose neighbour, a young man, was home recovering from having been served a rat in his bucket of Kentucky Fried Chicken. He had just finished watching that true-story movie where someone lets a little alligator go in the sewers of New York and it grows up to eat half the city. So anyway, he went to sleep and when he awoke he was in his bathtub and it was full of ice and he was sore all over.

When he got out of the tub he realized that HIS KIDNEYS HAD BEEN STOLEN and he saw a note on his mirror that said, "Call 911!" But he was afraid to use his phone because it was connected to his computer, and there was a virus on his computer that would destroy his hard drive if he opened an e-mail entitled, "Join the crew!" He knew it wasn't a hoax because he himself was a computer programmer who was working on software to save us from Armageddon when the year 2000 rolls around. His program will prevent a global disaster in which all the computers get together and distribute the $600 Nieman Marcus cookie recipe under the leadership of Bill Gates. (It's true – I read it all last week in a mass e-mail from BILL GATES HIMSELF, who was also promising me a free Disneyworld vacation and $5,000 if I would forward the e-mail to everyone I know.)

The poor man then tried to call 911 from a pay phone to report his missing kidneys but, reaching into the coin-return slot, he got jabbed with an HIV-infected needle around which was wrapped a note that said, "Welcome to the world of AIDS."

He tried to hail a pizza-delivery driver, but the driver didn't see him because he was too busy masturbating on the pizza he was delivering.

Luckily he was only a few blocks from the hospital – the one, actually, where that little boy who is dying of cancer is, the one whose last wish is for everyone in the world to send him an e-mail and the American Cancer Society has agreed to pay him a nickel for every e-mail he receives. I sent him two e-mails and one of them was a bunch of x's and o's in the shape of an angel (if you get it and forward it to twenty people you will have good luck, but if you send it to ten people you will only have OK luck and if you send it to less than ten people you will have BAD LUCK FOR SEVEN YEARS).

The poor guy tried to drive himself to the hospital, but on the way he noticed another car driving along without its lights on. To be helpful, he flashed his lights at him and was promptly shot as part of a gang initiation.

And it's a little-known fact that the Y1K problem caused the Dark Ages.

You must pass this letter on to ten people or you will be audited by the Inland Revenue.

❗ 📎 Why I'm Tired

I'm tired. For a couple years I've been blaming it on iron-poor blood, lack of vitamins, dieting and a dozen other maladies. But now I found out it ain't that. I'm tired because I'm overworked.

The population of this country is 237 million. 104 million are retired.

That leaves 133 million to do the work.

There are 85 million in school, which leaves 48 million to do the work.

Of this there are 29 million employed by the federal government. This leaves 19 million to do the work.

Four million are in the Armed Forces, which leaves 15 million to do the work.

Take from the total the 14,800,000 people who work for State and City Government and that leaves 200,000 to do the work.

There are 188,000 in hospitals, so that leaves 12,000 to do the work.

Now, there are 11,998 people in prisons. That leaves just two people to do the work. You and me.

And you're sitting there reading this. No wonder I'm tired, I'm the only one working.

....and finally ....

```
>            (__)                            .
>            (dd)                         .
>    /--------\/              U
>   / |        ||         /---V           .
> * ||----||          *  |--|
>      ^^        ^^                        .
> Cow that gives   Cow that gives   Cow that gives
> vitamin D milk.  condensed milk.      (gave)
>                                   evaporated milk.
>
```